Living
Aboard
Your
RV

Third Edition

Living Aboard Your RV

Janet Groene and Gordon Groene

 Ragged Mountain Press / McGraw-Hill

Camden, Maine • New York • Chicago • San Francisco •
Lisbon • London • Madrid • Mexico City • Milan • New
Delhi • San Juan • Seoul • Singapore • Sydney • Toronto

Ragged Mountain Press
A Division of The McGraw·Hill Companies

10 9 8 7 6 5

Library of Congress Cataloging-in-Publication Data
Groene, Janet.
    Living aboard your RV / Janet Groene and Gordon Groene.— 3rd ed.
        p.   cm.
    Includes index.
    ISBN 0-07-137724-7
 I. Recreational vehicle living. I. Groene, Gordon. II. Title.
    TX1110.G76 2001
    796.7'9—dc21   2001004996

Questions regarding the content of this book should be addressed to

Ragged Mountain Press
P.O. Box 220
Camden, ME 04843
www.raggedmountainpress.com

Questions regarding the ordering of this book should be addressed to

The McGraw-Hill Companies
Customer Service Department
P.O. Box 547
Blacklick, OH 43004
Retail customers: 1-800-262-4729
Bookstores: 1-800-722-4726

This book is printed on 60-lb. Computer Book by R. R. Donnelley & Sons, Crawfordsville, IN
Design by Lynda Chilton, Chilton Creative
Production by Dan Kirchoff and PerfecType
Edited by Jonathan Eaton and Joanne Allen

Contents

Preface to the Third Edition

The RV revolution is truly one of the wonders of our time. It grew out of the dream of traveling without leaving "home" and into the reality of today's fine-quality, fully equipped, and eminently roadable recreational vehicles.

People choose to travel in many ways and to live in many kinds of domiciles. However, it has always been difficult to combine nonstop travel with a real home. In the past, people who wanted to do both could hitch a prairie schooner to a team and shout, "Westward, ho!" For the wealthy there were private rail cars complete with kitchen and bath. No longer practical today, they have been replaced by the modern RV.

To those people who decry RVs as a desecration of the "camping" spirit, we suggest that RV fulltiming is not a replacement for tenting or backpacking. It is a replacement for house and garage, garden and grass, toolshed and cellar. The RV is a home as well as a base from which all other careers and activities—including primitive camping—can proceed.

As you consider fulltiming as a way of life, we wish you safe miles, a soft bunk, and a chance to brighten the many corners you'll encounter along the way.

Since the last edition of this book, dramatic changes have taken place: the Internet has revolutionized the ways we can communicate, pay bills, educate children, and earn a living; GPS navigation signals, telephone calls, and TV and subscription radio services are bounced to us from satellites; and thousands of RVers have joined the fulltiming ranks. Campgrounds are better than ever, RV clubs offer improved services, and RVs are more space and fuel efficient and more user-friendly—to veterans and first-timers alike.

There has never been a better time to hit the road!

ONE

Song of the
Open Road

We woke up to a thin, cold dawn and the pounding of a patrolman's fist on our camper door.

"Move along," he said, not unkindly. "I've let you sleep since two o'clock this morning, but it's six now and time you hit the road."

No, we weren't homeless alcoholics sleeping off a cheap drunk under a tent of yesterday's newspapers. We were young, able, self-sufficient adventurers who had stopped late the night before in a highway rest plaza, and we had overslept the two-hour limit.

Our visit from that policeman was just another in a long series of reminders that in shedding our old style of life and adopting a new role as full-time wanderers we had shed a lifelong mantle of respectability. Our new life baffled some people, amused others, and enraged more than a few.

What had we gotten ourselves into?

What It's Got, What It's Not

Close your eyes and picture the free, roving life on wheels. Immediately you imagine a cozy, self-contained camper beside a rushing, trout-packed brook. You have no deadlines, no lawn to mow, no leaves to rake, no committees, no neighbors to be stuck with year after year. You fantasize about a life with no ties, no traps, no taxes. The full-time RV life is all you hope for and much, much more. But it also means a break with treasured possessions, with status, with symbols, with your Place In Life.

1

Can you handle it?

The RV itself is a red flag in the faces of politicians in some cities, where special laws have been passed against RVs simply because they *are* RVs. In some communities you can't park an RV at the beach or the park even if it fits in a car-size parking place. Other communities have laws prohibiting RVs from staying within the city limits overnight, and a few don't want you in town *anytime*. There have been times when we have been hassled, threatened, vandalized, and humiliated.

It isn't our aim to talk you out of following our mud flaps, but we do want to prick your dream balloon enough to bring you back to treetop level. Knowing that there will be bitter with the better will help you to make necessary adjustments in yourself, in your dealings with society, and in your relationships with family and spouse.

In the Beginning

For us it all began in Danville, Illinois, where Gordon was a professional pilot for a large corporation. He liked the company and the job, and he valued his professional relationship with his coworkers. We both liked friendly little Danville, which was large enough to have good shopping and a nice mix of people, yet small enough that I could do most of my shopping by bicycle. We were only ten minutes from the airport, our church, or a night on the town and an hour from a major university town with theater and concerts.

Still, we began to toy with the idea of early retirement. One of our friends had died of a heart attack at 41, another of leukemia at 38. What if time ran out before the traditional retirement age of 65?

The Ties That Bind

You're probably wondering how we could even think of dropping off the edge of the world with all the family obligations one usually has at that stage in life. First it's the children, then the grandchildren, then the care of your elderly parents—an unending treadmill of obligations. However, people differ in how they handle such "obligations."

We met some young parents who became full-time travelers not *despite* their children but *because of* them—either because they wanted to spend precious years traveling and learning together while the kids were young or because they were determined to get their children out of an environment they perceived as too materialistic, too violent, or otherwise not up to the standards they wanted for their families.

Mail-order schooling, once just an oddball way of educating kids whose parents were missionaries or who traveled with the circus, is being used today by thousands of parents at home and on the go. Most feel that they can provide a better education than the schools can, citing such public-school problems as weapons, drugs, and overcrowded classrooms. With "home" schooling now available, affordable, and growing in popularity, children can travel full-time and still get a first-class education.

We've met many liveaboard children who have received some or all of their early schooling through homeschooling, and there wasn't a brat or a dunce in the bunch. Do an Internet search on "home school" or "homeschool" and you'll uncover a huge treasure trove of accredited schools, learning options, resources, and support groups. Do your homework to make sure you get the best program for the best price, with the most portable and credible credits for your child's future career or entry into college.

You might also check with your school district, which may offer schooling by mail, at least for a short time. Try your church too. Some denominations, such as the Seventh Day Adventists, provide homeschooling programs. Others, including the Lutheran Church–Missouri Synod, offer Sunday school by mail. For more on home-schooling, see chapter 12, Kids on Board.

It's true that many people prefer to stay put until their children are grown. Others feel that they must stay with elderly parents, a shut-in sibling, or a family business or farm. One of today's most common dilemmas is that of the "sandwich" generation, in which middle-aged people are saddled with the care of their aged parents just when their own children get divorced and move back home with *their* children.

We've heard just about all the reasons why you can't go. They range from very good ones to mere cop-outs. The truth is that you probably can take to the road in an RV if you and your spouse or companion(s) or family make the effort to work it out.

If you think you can't go because you don't *have* a spouse or family to travel with, think again. Legions of singles, both men and women—widowed, divorced, never married, available, and unavailable—are out there fulltiming and having the time of their lives.

Hundreds of examples show that you *can* do it—alone or together, young or old, as a couple or with a group—as long as everyone is on the same wavelength.

"But," you say, "I'm handicapped." Fulltiming is not only possible for you, it's some-times the *best* choice for persons with many types of disabilities. For one thing, it is the only lifestyle that allows the physically challenged of any age to enjoy their share of camping, fishing, and sightseeing in our state and national parks.

Financial problems? Fulltiming can cost pearls or peanuts, and we'll tell you how.

Career not portable? We've met fulltimers with a variety of professions, from pub-lishing to plant care, catering to wood carving. The Internet makes it possible to con-duct business in thousands of fields, no matter where you live.

In the pages that follow, we focus on the who, why, when, where, and how of this very possible dream.

What Kind of Fulltiming Life for You?

RV living is not one lifestyle but many. Much of your happiness and success in full-timing depends on finding just the right niche for yourself. For many people the camp-ing itself is the whole nine yards. They delight in camping clubs, camp meetings, RV shows, RV rallies, group caravans, and campground get-togethers.

At the opposite end of the spectrum are those who camp to get away from it all. They avoid destination campgrounds and memberships because they don't want to clump with other campers. They may be good neighbors, always willing to pitch in on a project or lend a hand with a repair problem, but they don't want to mingle with other RVers, either because they prefer to keep to themselves entirely or because they have a very full life quite separate from the camping scene.

Fulltimers come from all income and age brackets. Some are financially inde-pendent retirees; some have reached retirement age but must work at least part-time. Some work at professions that require them to live in one place for several months at a time. Others live in an RV because it provides a movable home while they pursue some special hobby or profession, such as sports car racing, fishing tournaments, surfing, lecturing, archaeology, working carnivals or rodeos, or creating and selling artwork or crafts.

Some fulltimers are constantly on the move, never content to stay in one spot for long and always excited about what they'll find around the next bend. Some camp in one campground each summer and in another every winter. Still others buy a campsite and rarely leave it. For us, the motorhome makes a comfortable home and office when we're on assignment as a travel-writing team, but we've never attended an RV rally (where thousands of rigs gather for a few days of trading tips and camaraderie) or participated in an RV caravan (where a group of RVers, led by a trailmaster, travel together).

For some, the RV is merely the vehicle (pardon the pun) that serves a particular lifestyle. For you, the RV alone may provide the life you're seeking. We're all part of the camping family, so *vive la différence*!

Exploding Some Myths

Before you get too far into your planning, we may as well hit you with some hard realities, the kinds of things you don't read about in the ads.

Myth: By living in an RV full time you can live on almost nothing.

Reality: Fuel, oil, tires, insurance, and turnpike fees cost more all the time. Campgrounds are rarely free; it's not uncommon now to pay $35 per night. You can't outrun the insatiable tax collector either. You'll pay taxes on almost everything you use or buy on the go: sales taxes when you buy the vehicle, yearly license fees, property taxes (because they are reflected in campground rates), and federal income taxes.

Myth: Wanderers have no responsibilities, no cares, no problems.

Reality: You'll have most of the same problems you've always had—staying on a diet, cooking and cleaning, making ends meet, doing the Christmas shopping, touching up the gray, grooming the poodle—plus many new ones, such as finding acceptable campsites, staying alive on the highway, and getting along with your mate in less space than a German shepherd is allotted at the dog pound. You'll be living in a very complex "house," that includes living quarters, sewer, waterworks, engine, and chassis, all of which you'll have to manage yourself.

Myth: It'll be like a second honeymoon, just the two of you on an endless highway of travel delights.

Reality: After a couple of weeks in close quarters you may start thinking about divorce, if not murder.

Myth: No more winter.

Reality: It is possible to follow the seasons, but so do crowds and high prices. On the other hand, if you stay in a cold climate in winter, heating costs will be high and comforts elusive. Each of us must find his or her own affordable, practical, geographic comfort zone.

Myth: Wide-open spaces.

Reality: Only in RV ads is one camper given exclusive rights to the entire Grand Canyon. In most campgrounds you'll be closer to your neighbors than you ever were back home.

Myth: Personal problems will melt away once you're on the road.

Reality: Troubles are an unseen trailer that follows all of us everywhere. If you're in a bad marriage, are in debt over your head, or are addicted to harmful substances or habits, fulltiming won't change you. Look at the RV life as an avenue to new adventures and successes, not as an escape. It isn't one.

We thrived on fulltiming for ten happy years. If there is a secret to our success, it's that we not only expected difficulties but welcomed new challenges. In exchange for the hardships of full-time travel we formed priceless friendships with folks in many states and nations, and we were freed from former careers to develop an entirely new life as freelance writers. Best of all, all those miles of roaming allowed us to live in many parts of the country and take a leisurely assessment of them before deciding where to put down roots.

No matter how flexible you are, changing your lifestyle is a tough assignment. In the following pages we'll try and help you through the roadblocks, breakdowns, detours, and potholes ahead.

TWO

Get
Ready

Exactly how can you begin preparing, right now, for a fulltiming life that may be months or even years away? First, get your priorities straight. Sit down with your loved ones and decide what really matters to you. Then take the following approach to making your dream a reality.

Test the Waters

If your goal really is to live and travel in your RV, stop fantasizing and try the real thing. Rent or borrow a suitable rig and take off for as long as possible. (For more on choosing an RV, see chapter 7, How to Choose a Home on Wheels.) A trial run may sound expensive, but it's a bargain compared with what it will cost to quit your job, sell everything you own, take off in an RV, and then find out you hate the new life and want to recapture the old one. We met one couple who took off with great zest and fanfare. They flitted across the country visiting all their friends and partying with old army buddies and then ran out of things to do and people to visit. Somehow, they never came to terms with fulltiming as an ongoing way of life. They sold their rig at a big loss.

Stay "out there" for at least three weeks—more if possible. During this time you'll encounter some of the realities of the fulltimer's life: rainy days when you're shut in until you could scream, mechanical breakdowns, finding campgrounds, putting up with campground neighbors, using coin laundries, getting mail and keeping in touch with your family or business, trying to cash personal checks in places where you're not known, walking the dog, living in very limited space, and filling your days with meaningful activities. (Believe it or not, some people find it boring not to have a job and a schedule.)

At the end of this time you'll also have a good idea what expenses you'll encounter over the long term as you slip into this new lifestyle: camp fees, pay phones, fuel costs, changes in food and entertainment costs, and probably some unpleasant surprises, such as an unexpected repair or replacement or a run-in with a nasty neighbor or uppity campground operator.

Even so, this is only a hint of true fulltiming. During this rehearsal you'll still have a home to retreat to if things get too rough. You'll still have an address, an identity, perhaps a job waiting for you, and lots more elbow room in the RV than you'll have when you're carrying everything you own. Still, it's enough of a preview to tell you, before you quit your job and sell the house, if fulltiming is what you expected it to be.

Live for Tomorrow, but Don't Sacrifice Today

From the moment we decided to change our lifestyle, we began shopping with resale in mind. Although we didn't have to give up a spacious home, good cars, occasional vacations—the good life in general—we weighed every purchase not only for its present value but for its resale potential. We could have afforded a higher mortgage in a swankier section of town, but we chose instead a big, old, five-bedroom house in a stable neighborhood near good schools, knowing that it would sell readily to a large family when we were ready to go.

Our car was an expensive German make famous for holding its value. Gordon groomed it meticulously, washed off the salt after every winter trip, kept it garaged, and generally treated it royally. It gave us endless hours of fun and good service and then sold for the plum it was.

Our furniture was in solid woods, not veneers, in traditional styles that never lose their popularity. Many pieces were antiques that we had refinished ourselves. Our appliances were good brand names. When the time came to sell out, everything brought top dollar.

That money was only part of our nest egg, but we met one family from Vermont who bankrolled an entire two-year trip for themselves and their two small daughters with money they got by renovating and selling an old house and its antique furnishings.

Get Your Financial Picture in Order

It's easier said than done, but get out of debt. Start by hiding your credit cards. Don't borrow another cent for anything but a real emergency. Start mopping up all the little obligations—credit cards, time payments, petty loans. Keep your eye on the real goal, which is fulltiming, and impulse purchases will lose some of their luster.

Do financial planning for today and for a long line of tomorrows. One couple didn't cut loose from "real life" until they had established trust funds to pay their children's college tuition. Before another couple hit the road, they helped their elderly parents to sell a home they could no longer maintain properly and to get into a life-care facility.

Such planning usually benefits from professional help. There are all kinds of planners, and the letters that follow their names can provide some clues to their backgrounds and experience: an APFS is an accredited personal financial specialist (a CPA who has done further study); a CFP is a certified financial planner; a CPA is a certified public accountant (be sure to find one who has additional training in financial planning); and an MFS, or master of financial science, has a master's degree in investment planning. Financial advisors may have other credentials, but often these apply to specialties, such as pensions or insurance. Be sure to choose a reputable planner; try asking friends for a recommendation.

We went to a fee-only financial planner—one who doesn't also sell stocks, insurance, or other financial products—to get unbiased advice. The National Association of Personal Financial Advisors recommends interviewing at least two individuals from different fee-only firms before making a choice. Fees are usually per hour or per consultation; we paid $1,200 for a onetime financial inventory.

While you may want to consult an attorney as well as a CFP, especially where taxes or inheritance are concerned, keep in mind that lawyers usually are not qualified to give investment advice. Don't rely on one as your sole financial consultant.

Some planners don't want to bother with people whose net worth is less than $250,000 to $500,000, although none of those we interviewed had any such limits. In fact, none even asked our net worth. CFPs charge about $150 per hour, so this service doesn't come cheap. However, you're buying a strategy that can get you started on the right track for the rest of your life.

Free advice is available too. You can solicit complete workups from individuals who sell insurance, annuities, precious metals, or mutual funds. The result will no doubt be skewed because these advisors work on commission in their fields and are unlikely to suggest a balanced portfolio. Still, a certain pattern will probably emerge after you've consulted three or four.

If you're in debt over your head, nonprofit credit-repair advisors will work with you. Check with your local volunteer bureau or community service agencies and in the Yellow Pages under "Credit and Debt Counseling."

If you're willing to reveal every penny of your assets, expenditures, and debts, to be published for all the world to see, there's one more way to get professional financial planning advice, absolutely free. Some large newspapers, including the *Orlando Sentinel*, and many magazines, including *Money*, have regular features in which they outline a family's financial situation and have it analyzed by two or three experts, who tell the family, and the reading audience, how to reach their goals. If you're not concerned about privacy, volunteer for such treatment. The advice is likely to be excellent, but read the next issue's letters to the editor, where you may learn even more from readers who agree or disagree with the advice you received.

Don't Burn Your Bridges

We've all dreamed about walking into the boss's office someday and saying, "Take this job and shove it." Unless you're retiring permanently, however, keep in mind that someday you may want to go back to the same company for a recommendation or a reference if not for a job.

If possible, take a leave of absence. You can always resign later, but you will have left the door open in case circumstances change. Keep as many ties as possible. For example, you are permitted by law to keep your group health insurance for a stated period after you leave. You may also be able to leave your pension plan in place for investment and tax advantages, or get free, expert help in rolling it over. If your company has a good human resources department, consult personnel there about your options.

It's a good idea to make your first trip a short one so you won't be in Alaska or Baja if you find fulltiming isn't for you. Once you've made the decision to go, set milestones at which to reevaluate your plans so you won't feel that you've made an irrevocable break with your past life. For instance, you and your mate might agree to a serious rethinking after two years. Or when you reach a certain age. Or when your savings get down to so many dollars.

Take It Slow

The RV of your dreams may beckon you to the showroom, but don't buy that rig before you're able to enjoy it, maintain it, and afford it. Timing is very difficult. If you purchase the RV too early and can't sell your home, double payments could break your back. If your home sells too quickly, you could make too rash a decision on an RV.

Most of us want to do a lot of customizing in a new RV, so it's handy to have your home workshop and tools available for most of the work. Lots of things have to dovetail, so don't act in haste.

Don't Let Possessions Run Your Life

Many people have told us they'd love to go fulltiming but can't part with their library, Hummel collection, or billiard table. Your fulltiming life can't get off the ground until you can jettison all the pounds of impedimenta that clutter your life. When you're living in tight quarters, tempers can flare over whose straw is breaking the camel's back.

Develop Interests and Hobbies

Shifting into the fulltiming life may still be more of a jolt than you think. Travel alone may not be enough to fill your days. There may be times when you are delayed by weather, holed up for repairs, or simply too far over your budget to fill the fuel tank as often as you'd like.

The travel life can lead to countless hobbies: ham radio, gravestone rubbing, postcard collecting, square dancing, photography, letter writing. Hobbies give you purpose and identity, something to do on rainy days, and social focus when you're in areas where you don't know anyone.

Network

Join national camping clubs, retiree groups, professional organizations, and hobby groups. By networking you can keep current on the job picture in your field or get the latest information on treatment for your handicap, on where the season's best jazz festivals will be held, or on steps to take to further your favorite political cause. It may be difficult to connect after you take off, so join before you go.

Compute Your Launch Value

When you stand ready on the launch pad of your fulltiming life, what will your net worth be? The closer you are to leaving, the more accurate your figures will be, but here are some tips on adding up your net worth as of today.

Keep in mind that net worth is not monthly income. For example, social security is not included in net worth. It may have a value to you, but only month by month, depending on your age and your lifetime earnings. Since it has no lump-sum value for the purposes of a net-worth statement, it doesn't figure in this ledger.

Get out a pad and pencil and start a list. The object is to come up with a figure that tells you what you would have in hand today if you liquidated everything. In the process, you will gain an overview of how independent you are right now.

Ready Cash

In the ready-cash column list both liquid assets and other assets that are fairly well assured. These include bank accounts, money market funds, CDs, cash on hand, and monies that you are fairly certain to collect soon (such as a maturing insurance policy or a tax refund).

Add in any sums that you intend to have on hand by your upcoming takeoff date, such as a retirement bonus or lump-sum settlement, IRA or Keogh, vested interest in a profit-sharing or other retirement plan, insurance settlement, or maturing bonds or other investment.

Today's Value

In this column you should list only the present value of items that could be worth much more or much less tomorrow. Include stocks, mutual funds, trusts, and tangible deposits such as silver bars or gold bullion. Add in the cash value of your life-insurance policy—not the loan value, but today's cash-in or rollover value.

If you have a business partner, get a professional appraisal of what your share of the

Assets and Debts

Make a list of your assets and debts to get an idea of your worth. Here's an example for a couple with grown children.

Assets		Debts	
Home equity	$150,000	Owed on RV	$150,000
Combined IRAs	114,000	Mortgage	50,000
Combined 401ks	89,000	Personal loan from parent	9,000
T-bills	30,000	Margin account, broker	8,700
Stocks, mutual funds	14,500	Owed on credit cards	8,500
Bank CDs	12,000	Owed on car	8,000
Paid-up life insurance	10,000	Student loan	6,500
Furniture	8,000	Note co-signed with son	4,500
Car equity	1,400	Owed on prepaid funeral	3,500
total assets:	$428,900	total debts:	$248,700
launch value:	$180,200		

business is worth on today's market. Add in the current market value of your car, boat, home (its fair market value, not your equity), and furnishings, as well as the garage-sale value of items you could liquidate easily.

The total will probably be impressive if yours is a typical household complete with appliances, yard care equipment, shop tools, electronics, sporting equipment, and so on. If you don't have an inventory of these items, do one immediately. Even if you don't sell out and go, you'll need it to collect your insurance if your home burns down or is robbed.

Now add in the present worth of valuables, including jewelry, Oriental rugs, guns, sterling silver and china, antiques, artwork, furs, and collectibles of all kinds. Again, if you have no idea of their value, have them appraised and inventoried immediately. You'll need a professional appraisal to sell them at the best price. And if you plan to keep them, you'll need an appraisal before insuring them to take with you or to leave behind in storage.

The Debt Ledger

This is the tough part. Just when you thought you were riding high, you start listing your obligations. They include the balance due on your home mortgage, unpaid taxes, the unpaid balance on the cars and RV, the full balance due (not the monthly payment) on all credit cards, and the balance due on any other loans.

Don't forget any lump-sum expenditures that are coming up, such as a balloon payment, maturing of an auto lease, annual real estate taxes, college tuition, or insurance premiums.

If you have any debts to your broker, such as a margin account, list them too. If you have debts in partnership with someone else, don't forget them. If, for example, you have co-signed a note with one of your children or have made bail for someone, you'll have that hanging over you until it is paid off or resolved. No matter how well intentioned you or the other party is, something could go awry.

You're now ready to subtract the little number from the big one to find out whether you're ahead of the game, and how far. Once you've looked over the figures, you'll be better equipped to decide whether to sell the house or keep it, to use your available funds to pay off the RV or to keep making payments, or to sell the Oriental rugs and keep the coin collection.

You can start making decisions about which assets to roll over, which to sell now (consider the tax consequences), and which to convert into assets that will contribute more income, more security, or more growth potential.

When you're on the road full time, it can be harder (and a lot less fun since you'll have better things to do) to shift your funds constantly to squeeze another ¼ percent interest out of a CD or to keep abreast of the stock market. The time to strategize is now. And that process begins with knowing just where on the great fiduciary treadmill of life you are trotting at this moment.

Keep reassessing your goals, your changes and chances, your pleasures, your future. Keep learning, searching, growing. Go. Do. Enjoy.

THREE

Fulltimer Case Histories

It's always useful to read about how others have handled something you are contemplating. Here are some case histories of fulltimers who were kind enough to share their stories and secrets with us. Names and some details have been altered, but the stories are true. Once on the road, you'll hear dozens of absorbing, inspiring stories from people who have paved the way before you. In fact, swapping yarns around the campfire—especially yarns about where you came from and how you got into fulltiming—is one of the best things about life on the go.

RV travelers are among the finest folks anywhere. To become one of them, especially full time, is a privilege and a joy. We hope you'll be lucky enough to run across people like those whose stories are told below.

Cliff and Marie

Aged 58 and 60, Cliff and Marie live in an 8-year-old motorhome, tow a Jeep Cherokee, and have a combined annual income from their investments of about $50,000. They do all their own maintenance except for changing tires and the computer work on engine controls. Each year, they travel 10,000–15,000 miles, returning to the same clinic for their annual physical checkups.

Advances in technology have benefited them, as they have most fulltimers. They rely exclusively on electronic banking and bill paying, have satellite TV reception, use a cell phone with a monthly plan that has no long distance or roaming fees, and keep in touch with their families by cell phone and e-mail. "Things get easier for mobile folks every year," Cliff enthuses.

George

George is single, 47 years old, and works for a company that pays him $75,000 a year as a traveling consultant and trainer. The job meshes perfectly with his life as a full-timer, living in a class A motorhome with washer, dryer, and a motorcycle carrier. He does most of his own maintenance, gets his mail at a post office box in his home-town, and travels 15,000–20,000 miles a year, rarely staying more than a week in each spot.

He is techno-savvy but prefers to pay bills by mail, and he uses a debit card for cash and groceries. He uses e-mail for work but not for personal correspondence. "Living and working in an RV is an 11 on a scale of 1–10," he finds.

Jerry and Eileen

After camping with their five children, Jerry and Eileen knew they liked the informal-ity of the RV lifestyle. Three years before Jerry planned to retire, they began plotting their Great Getaway. In October of the third year, their house on Long Island sold; in November, they bought a late-model 32-foot Winnebago; and by 6:00 P.M. on Decem-ber 20 they had hit the road, ready for their January retirement. The last we heard, they were still fulltiming and loving the RV life.

Costs? Jerry says that "like many Americans, we spend every penny we make," so they use their $28,500 annual retirement income for all it's worth. Jerry started draw-ing social security at 62, adding $9,600 to their income, but at 51, Eileen still has some years to go before she can collect social security.

Proceeds from the house paid for the motorhome, finished paying for the five kids' college educations, and were invested in a duplex that is just breaking even as a rental property. Among their expenses are $1,200 a year to insure their RV and car; life insurance at $275 per year; and $110 monthly on phone bills. They've also built a retirement cottage in the foothills of the Catskills in anticipation of the time when they decide to give up fulltiming.

Harry and Teddi

With their fourteen-month-old daughter, Harry and Teddi started fulltiming two years after they began planning, liquidating Harry's business, and consolidating. They went fulltiming not *despite* having a child but largely *because of* her.

"Day care (for children) doesn't make sense to me," says Harry. "All that effort is put into creating a child, and then during their most formative years they are turned over to someone else to raise. I understand that 80 percent of all learning is done in the first three years of life. If this is correct, then we do not want someone else teaching our child the basics of humanity."

The couple bought an older motorhome and set out to see if three people could live in a 200-square-foot domicile. They say that they managed, "by unloading everything that we could not carry with us," to get the payload aboard their rolling home down to about 1,500 pounds, which Harry finds "a most economical way to live." He says, happily, "our passion is travel and the unknown."

David and Francie

Ask Francie what turned her and her husband into fulltimers, and she replies, "grass cutting and home maintenance." After David retired, the couple traveled extensively but had to keep coming home to take care of the house and yard. The more they worked at it, the more they hated it. So one day they put the house on the market, and suddenly they were on the road full time.

Francie couldn't bear to part with the belongings of a lifetime, so many of their things were passed along to the kids or put in storage. "Our original plan was to full-time it for a year, then buy another house on the lake or beach," Francie says. But after one year they decided to try another year, then another. The last we heard, they were still fulltiming.

One of the low points came when David had a heart attack and ended up in an intensive care unit, leaving Francie to live alone in the RV. "It took me three hours to do a thirty-minute job," she says in describing the first time she had to do the hooking and unhooking. Her stories, though, are heartwarming. The hospital invited her to stay in its own RV lot, which had full hookups. People appeared out of nowhere to help her hook up and to get the car off the dolly she was towing. "I love them to this day," she says.

The happy ending is that David had bypass surgery, recovered fully, and went back on the road. "We have never looked back," says Francie.

David and Francie cite among their best investments their membership in Coast to Coast (CTC) Resorts (see chapter 16, Home, Sweet Campground, for details). They use member campgrounds almost exclusively, except in state or national parks or when they are in areas that have no CTC resorts, so their camping costs average only about $100 monthly. They have a debit card with their broker and get most of their cash through a nationwide ATM card. Their biggest expense, reports Francie, is fuel because they stay on the go, spending a week here and a week there. (About twice a year they get "home" to Tennessee to see the family, doctors, and dentists.) Their RV gets 7.3 miles per gallon; the little car they tow for sightseeing and errands gets 40 mpg.

Among their biggest problems they list getting quality repairs for the RV and car, finding dentists and doctors on the road, carrying too many clothes and shoes, and using public telephones. Like many fulltimers, they found cell phones too costly, although the wireless revolution is gradually changing all that.

The couple eat out at least four times a week, usually at lunchtime. Francie likes crockpot cooking and quick recipes. "When I cook in the RV, it's those good Southern dishes we can't get in restaurants: garlic-cheese grits soufflé, beans and cornbread, and gumbo," she says. Mail is forwarded via FedEx. "It's expensive but worth it," they say.

"My biggest advice to fulltimers is to make sure both partners can drive (the RV) and do every chore that needs to be done. I know many women who refuse to drive. Take it from someone who has been there, it may save your life or your spouse's," says Francie.

John and Barbara

As part-time campers, John and Barbara began easing into fulltiming with a slide-in camper mounted on the frame of a cargo van. One RV led to a larger one, and soon they had been fulltiming for five years and "enjoying every minute" in their 33-foot motorhome, towing a small truck.

Discovering that house payments would be little more than what they were paying to store their household goods, they bought a home in the hills of Texas. They can get by on $24,000 a year, which covers both their travel and about five months a year in their house. They too consider their CTC membership one of their best investments.

John and Barbara work part of each year, partly to earn extra funds and partly to "add spice" to their lives, John says. They recommend doing something in a field other than the one you were in before retirement. "There's comfort in knowing you only have to do whatever it is for a few months, and then continue on your way," they report.

They've been lucky with repairs. They are faithful about having the motorhome serviced on schedule and try to use factory-authorized repair locations for RV components. They're both in good health, and they get their medications by mail through the American Association of Retired Persons (AARP) pharmacy at discount prices. For their few medical emergencies they have used 24-hour walk-in clinics.

Mail hasn't been a problem; they know it will be slow, and they plan accordingly. They keep track of all their bills, so they know at once if one goes astray, and they prepay whenever possible.

Fran and Pete: Two Fulltimers Look Back

As former fulltimers, Fran and Pete rhapsodize about once again having a telephone, a mailbox, a porch, a small yard, and a full-size sink and stove. When fulltiming, they didn't purchase a cell phone because their daughter, who lived in a remote part of the United States, didn't get good reception. Like other fulltimers, they found that pay phones were a pain. "Use whatever phone cards are available, and pay," Fran advises. She found that it just wasn't worth it to jump through hoops and switch carriers constantly to save a few cents per minute.

As fulltimers, this couple's luxury was eating out four or five times a week. When she cooked in the RV, Fran favored pastas, green salads, and whole grains.

Kathleen and Marilyn

This is one of our favorite fulltimer case histories because Kathleen and Marilyn were the only mother–daughter fulltimer team we met. And what a dynamic duo they make!

Marilyn was a Chicago-area tax appraiser for eleven years; her daughter Kathleen, who lived in her own apartment in another Chicago suburb, was reaching burnout in her high-pressure career in police work. Her five children raised and her house too big, the widowed Marilyn phoned Kathy and suggested, "Why don't we go into business for ourselves?" Kathy's immediate reply: "I'll give notice at work tomorrow."

Marilyn, who was still in her 50s, and Kathy, just turned 30, began making plans. They wanted to see more of the country before settling down. Marilyn sold her house, Kathy gave up her apartment, both women put their furniture in storage, and they took off in their new, 27-foot Fleetwood motorhome.

Kathy is bright and bubbly; Marilyn is serene, unflappable, and practical. They left shivery Chicago in January, headed south toward Florida, and drove along the coast into Texas, following what Kathy calls "perpetual springtime." During the next seventeen months, they visited every national park in the United States, every province in Canada, and a few areas of Mexico.

How did the family take the news that the two were hitting the road? "My mother thought we were crazy," admits Marilyn. "But our friends were happy for us," remembers Kathy. "They knew it was the chance of a lifetime."

Adjusting to the new lifestyle was easier than either had hoped. Kathy did most of the driving, especially after Marilyn broke a foot in Oregon. Marilyn, who is a detail person, made a good navigator and planner.

Kathy, an amateur artist like her father, brought along her art equipment and cameras. Both women brought motor scooters. They also packed a sewing machine, an inflatable canoe, a typewriter, and "tons" of reading material.

They loved the RV lifestyle so much that they decided to buy a campground in the Great Smoky Mountains. Working twenty-hour days, seven days a week, they waded in. "I like cleaning," enthuses Kathy, "so I started in on the dust and dirt while Mom learned to run the cash register. The day after we arrived, school was out and the crowds arrived. We've been going gangbusters ever since."

Ellen and Les

Like many early retirees, Ellen and Les became "fed up" with jobs that had changed with the times and just weren't "fun" anymore. They fulltimed for two years in a truck-cum-camper before they bought a motorhome and became a one-vehicle family. "Our insurance costs went from $512 for the truck and camper to $360 for the motorhome, with better coverage," they wrote.

Newlyweds at ages 62 and 52, they have six children and three grandchildren between them, and they find that gifts for all the birthdays really add up. Still, they're able to save money while living on their combined pensions of about $26,400 annually. Fortunately, Les's pension includes COLAs (cost-of-living allowances) and medical-dental insurance, so they have few worries about inflation or the cost of treating an illness.

Campsite fees amount to very little thanks to campground memberships they bought at highly discounted resale prices and because they spend many nights in free boondocks campsites without hookups. (Look for information on discounted memberships in camping magazine ads or do an Internet search on "camping + membership + resale" to locate resale brokers.) To keep their battery fully charged while in the boonies, they have a solar panel that gives them 88 watts of juice in full sun.

"Problems? We haven't had any," they write.

"We left to get away from strange people, but they are out here too," they admit. "But, we've also made some of our closest friends while fulltiming. Everyone has a story to tell, and all are interesting."

Jim's Story

Jim wrote us from Texas with thoughtful advice, bright observations, and a wonderfully upbeat story he calls "Confessions of a Rookie Fulltimer: My First Year on the Road in the Old Soldier's Home on Wheels."

After twenty-five years of military service, Jim retired at the age of 47, not realizing that he would soon lose his wife to lupus. Unable to face life alone in a big house, he donated the furniture to charity, rented out the house, studied floor plans of several RVs, and ordered a brand-new 33-foot Itasca by phone. Six weeks later he was hooked on fulltiming.

Now both older and wiser, he has invaluable advice for would-be fulltimers. Military life had put Jim in a lot of large vehicles, but "nothing prepared me for the agonizing thrill of driving a 33-foot, 16,000-pound vehicle," he says. "The unexpected influence of wind currents on the steering was shocking."

He pored over the five pounds of reference material that came with his rig. "When all else fails, read the operator's manual," he advises. When he found one manual missing—the one for the dash radio—he called Winnebago, which sent it promptly. Without it, he couldn't set the clock radio.

In the driver's area of the cockpit alone Jim has twenty-nine controls plus a rearview closed-circuit TV monitor, a cell phone, and a CB radio. "The operator's manual effectively explained the proper function of each," he says.

"There is no substitute for experience when it comes to operating a motorhome," Jim says. He had minor problems at first, most of which were corrected by the dealer. One of his own additions is a Plexiglas shield on the wall next to the stovetop, which allows him to wipe off spatters easily.

On the road, he had antirock shocks installed, added an awning, and toured the factory where his RV had been made—a visit he recommends to everyone. After 10,000 miles he decided that he needed to tow a car, and he did extensive research into his options. "Four wheels down is the most cost-effective way to tow," he finds, but the dolly method is the most practical, as well as the one RV owners complain about most. More research is definitely needed, he says.

Costs? He spends $235 per month for long-term campsite rentals, $350 per month when on the go. Payments on the RV, food, telephone, and laundry add up to just over $1,700 monthly, not including maintenance, propane, storage, and medical expenses. There's also a big outlay for fuel, which is rising sharply.

Among his suggestions to motorcoach builders: add more wardrobe and bathroom space, bigger air conditioners, a curtain behind the driver for night driving, and water purification as standard equipment. Add leveling jacks to all class A motorhomes; offer telephone jacks as an option.

His advice to prospective fulltimers: the minimum size of the liveaboard RV should be 36 feet (we manage in 21 feet); stick to back roads to find the real America; keep the galley area carpet-free; try winter camping for special opportunities and challenges; and don't get an awning without a metal cover or it will unroll in highway winds.

"After a year on the road, fulltiming is not the dream I envisioned," Jim admits. "The decision to keep my house emerges as the best of the year." (We agree, not because we believe that fulltimers should keep their homes—we didn't, and we're glad—but because Jim had been newly widowed. He was wise not to burn all his bridges at once.)

"Freedom is not free," he concludes. "Fulltiming demands a high price in dollars and emotional expense . . . periods of highs, followed by lows, fueled by boredom and idleness." However, there is a happy ending: on the road Jim found a new traveling companion.

A Case of Case Histories

Each year we informally survey fulltimers who read our monthly column in *Family Motor Coaching* magazine and return a form provided. Membership in Family Motor Coach Association (FMCA) is open only to people who have motorhomes, not travel trailers or other types of RVs, so the survey doesn't represent all forms of RVing. Still, these fulltimers are seasoned road warriors who reveal a lot about the RV lifestyle.

In the 2000 survey, most of the 600 people represented by the 320 responses were twosomes, but 27 respondents, aged 41 to 78, traveled alone. One had been fulltiming for 48 years. The youngest were a couple aged 37 and 38 with a 10-year-old son, and the oldest was 90. The median age was 62. Forty-four were under age 50, nearly 200 were between the ages of 50 and 60, and 80 were over age 70.

One question asked whether fulltimers had ever been hassled when boondocking or dry camping (without hookups). Many had, to the point where they were disheartened. Most, however, including a 70-year-old woman who travels alone, had not. Many praised Flying J, Sam's Club, and Wal-Mart parking lots as free places to stay. (Some communities now prohibit overnight parking, by posting "No RV Parking" signs, even if the host, such as Wal-Mart, permits it.) One respondent reported that "too many inconsiderate RVers have ruined it for the rest of us," and 28 said that it was getting harder each year to find free, safe camping. Many noted that they rarely dry camped, and a few were hostile to the idea of "freeloading."

Two dozen of the respondents had new motorhomes, chiefly because they wanted to trade up to a model with one or more slide-outs, where one or more portions of the body slide out when parked to increase interior space. The oldest RV listed was a 1941 model, but the writer was about to replace it with a 1952 unit. Many reported that they traded regularly every two, five, or ten years. Most others said that they would trade when they found something they liked better, but one of the biggest reasons why these fulltimers were hanging on to an RV was that they just couldn't face "getting the bugs out of a new one and customizing it our way." Two dozen said they would never replace their present coaches.

Four said they would replace their coaches "when they win the lottery," and some fulltimers said that they religiously changed coaches every 50,000 miles or so, although one commented, "Our 23-year-old bus conversion is up to 500,000 miles and we expect it to go to two million." A few were thinking of getting a smaller RV, not a larger one, to save on fuel, or for easier handling.

Incomes were as low as just over $8,000 a year for a lone fulltimer who said that was enough for his needs. Thirteen members reported incomes of $100,000 and over, and one as high as $800,000. Many supplemented their incomes with full- or part-time jobs, and others dipped into savings as necessary. Of the seven respondents whose income was $18,000 a year, two said that amount was marginal, a single and two couples said that it wasn't enough, and two couples found it adequate.

Of the 110 respondents with incomes of $36,000 a year and less, mostly couples, most wished for more income. A few were emphatic about "getting by just fine," but others said that they had to work along the way, do without, or stick to a strict budget. Only those respondents who earned $60,000 a year and up reported that they really had enough to meet their needs. Even so, some of them reported concerns about inflation, unexpected bills, or other setbacks.

Some fulltimers reported that they did none of their own maintenance, but most did 90–100 percent of the fixing and cleaning themselves. A 71-year-old woman who travels alone does 90 percent of her maintenance and is taking courses so that she can do more. An 82-year-old woman does everything but major engine work.

While this 2000 survey was informal and unofficial—and anonymous, except for the 10 percent who gave their names and addresses—it's clear that fulltiming is highly satisfying, doable at almost any income level, and attracts people of all ages.

FOUR

The Cost of RV Living

It is surprising how often we are asked how much it costs to "get by" when you live in an RV. We usually counter with another question: "How much does it cost to live in a house?" Immediately, people realize the complexity of the question and the impossibility of giving pat, bottom-line answers.

The full cost of RV life can't be gauged in advance, any more than you can tell, right now, what it will cost to live for the next few years on a farm or in a co-op apartment. You can't predict whether you'll have a medical disaster, a sudden need for gum surgery, or a family emergency that throws all your plans into a cocked hat. Nor can you measure the cost of missed career opportunities or income lost because you chose early retirement.

Other fulltimers can tell you what they spend, but their figures have little meaning for you if your needs or standards are different. We know people who are happy if they have five dollars in their jeans, and others who wouldn't consider fulltiming until they had $100,000 in the bank. You can live in a modest RV or a rolling mansion, eat hamburger or high on the hog, save your pennies or play the ponies. We all have our own ideas about what is luxury and rock-bottom necessity, emergency and economy, splurge and sensible.

What You Spend Now

To project *your* actual fulltiming costs, first determine your current living expenses. Make a list of weekly, monthly, and yearly expenditures; you need to know where your money goes now and what will change when you go fulltiming.

List everything on your worksheet, including those expenses that are sure to stop after you start fulltiming. Work from the top of your head, thinking it through day by day. Then use credit card bills, check stubs, receipts, and other records to fine-tune the list as accurately as possible.

Weekly: List here everything you buy in a week, such as groceries, bus fare, church donations, lunches, lottery tickets, newspapers, magazines, fuel, Friday night bowling, or Sunday dinner in a restaurant.

Monthly: This list should include time payments of all kinds, credit card bills, utilities, rent or mortgage, child support, and so on.

Yearly: These expenses include insurance, annual medical checkups, maintenance contracts, dental care, eyeglasses, subscriptions, dues, and Christmas and birthday gifts.

Continuing Costs

When your list is finished, mark those expenses that are unlikely to change when you go fulltiming, such as life and health insurance, clothing and linens, magazines and newspapers, church contributions, care of a parent, medicines and eyeglasses, family gift occasions, dentistry, veterinary care, time payments (cemetery lots, credit card debt, college loans), greens fees, club dues, alimony and child support, and food.

Add 5 percent to your food bill. When you are fulltiming, you'll buy smaller, less economical quantities, and you'll probably eat out more often. You also may not always find the most economical supermarkets. If your food bill is now low because you do a lot of gardening and home canning, add 10 percent or more to your projections.

Don't be too quick to cross out expenses you think will be left behind. For example, you'll probably still have utility costs. Electricity is extra at some campgrounds. In monthly or annual site rentals you may have your own meter. When you dry camp, you'll have the expense of maintaining and fueling a generator.

Telephone charges may be higher than before, especially if you have a cell phone. You'll be buying your own propane for cooking and heating and even paying for sewage in the form of dump stations or full hookups. Water is usually the only free utility in the roaming life, and sometimes you even have to pay for it.

Current expenses that may stop when you hit the road include mortgage payments, home insurance and maintenance, a second car, lunches at work, commuting, and business clothes. However, if you're financing the RV, payments can be as much as house payments, perhaps even more. If you tow a car or boat with your RV, or use a car or truck to tow a travel trailer, you'll continue to have expenses for a second vehicle.

New Expenses

By making a few phone calls you can come up with a lot of projections, even if your plans are still hypothetical. Call a bank and ask what monthly payments would be on an $80,000 RV for five years or a $100,000 RV for ten years. Get a quote from your insurance agent on all the policies you'll need for an RV, its contents, and its tow vehicle. Get quotes from a couple of mail forwarding services. Check into monthly costs for a cell phone with nationwide roaming, an answering service, a pager, an Internet service provider, and satellite TV service.

Now list other new expenses: coin laundries at $8–$10 a week, management fees if you intend to rent out your house, furniture storage, legal fees if someone is managing your business or affairs back home, and the special expenses, discussed below, associated with life aboard.

Energy and Fuel

You'll need a generator for when you're camping without hookups (dry camping). To estimate your fuel costs, calculate how many gallons your generator burns per hour, then multiply that by the number of hours per day you'll be running it—say, twelve; that's how many gallons of fuel you'll use per day. Our 3.5 kilowatt generator burns 3.5 gallons of gasoline per hour. Your fuel costs will also depend on the size of your generator and what type of fuel it uses. If you travel in cold climates and run a gas furnace, your costs will be much higher.

To estimate traveling fuel costs, work out several travel scenarios. For example, if you drive 10,000 miles a year in an RV that gets 8 miles per gallon and buy fuel at $1.50–$1.60 per gallon, your fuel costs will be about $2,000 a year (10,000 ÷ 8 × 1.60 = $2,000).

Add costs for oil and other fluids; the driver's manual will tell you how many quarts are needed after how many miles.

"Rent"

Campground fees can vary from almost nothing to $60 or more per night. Many full-timers bless the day they bought a membership in one of the nationwide camping resort chains. Memberships can involve an initial investment of $5,000 or more, but it's a lifetime deal that entitles you to camp in any member campground for only a few dollars per night. For more on camping resorts, see chapter 16, Home, Sweet Campground.

Before investing in a resort membership or a condo campsite, read the contract very carefully and be sure the deal is for you—financially, geographically, and socially.

Campground discounts go with membership in almost any of the camping clubs (see chapter 16, Home, Sweet Campground for details). KOA (Kampgrounds of America), among others, has its own membership discount card. Senior citizens receive widespread discounts, including for camping in state and national parks. Ask as you go, especially if you're age 50 or over or are a member of AARP.

We suggest that you try lots of different options your first year; by then you should have a better idea of what kinds of campgrounds best suit your fulltimer lifestyle. You may find that you want the luxury and security of a full-facility camping resort, or you may find yourself seeking out the most remote, primitive campsites, far from the nearest neighbors and free of charge. For now, minimize nightly costs by taking weekly or monthly rates, staying in free or very inexpensive state and county parks, parking here and there with friends and relatives, or working by the season in a campground that gives you a free site in exchange for doing chores.

Maintenance and Repairs

Costs for RV care and repair are a huge question mark. You may be lucky enough not to have accidents or catastrophic failures; if you can do routine maintenance yourself

What RVers Spend

Retirees

According to the Bureau of Labor Statistics, the average retired couple spends their money as follows:

Food:	29.3%
Housing (RV, campsite):	33.6%*
Transportation:	8.9%*
Clothing:	4.7%
Personal care:	2.9%
Medical care:	9.8% (but rising)
Other family needs:	4.6%
Other:	6.2%

*To stick to this guideline, the total cost of RV, campsites, tow car or taxis, fuel, and repairs should equal the sum of these two, or 42.5%.

If you have a net monthly income of $1,500, your monthly budget according to the formula above would break down as follows:

Food:	$439.50
RV, fuel, campsite, supplies, repairs:	$637.50**
Clothing:	$70.50
Personal care:	$43.50
Medical, dental, optical:	$147
Other family needs:	$69
Other:	$93

**From this, also contribute to the reserve fund mentioned above.

If your net monthly income is $2,000, your monthly budget might look more like this:

Food:	$586
RV, fuel, campsite, supplies, repairs:	$850
Clothing:	$94
Personal care:	$58
Medical, dental, optical:	$196
Other family needs:	$92
Other:	$124

Keep in mind that these figures apply to retirees, not fulltimer families who are educating children, caring for elderly parents, completing their own education, or taking a sabbatical before returning to careers.

(continued on page 24)

(continued from page 23)

Part-Timers

Here is what one couple told us they spent during a recent 16-month RV experience. They were on sabbatical, so this was a temporary getaway and not a way of life they planned to pursue indefinitely. If it had been, they might have traveled more slowly and spent less money. We have separated their figures into three categories: yearly expenses, monthly expenses, and one-time costs. Their annual costs totaled about $1,300 for insurances, licenses, and once-a-year fees. Unplanned purchases (not counting emergencies or repairs over which they had no control) totaled just over $1,200 for the entire 16 months.

They also had the following average monthly costs, rounded off to within $5.

Other insurances (including health):	$325
Campsites:	$155
Cell phone:	$90
Food and drink (groceries):	$450
Food and drink (restaurants):	$200
Fuel—engine, generator, propane:	$260
Laundry:	$15
Mail forwarding:	$15
Maintenance, repairs:	$105
Maps, guidebooks:	$125
Personal storage unit:	$55
Postage, stationery, postcards:	$35
Sightseeing, entertainment:	$80
Unplanned purchases, fees, tolls:	$100

Totals: $2,010 per month; plus $1,300 per year; plus $1,200 for one-time expenses (over the 16-month trip).

The couple reported that they could have spent more for campsites but chose to dry camp much of the time. They could have spent less for sightseeing, entertainment, and restaurants but considered them to be an important part of the travel experience. One of their biggest surprises was the cost of maps and guidebooks, but they considered these expenses important to their travel experience too.

They found a great range of fuel costs around the country, with more than a dollar per gallon difference between one area and another.

They used pay phones at first but changed to a cell phone and a one-rate plan. They found that many expenses, including food, restaurants, insurances, and entertainment, were about the same in fulltiming as in their home-based budget.

Most fulltimers will also have expenses that this couple didn't mention, such as gifts, dues and memberships, church and charity, hobbies, souvenirs or photography, towing a car, and regular obligations such as a retirement plan, prescriptions, medical and dental care, eye exams and other health care expenses that usually are not covered by insurance. They also didn't mention whether they had to make payments on an annuity or on disability or long-term health care insurance, whether they had to make time-sensitive payments of any kind, or whether they had to support an elderly parent or a child in college.

Their mail forwarding costs seem low, but they didn't specify whether they did most of their correspondence and bill paying online. They weren't fulltiming long enough to have to replace consumables such as clothing, towels, bed linens, and start batteries (for the engine) and house batteries (for 12-volt lights, TV, etc.). Things eventually wear out or break down, often requiring major expenditures. Still, their experience is an interesting one that gives plenty of food for thought.

(changing the oil, cleaning, etc.), it should cost very little. If you have to pay for every little service and your RV proves to be a lemon, your savings will melt away in mere months.

We recommend adding an amount equal to 5–10 percent of the value of the vehicle to a reserve fund each year. As the RV ages and its needs accelerate, you'll need these reserves for major replacements: upholstery, generator overhauls, engine and transmission work, and so on. As long as you don't need these reserves, they will continue to grow toward the day when you need really major repairs or a newer or larger RV. Some years you may hardly draw on the account all. Nevertheless, continue adding to it at a steady rate because time will inevitably take its toll.

Entertainment and Admissions

Estimating expenses for entertainment and admissions is pure guesswork, and the sky is the limit. A couple of days at Disney World or a few days' ski lift tickets can cost $300 or more per couple.

Even if you're a careful spender, the travel life demands certain expenses—museums, attractions, theme parks, restaurants, guided tours, guidebooks, maps, and the like. Presumably, the reason you're traveling is to see and do things, and some of the best things in life, such as a whitewater trip down the New River, or a helicopter tour of the Grand Canyon, aren't free.

Workamper News

If you want to start fulltiming but need to work for a living, subscribe to *Workamper News,* a print and electronic newsletter that matches up RV travelers with jobs throughout North America. Most jobs are temporary or seasonal, which gives you the freedom to travel, and most include a free campsite. Contact information: 201 Hiram Road, Heber Springs, AR 72543; 501-362-2637; info@workamper.com; www.workamper.com.

As much as we'd like to give you definite answers, nobody can tell you how far your dollars will go, literally or figuratively. Full-time life on the go is as unpredictable, as cheap, or as expensive as your life has always been but infinitely more rewarding than the *things* money can buy. When you're living out your dreams, experiencing the joy of travel, you're creating a bank account's worth of memories that no one can ever take away from you.

The total cost of fulltiming begins on your first visit to an RV showroom and ends on the day you sell your coach. If you start out with a new, paid-up RV and all new soft goods, it could be years before serious refurbishing and replacements have to be budgeted for. If you stay on the road long enough, however, you can have huge, expensive surprises, such as when you need a new generator, transmission, or refrigerator, or new upholstery or tires. Eventually, you'll probably need a new rig.

Only when your fulltiming days are over and you have sold the RV at whatever profit or loss can you put a dollar figure on the entire experience. But who cares? You will have pocketed uncounted riches in good times and new friends.

FIVE

Where's Home?

M ost fulltimers find it easier to select one state as a home base where they can vote, pay taxes, license their RV, and renew their driver's licenses. But creative planning can greatly reduce fulltiming costs; as long as you live nowhere in particular, you can "live" wherever you can get the best deal. The truly stateless fulltimer can use several addresses to maximize benefits and minimize costs.

To avoid paying state income tax, look into mail forwarding services based in states that have no such tax. When their address becomes your address, their tax haven becomes your tax haven (see chapter 11, Keeping in Touch).

Health insurance rates are determined by your home address as well as by your age, state of health, groups you belong to (such as a professional organization or union) that qualify you for group rates, and the size of your deductible or co-payment. It's an enormous puzzle that you can sort out by visiting insurance offices or searching the Internet using the key words "health insurance quote." If you're retired from the military or are an honorably discharged veteran of any age, many benefits apply, and they are portable throughout the United States and its possessions. So are Medicare benefits, but not all Medicare supplemental policies.

The rates you pay to insure your RV and other vehicles are also determined by your home address, and it's very possible that the cheapest place for health care is not the cheapest for highway insurance. Also determined by your "home" address are state and local income taxes, inheritance taxes, and the cost of licensing the RV yearly.

States that have no sales tax, such as Alaska, Delaware, Montana, New Hampshire, and Oregon, are good places to begin a fulltiming life because you can save hundreds of dollars by buying your RV in one of them. Contrast this with a state that has a 7 percent sales tax, where you'd pay an additional $10,500 on a motorhome priced at $150,000.

Even if you *buy* the RV in a no-tax state, though, you'll have to pay the tax if you *register* it in a state that does have sales tax. As long as you're on the go and can keep the rig licensed in a no-tax state, you're ahead of the game, but if you start putting down roots, it's just a matter of time until you get nailed and have to pay up. Meanwhile, the RV continues to depreciate, so the day may come when you're better off registering it in a sales-tax state and paying the taxes on the RV's current value, which is substantially less than it cost new.

Nevada, New Jersey, and Rhode Island have the highest *state* sales tax rates, but the total bite in a given locale may be far higher because of additional city and county levies. In Florida, for example, the state sales tax is 6 percent, which can be hiked another 1 percent by county option. In addition, some counties, such as Volusia County (Daytona Beach), have fuel taxes of 5 cents per gallon.

At one time, we licensed our RV in one state and our boat in another, bought health insurance in a third, and paid income taxes in a fourth. We were truly homeless and used many different addresses to different advantages. While summering in one state we opened a bank account there, but we yanked it out quickly when we started getting state income tax bills for the interest earned. If you open a bank or brokerage account in any state that has an inheritance tax and your partner dies, you may have to pay taxes on half of the assets even if you earned 100 percent of them.

We never rented a safe-deposit box without first learning whether it would be sealed if one of us died. Some state regulations require the freezing of bank accounts and the sealing of safe-deposit boxes if one signatory dies. Before opening any account, ask lots of questions.

However, too much finagling with different addresses can land you in trouble with the government and could void your insurance coverage, too. It's a felony to misrepresent your address when voting, for example, so once you have selected one legal address, you're on thin ice if you claim others to suit your own purposes.

Local, county, and state taxes and fees can change constantly, depending on the whim of politicians, whose appetites seem insatiable. So juggling your addresses requires careful study and constant vigilance. Taxes change, and so does your personal situation, depending on the source of your income, your age, your net worth, and any emergency help you might need from state agencies.

Some states have lower taxes but charge higher fees for licenses and services such as vehicle inspections. And some states seem generous while you're alive but will torque your spouse for inheritance taxes on half of your jointly owned RV and savings if you die.

Some tax angles to investigate:

Senior citizen benefits. Once you're 65, your state income tax might be reduced.

Source tax. Some states are now reaching out beyond their borders to tax pensions earned in that state. This is one you may not be able to outrun.

Inheritance and estate taxes. You may have to pay tax on inherited assets (including, in some cases, your half of your own motorhome if you and your spouse owned it jointly, as well as joint bank and brokerage accounts). Not all states charge inheritance taxes, and the federal tax rules have recently undergone some changes. See a tax advisor about how to pass some of your wealth along to your heirs tax free.

Personal property tax. More insidious than a one-time sales tax, some states charge a personal property tax that must be paid each year on the worth of such things as household furnishings, collectibles, keepsakes, and other valuables, including your wedding rings.

Intangible assets tax. Certain assets are taxed yearly in some states. Florida, for example, has no income tax but will tax you yearly on the value of stocks, mutual funds, accounts receivable, and certain other holdings according to what they were worth on December 31 of the previous year—regardless of their worth at the time the tax is due. This complicated tax has snagged many an unwary retiree with a large stock portfolio.

For optimal tax avoidance, it isn't enough just to pick a state known for its low per capita taxes. You should try to find the one that charges least according to your own needs, source of income, net worth, age, and changing circumstances.

Tax avoidance is, of course, only part of the fulltiming picture. Most of us choose a home base first for personal considerations, such as having family nearby, or familiarity with a region. Other considerations are climate, crime rate, cost of living, availability of good medical care, cultural amenities, and leisure activities.

Look for annual retirement guides that rate areas for these advantages. Find them in any bookstore. A reference librarian can also help you find the most recent articles in retirement and financial magazines on state taxes and retirement havens. The Internet is also a good resource for online articles and state-by-state searches.

Down to Brass Tacks

Bookstores offer many books on the best places to retire, raise children, or find "quality" life, but we are all different. It may be impossible to find a rating for the exact combination of climate, health care, schools, taxes, and career opportunities that will determine your choice of a home base.

According to the May 2001 issue of *Bloomberg Personal Finance* magazine, for example, New Hampshire has many tax advantages, but it ranks a dismal thirty-seventh for retirees because it taxes interest and dividends, which seniors rely on for much of their income. Louisiana ranks second in the nation for retirees because it exempts all social security and public pension income, as well as the first $6,000 of private pension income, from state income taxes.

According to the article, the ten best states for retirees are Alabama, Alaska, Delaware, Florida, Louisiana, Mississippi, Nevada, Tennessee, Washington, and Wyoming. The ten worst are Connecticut, Kansas, Maine, Minnesota, Montana, Nebraska, New York, Rhode Island, Vermont, and Wisconsin.

Things change with the political winds, of course. Florida continues to phase out its intangible assets tax, the state of Georgia sends state funds to some communities to provide local property tax relief to seniors, and Oklahoma has replaced its value-based vehicle tax with a flat fee based on the age of the vehicle. That could be good news for some fulltimers but bad news for others.

Even though you can park your RV anywhere you choose and may never even see your home-base state, choosing an official address still depends on whether you are retired or working, whether state inheritance taxes will affect your spouse if you die, whether your income comes from pensions or stock dividends, and much more. The more homework you do, and the more questions you ask along the way, the more you'll be able to make informed choices.

Six

Making
the
Break

As one man commented to a friend who was about to step off the tenth floor into an open elevator shaft, "Watch that first step. It's a big one."

The decision to leave behind a conventional house and belongings to become a homeless wanderer is not unlike taking that ten-story jump. In the process of leaping off the edge, there may be missteps, blunders, and stumbles.

Which possessions should you keep? sell? give away? As you begin your pullout, what do you tell your family, your neighbors, your closest friends—and when?

Three hackneyed expressions make excellent advice:

- Don't burn your bridges.
- Don't go away mad.
- Make your words sweet because you may have to eat them later.

For many people, the big decision to go fulltiming comes at a pivotal time of life, such as retirement, graduation, marriage, divorce, or when the last child marries or goes away to college. We met one couple who went fulltiming because they'd lost everything they owned in a house fire and were forced to make a new start immediately.

For us, things evolved very slowly and thoughtfully. There was no great, beckoning opportunity, such as winning the lottery. Nor did any significant milestone enable or prevent our breakaway.

31

Gordon was decades away from retirement or pension, so money would be a problem. On the other hand, we hadn't suffered any precipitating cataclysms. In some ways this made things easier for us because the timetable was ours. In other ways it was harder because, like everyone else, we found it easy to procrastinate and difficult to give up possessions, old habits, and hard-won careers.

Our first decision was that we wanted our parting with Gordon's job to be a happy one. We liked the company and are still friends with many of his former coworkers. We were fond of our neighbors too and wanted to sell our home to nice people for their sake. Gordon gave three months' notice at work, allowing plenty of time for the company to replace him.

Keep in mind that we were still in our early thirties. We were sure we'd have to get jobs again when our meager savings were gone, so we wanted the transition to be smooth and amicable.

Because our families lived elsewhere, we decided to break all our bonds with Danville, Illinois, where we were living at the time, and sell out completely. However, you may prefer to leave more doors ajar, with the hope of returning to your hometown someday.

Some options (check with an accountant; circumstances vary):

- Sell the house at a profit and make a tax-free exchange for an RV.
- Sell the house at a profit and take the capital-gains exclusion available to homeowners.
- Get rid of the house, even if you must take a loss, so you'll be totally free.
- Rent or lease the house. Its value will probably keep up with inflation better than most other investments you could make. However, look carefully into the cost of landlord insurance, professional management while you're away, and income tax pluses and minuses. (In Florida, where every householder gets a $25,000 homestead exemption plus added exemptions for a handicap or widowhood, taxes on a modest-size home would double if you moved out and renters moved in.)
- Let the house stand empty, which means you can use it any time you like. However, you'll also have the expense of upkeep, insurances, taxes, and security. Be certain the house is well protected and looks lived in while you're gone. Otherwise, the insurance company may claim "abandonment" and refuse to pay a claim if the house is robbed or vandalized.

If you sell your house, you'll no longer have to worry about mortgage payments, skyrocketing local taxes, tenants who run off without paying, repairs, insurance, vandalism, or coming home to find that some sharp politician has sneaked through a variance that rezoned your neighborhood as a toxic-waste site.

We met one couple who were having a wonderful winter in Mexico when they heard from a former neighbor that their tenants had moved out, leaving the house a shambles. They had to leave their RV, fly home, make major repairs to the house, and find new tenants. It took three awful, expensive, frustrating months. Let's take a closer look at making one of the biggest decisions of your fulltiming life.

To Sell or to Keep

Only you can decide whether to sell the house now or keep it for the time when you want to settle down again. Make your own list of pros and cons, never forgetting the "primary residence" rule, which could make a big difference if you rent out the house for the next few years and then sell at a huge profit.

Why to Sell Now

■ You can figure the house money into your whole financial picture. Set your own agenda for selling the house and furnishings before you leave town, while you're still in control.

■ The money will be in your bank account, not tied up in real estate. Property values in your area could drop.

■ You won't have to worry about maintenance, mowing the lawn, rental management fees, taxes, repairs, vandalism, insurances, and tenants that skip town owing you money.

■ As a full-time roamer with ample time to sample a great many climates and communities, you might find a region where you'd rather live if and when you settle down.

■ It's a psychological thing. You're determined to succeed at fulltiming, and you fear that you may not be able to resist the pull of a home and garden waiting for you.

Why to Keep the House

■ RVs rarely increase in value, but houses usually do. Take a big mortgage at today's low interest rates and let renters make the payments. Meanwhile, you'll get the tax deduction for interest, taxes, maintenance, and repairs.

■ Will the house bring in more in rent, even after allowing for expenses and repairs, than you'd get by putting the money in T-bills or CDs at today's interest rates?

■ This is your home. Even if all the neighbors and every family member moves away while you're gone, you'll come back here someday.

■ It's too much to leave your home and hometown all at once. Hang the tax consequences; you'll fulltime for a trial period and then decide what to do next.

■ You may be one of those lucky people who can afford to keep the house and furnishings intact, fully insured and maintained, to come back to any time you choose.

To Sell or Not to Sell

We don't claim to be advisors on taxes or legal matters, but we do know that it's important to get expert advice if you are selling your house and using the profits to bankroll a life of full-time RV travel. If you sell out at a big profit, capital-gains taxes may take a big bite out of your grubstake if you don't do things right.

You can claim an exclusion of $250,000 if you're single or $500,000 if you're married and filing jointly *if the home has been your primary residence*. It gets more complicated if you are divorced or divorcing, are newly widowed and the house was in the name of your deceased spouse, are married but file separately, or previously claimed an exception when single or married to someone else. Remember the words "primary residence."

If you own two homes, you can claim the exclusion only if the house you are selling was your principal residence for a total of at least twenty-four months out of the last five years that you owned the place. If this is the address where you vote, get mail, and pay taxes, you have a strong case. Also counted is any time spent in a nursing facility, but time spent in your RV or your beach house doesn't count. You also get credit toward the twenty-four months if you're separated but still own the house occupied by the spouse you're divorcing.

Things get more complicated if you're recently widowed and your spouse's name was on the deed. Selling the house in the tax year of your spouse's death or waiting until the next year could make all the difference, depending on how long you lived in the house and how long you were married to the homeowner.

State taxes also should be considered in your decision, so go to an advisor who knows both federal and state law. Even if you don't qualify for the capital-gains break, consider the difference between quitting your job this year and selling out next year, after you have retired and are in a lower tax bracket. Collect all the paperwork and start a file that contains the closing statement showing the total purchase cost of the property, including closing costs. Save receipts for all costs and capital improvements related to the home. A good tax advisor can lead you through the drill. You can also go to the IRS Web site, www.irs.gov, and download publication no. 523, *Selling Your Home*. It is a guide to the records you'll need and when to sell.

To Sell or to Store?

We kept only a few family heirlooms and some antiques Gordon had restored to showcase condition. We had happy memories of starting our marriage with nothing and then saving, dollar by dollar, to buy the things we had accumulated. We knew that someday, when and if we settled down again in a house or apartment, it would be just as much fun the second time around.

When you sell out completely, you have the money in hand to spend on today's fun. You'll be free to settle down again according to your new ideas about location, decor, furnishings, and neighborhood. If you sell all the furniture, you don't have to worry about storage costs, fire, deterioration, changing fashions, and mildew.

The Sellout

We allowed six months for our home to sell, but a lot will depend on your neighborhood and on the economy in your area. We did learn that it pays to shop around for a

Realtor who will work for less than standard commissions. Interviewing several agencies, we bargained for lower commissions, a higher advertising budget, and other promotional gimmicks, such as how many open houses would be held. The result was that our house sold in only a few weeks.

We were glad we hadn't signed with the first Realtor we talked to. Play it cool and create your own timetable. If you mention to a close friend that you're thinking about selling out to go live in an RV, and she tells her Realtor friend, you soon will be under siege. Remember, *you* are in control.

When the house went on the market, we began running newspaper ads for a few of our largest, least-used items. We didn't want to denude the house too soon because the Realtor had told us that fully furnished homes sell more readily. By advertising only a few things at a time, we avoided being overwhelmed by phone calls, dealers, and the merely curious. We sold some extra furniture, the second car, the slide projector, and other specialty items through individual ads, showing the items by appointment only.

As soon as we had a contract on the house, we began going through the inventory that filled ten rooms, a basement, the attic, and a 2½-car garage, in inverse order to our need for each item. Guest room furniture went first. Then hobby equipment; the extra freezer, the largest shop tools, the dining room furniture, and the living room furniture. Last to go were the washer and dryer, kitchen appliances, and our bedroom furniture.

Finally the time came when we had to open the floodgates. During the final weeks we had massive weekend garage sales. If you're not a yard sale follower, attend a few to get an idea of how they work. The most common mistake for neophytes is to price things too low. Forget what you paid for an item back in the 1960s or 1970s. While some of it is now worthless junk, other things are worth much more than you paid.

Be forewarned that garage sale stalwarts can overwhelm you unless you stand firm. People started ringing our doorbell the night before each sale; others showed up for a 9 A.M. sale at dawn. Fortunately, we were able to price our things, arrange them in the garage, and keep the door locked until our advertised sale hours.

This is a nerve-racking period in your life, so try to keep calm. Provide crowd control, if possible, by confining the sale to the garage, porch, or a roped-off section of yard. Lock the house while you're selling. Our sales brought huge crowds, and things could have gotten out of hand.

Start the day with plenty of change, preferably in a carpenter's apron so you'll have everything on your person. If you keep all the cash in a cigar box, it's too easy for someone to walk off with it while you're demonstrating how well the lawnmower works or helping someone try on your roller skates.

Some other suggestions:

■   Put a price tag on everything. It eliminates confusion, not just for the customer but for your spouse and anyone else who is helping you sell. Bits of masking tape work well and cost almost nothing.

■   Have on hand a supply of paper bags, newspaper for wrapping breakables, and boxes for packing large purchases.

■   If you have a lot of items to sell, as we did, don't put out everything at once. It's easier to keep control if you spread the sale over several days. Also, you can adjust prices upward for items that sell better than expected and lower the prices on wallflowers.

■   Beware of dealers who arrive early and offer a flat rate for everything. It may sound like a lot of money, but we made far more by extending the sale and lowering our prices on the last day. Yard sale regulars are great bargainers, but we held firm to our prices. When someone made a lowball offer, we invited them to come back on the final day. Most paid our asking prices rather than wait.

Other Sellout Choices

Garage sales are a gold mine, but you may be wiser to give some items to nonprofit causes and take a tax deduction; check with your accountant. Giving antiques or good jewelry to a museum can bring a handsome deduction. We donated our expensive books and records to a library. Gordon's high-ticket business suits went to a charity. The last of our unsold items we donated to a thrift shop, and we obtained a receipt for the IRS. Don't leave anything salable or usable for the trash collector.

Another choice is to hold an auction. It can be painful to sell off bits and pieces of your life at garage sales. By turning everything over to an auctioneer you can simply walk away and trust that the professional will work the crowd for the highest dollars. You're spared much of the work and sadness of selling. However, the auctioneer's commission is usually a hefty 25 percent. Consignment shops are another option but can charge up to 60 percent.

As a last choice, you can call in a dealer who will haul everything away and pay you a flat fee. It's quick and neat, and you're spared the heavy labor of hauling, the annoyance of crowds and phone calls, and the hassle of haggling.

We found secondhand dealers to be the most rapacious, underhanded people we had to work with in the entire agonizing process of selling out. They sniffed over our goods like turkey vultures over roadkill, hoping we didn't know the value of our hobnail glass, old baseball cards, or antique toys. Certainly some dealers are honest and perhaps even generous, but if you must deal with one, call in a licensed appraiser—not the same one who is also trying to buy your goods—to give you a fair picture of what things are worth.

Storage: What's in Store

If you decide to keep some or all of your furnishings, you have several options. You can rent your home fully or partially furnished or pile everything into the attic or spare room, lock that part of the house, and rent out the rest of the house. (When you buy landlord's insurance, don't forget to insure your personal belongings separately.)

You might ask friends and relatives to store whatever they have room for. It's free, and a trusted relative could even be enlisted to go through your things on your behalf if, say, you're in New Mexico when you need an old medical record that's stored in the attic back in New Hampshire. Or you might run short of cash and want Aunt Sue to sell the heirloom silver you've stored in her attic. If Aunt Sue has free access to your stuff, she can do more for you than just warehouse it.

This solution also has its drawbacks. First, you have the expense or labor of moving everything to Muffy and Bob's basement or to Aunt Sue's attic. Then, when Muffy and Bob are transferred to South America, someone has to find a new place and move your things there. The precious possessions that you thought were resting secure in that basement are now being shuffled around by heaven-knows-whom to who-knows-where.

There is sure to be a wrangle if the house your goods are stored in is burgled or hit by a natural disaster, which would bring the homeowner's insurance into the matter. And the day may come when Uncle Leftie swears that your stamp collection was not a loan but a gift.

It may cost more to deal with professional storage companies, but it's often worth it. The good news is that with so many people today living in small apartments and in homes with no attics or basements, there has been an explosion in the building of self-storage facilities. You see them everywhere. They look like long, windowless buildings faced with row after row of doors and "garage" doors. You lock your own warehouse door, visit your goods whenever you please, and pay a modest monthly, seasonal, or yearly storage fee.

Typical self-storage areas range from bins as small as 4 by 8 by 4 feet to full-size rooms about 10 by 22 by 8 feet. The smallest of these minis, only 4 feet high, is suitable only for things like piled boxes, a motorcycle, or other small items. It rents for $40 or less a month in most places. At the upper end of the scale, you'll pay $150 a month or more for a large room, and more still if you use electricity to run a dehumidifier.

Most self-storage facilities are well fenced and may also have 24-hour security. Some have their own locks; for others, you supply the padlock. Some allow you access only during business hours; others are always accessible. When you're shopping for self-storage, compare not just price and size but access, security features, and whether electricity is available. And don't forget that you'll need your own insurance.

If you deal with a moving and storage company, you have the protection and convenience of working with professionals. They pick up everything at your house, install it in their warehouse, and deliver it wherever and whenever you want. A good mover will put your household into individual plywood containers to prevent wear and tear and will put upholstered pieces on racks where they'll get good air circulation.

Look for a company that is bonded, that has a sprinkler system and circulation fans, and that stores furniture on platforms rather than on cold, damp cement floors.

Prices for such a service are high and are charged by the hundredweight (cwt), which usually works out to about $60 per room per month. Insurance provided by the storage company is also figured by the cwt and is usually well under your household's actual worth. Get additional coverage from your own insurer. The cost of moving into and out of storage is also high, charged at typical moving van prices.

The biggest problem with any storage facility, but especially an unventilated or unheated self-storage facility, is that moisture, heat, and cold continue to batter your belongings. In the north, do not put any liquids in with goods stored in unheated warehouses—freezing will result in breakage and inevitable damage to nearby goods.

Before storing any fabrics, wash and dry them thoroughly. Atmospheric stains appear out of nowhere after several months of storage in even the driest attic. One of our friends retrieved her stored linens from a humid Florida warehouse to find that they had turned to dust in a few months. We had better luck in storing freshly washed, dried fabrics that were sealed into plastic bags on a dry day.

Make sure, too, that all batteries are removed from stored items. We use so many batteries today that it's easy to overlook one in a camera, wristwatch, calculator, toy, or flashlight. When batteries discharge and begin to leak, they ruin the item they are in and can damage surrounding items as well.

The Final Cut

At long last, you're ready to move into the RV. We thought we'd pared our possessions to the bone when we sold out, but once we started moving, we saw we'd have to become even more ruthless about what to keep and what to get rid of. Even if you can find room for your custom-made bowling ball and the marble bust of Beethoven, keep in mind that every ounce costs you fuel dollars.

Clothing, books, hobby gear—everything should be looked at with unprejudiced eyes. It's better to sell your wardrobe down to the bare skin and use the money to buy one or two versatile and practical new outfits than to start out with closets filled with unmatched separates and shirts that need ironing.

Still, you'll take too much. We all do. And that's when the battles begin over his space, her space, and our space. We'll get into that in chapter 8, Equipping Your RV Home Your Way.

Parting Is Such Sweet Sorrow

No matter how you choose to unload your household goods, you'll have to make difficult decisions. You and your mate may disagree over what to keep, what to give away, and what to sell. And if you decide to sell something, you may argue over pricing. Steel yourself for some rocky times.

Suddenly you will realize how many good times you had in this house, how comfortable you were in that old overcoat, and how much you both like the silly little lamp you bought on a trip to Atlantic City.

You'll agonize over how much you'll miss the morning sun coming in through the bay windows to kiss the African violets. You'll worry about managing without this or that. You'll cry together, and you'll cry alone.

In addition to your own bittersweet partings with things that you and your spouse love, expect some ugly pressures from other people too. Relatives may get huffy if they see you selling things they gave you as gifts or things they think of as family pieces that should be given (never sold, of course) to Little Barney or Cousin Sue.

Many friends and neighbors may expect you to give things to them, and in fact you may be embarrassed to put a price tag on the handmade quilt that Betsy has always admired or the garden tool that Harvey always borrowed from you.

This is a time of great mental, physical, and financial vulnerability. Be ready for hurts of all kinds. This is the tough part, but it's soon over.

Now let the good times roll!

SEVEN

Choosing a Home on Wheels

Camping on weekends and vacations is one thing; living aboard is quite another. Part-timers don't mind roughing it for a few days. If the bed is too hard or too short, they laugh it off. They can breakfast on cold beans if it means getting out on the lake earlier. And taking the path to the bath is simply a quaint camping necessity.

Forget maintenance, cleaning, and costs—the piper can be paid later. When part-timers get home, they can dump all the dirty clothes and bedding into the automatic washer and dryer, soak off the grime in a full-size bathtub, and turn the rig over to a trusted hometown mechanic for a checkup. They can pay the bills as they straggle in and luxuriate in household living until it's time to go camping again.

Fulltimers, by contrast, have to find their own luxury, fulfillment, and comfort aboard because the *RV* is home sweet home. The bubble bath or laundry or fall housecleaning can't wait until you get home because you *are* home. The piper must be paid one tune at a time.

The RV has to hold everything you need, year in and year out. That includes the income tax records, holiday decorations, off-season clothes, hobby and entertainment paraphernalia, tools and spares for the plumbing and wiring and drive train, as well as such homemaking supplies as the mending basket and the jelly jars.

Within these four walls you'll have to eat, drink, and be merry. Here's where you'll recuperate from the flu, play cards with your friends on Saturday night, get dressed for the hoedown, pay the bills and do the bookkeeping, soak your corns, settle spats with your spouse, do the spring cleaning, and plan, take, and recover from trips.

39

The part-timer is probably concerned with how many folks the RV will sleep—the more, the merrier. Fulltimers, by contrast, usually need sleeping accommodations only for themselves, but the bed(s) must be exactly the right length, width, and firmness—and don't forget about room for the TV, reading lamps, and bedside books.

The part-timer carries gear for a week or two, and only for the purpose of the current trip—bass fishing this time, photographing the bald eagle migration next time, snowmobiling the time after that. The fulltimer needs freshwater tackle and saltwater tackle, snow skis and water skis, old clothes and Sunday clothes—everything, *including* the kitchen sink.

Vacationers take dining shortcuts, eating in restaurants and cooking with convenience foods. The fulltimer needs a real kitchen where economical, nutritious meals can be created and served attractively in a comfortable dinette seven days a week.

In recognition of these needs, indeed in *celebration* of these needs, let's take a look at the RV marketplace.

Types of Recreational Vehicles

Even longtime campers may confuse some of the terms used in the RV world, so let's define them.

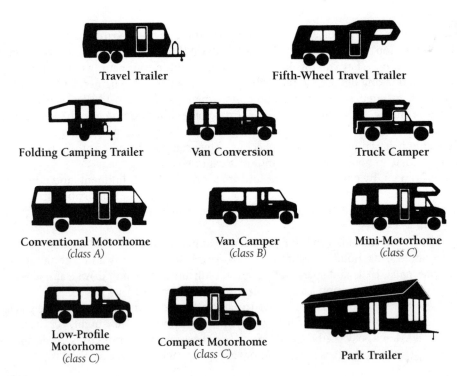

Travel Trailer   Fifth-Wheel Travel Trailer

Folding Camping Trailer   Van Conversion   Truck Camper

Conventional Motorhome   Van Camper   Mini-Motorhome
(class A)   (class B)   (class C)

Low-Profile
Motorhome   Compact Motorhome
(class C)   (class C)   Park Trailer

RV categories. (RVIA)

First of all, this book is about homes that are mobile, not mobile homes. *Mobile homes* (or *manufactured houses*, as they are sometimes called) are large houses on wheels, with no engine. They are towed by a hired truck and installed permanently in a trailer park or on a plot of land, and they are about as agile as an anvil.

The subject of this book is the *recreational vehicle (RV)*, a vehicle designed to go places while also providing a place to eat and sleep. RVs fall into several categories.

Pickup campers are camper units that slide into pickup truck beds. Also called *truck campers*, they range from simple shells to elaborate units that include kitchen, bath, bunks, and dinette. Camper add-ons are available at prices from under $5,000 to $15,000 or more.

Van campers (van conversions) may contain a microwave oven or tiny bathroom but generally are suitable only for solitary RVers. They usually cost $40,000 and up.

Travel trailers are complete living units towed by a car or truck. They come in many shapes and sizes, from little folding trailers that can be towed by very small cars to enormous wheeled estates measuring 35 feet long or longer. Folding campers start at under $10,000; travel trailers start at about $10,000 and average about $25,000.

Truck camper. (RVIA photo archives)

Variously called van campers, van conversions, or class B RVs, these small units have all the essentials for single fulltimers. (RVIA photo archives)

Travel trailers are available in a wide range of sizes and prices. (RVIA photo archives)

Fifth-wheel trailers are a subcategory of travel trailers with an extension that fits over the bed of a pickup truck for easier maneuvering and towing. These sell for about the same prices as conventional trailers. Larger models are $35,000 and up.

Park trailers also are travel trailers, but they are not designed for extensive towing. Most have peak roofs and expanding sections that can add a dining room or double the width of the living room. Larger park models may be single or double width, sporting such features as cathedral ceilings and bay windows, so the largest ones resemble mobile homes more than they do RVs. Expect to pay $35,000 or more.

Fifth–wheel trailers have a special design that makes it easier to tow a big rig. (RVIA photo archives)

Class A motorhome. (RVIA photo archives)

Class C motorhome. (RVIA photo archives)

Motorhomes are complete units containing living quarters, engine, and chassis. They range from mini-motorhomes to large (class A) motorhomes (or motorcoaches). Class (or type) A motorhomes start in the $65,000 range; better models with expensive rear-engine diesel power sell for $150,000 to $250,000 or more.

Some Basic Choices

Your first decision should not be about the size, price, or shape of your rolling home but whether you will drive it or tow it. For all their cute and fetching features in the showroom, RVs are *vehicles*. Safety, handling, weight, and fuel economy are paramount considerations. So is the cost of one vehicle versus two.

You can have

- one vehicle, such as a pickup camper or motorhome
- an RV trailer plus a car or truck to tow it
- a motorhome that tows a small car

The Case for Towing

Any RV that doesn't have an engine will naturally be cheaper than one that does. Because there are nearly five times the number of trailers than there are class A motorhomes, the choice of trailer brands, sizes, layouts, styles, and decors is better than in any other category.

When you get to the campground, you unhitch the trailer and you're home. Your car (or van or truck) is now free for local shopping and sightseeing.

There's an advantage to being able to trade or upgrade the trailer and the tow vehicle separately, with a choice of diesel or gasoline, as needed. And the tow vehicle can also provide extra storage, workshop space, or even, in some cases, an extra camper. If you tow a large trailer with a large truck that also has modest accommodations aboard, the trailer can be left in base camp while you make expeditions into more remote areas in the truck.

The Case against Towing

For anyone who is reluctant to hassle with a tow on the highway and con it into and out of tiny campsites, there is no argument at all: towing is out, period. And even if you and your traveling companion(s) are adroit and skilled drivers who love towing, there are other drawbacks.

If you decide to tow, and you cover a great many miles each year, fuel costs will probably be higher than in a single, aerodynamically efficient vehicle. So will costs for tires, because you have more skins on the road. And because tolls are charged per axle, you'll pay more to drive toll roads. Check with your insurance carrier to compare the costs for coverage of a car and trailer, of a motorhome, and of a motorhome that tows a small car.

When you have a single, walk-through unit, you can pull over to the side of the road to take a nap or make lunch without going outdoors. If you have a trailer, you have to go out into the weather to enter your living quarters. Heat and air are separate, so it may be a nuisance (or impossible, if you don't have a generator) to start the air conditioner or furnace each time you stop for lunch. In a motorhome, by contrast, you can opt to leave the engine idling for short periods to run the heat or air.

It's illegal in most states to ride in a trailer under tow. That means your spouse has to be in the tow car with you when you are under way even if he or she would rather be snoozing in the bedroom or doing needlepoint in the living room.

Gordon Groene

Narrowing the Choice

Only you can decide which rolling lifestyle best suits your comforts, your frequency of travel, your budget, and your driving abilities. What we'd all like to have, of course, is a three-bedroom RV with garage, basement, attic, and vegetable garden. What we must settle for is a compromise: between fuel economy and responsive handling on the one hand and space and weight on the other; between one vehicle and two; between the RV we covet and the RV we can afford.

Our RV is a 21-foot diesel mini-motorhome. It's small compared with what most fulltimers choose, but keep in mind that we're not retired. We travel quick and light, make a living on the go, and rarely stay in a campground for more than a few nights at a time. We like having everything with us everywhere we go.

Our 21-footer is large enough to have kitchen essentials, a comfortable dinette, a double bed, and a bathroom with a shower. Yet it's short enough to park in city parking lots, in the yards of friends and relatives, and on the street outside a friend's home.

When we're doing television appearances in connection with our books, it's no problem to make the morning show. We sleep in the parking lot, have breakfast, dress, and walk in. We have slept in city parking lots after the theater, at trade shows, and at airports.

A larger, more complex rig that wouldn't fit into a car-size parking space would make our business life more complicated and costly. The retiree, on the other hand, would probably prefer more living space and less driving. In fact, there are retiree-only RV parks where you can stay by the season, the year, or the lifetime.

Here are some pros and cons of different types of RVs.

Pickup Campers

Pros: If you will be combining the fulltiming life with a business in which you'll use a pickup truck, this camper can be offloaded in the campground to form a wheelless, slightly odd-looking, but complete and cozy home while you take off in the truck. These campers are inexpensive to buy and because you have a separate truck and camper, you can change or upgrade either one when the time comes.

Cons: Because it was designed as a removable addition to an existing pickup truck, the truck camper gives you the poorest space utilization, weight distribution, handling, and riding ease of any camper you could choose. And you have to get out of the cab and go to the rear to enter the living quarters.

Van Conversions

Pros: Vans are stylish, lean, and mean on the highway, have a low profile that fits under canopies at gas stations, are agile on back roads and hills, and provide excellent riding comfort. A van can be fitted with an attached tent for an extra room. For the single fulltimer with minimalist tastes and few belongings, the van provides unlimited possibilities.

Cons: Although many vans have toilets, you'll probably still be dependent on campgrounds for showers. Van kitchens are adequate for warming up convenience foods but not for serious cooking. There isn't space, or water tankage, for much dishwashing or bathing. Some vans don't have standup headroom, and most have convertible beds that are awkward to make and uncomfortable to sleep in.

Travel Trailers

Pros: A lot of "house" for the money. If it can be towed with a car or truck you already own and trust, you're off and running. Travel trailers come in so many types and qualities, you can shop for good, better, or best in any size from compact to queen. Get the trailer that exactly matches your needs, and just the right tow vehicle for the power, layout, seating, storage, and comfort you want. You can have the best of both worlds, leaving the trailer behind when you're touring.

Cons: In addition to the challenges of towing, as mentioned above, trailers are usually light in relation to their size, so windage can be a problem. The sheer size of a trailer-cum-car makes it difficult to "anchor out," which is what we call it when we overnight free in a friend's yard or driveway. And the larger and more awkward the rig, the less able you are to reach smaller, more remote beach or mountain campgrounds.

You'll probably be more dependent on campground hookups, especially electricity, because 110-volt generators are not installed as commonly in trailers as they are in motorhomes. Most travel trailers now have simplified electrical management, in which the "house" battery is charged from the vehicle's alternator, but lighting and other 12-volt needs must be provided for.

Pop–Up and Folding Camp Trailers

Pros: The lightest, most towable, and least expensive of all camping trailers, the fold-out (or pop-up) is a good way to try out the RV life. They are available in many configurations, in canvas and hard-bodied models. Larger pop-ups have rudimentary kitchens and baths and can be fitted with air-conditioning.

Cons: These are really a good fulltiming choice only for special situations and the most severely strapped budgets. In a typical layout, two double-bunk "wings" unfold

Pop–up trailers are a good way to get started in RV touring. (RVIA photo archives)

from the body of the camper. Unless you need both as bunks, they have little use except as space to spread out gear while you're in camp. Living comforts are few, campground dependence almost total. Until you unfold the camper, you have no access to any of your own facilities. And setting up or breaking camp in bad weather is a burden.

Motorhomes

Pros: There is a large choice of sizes, styles, and prices. You can have everything with you, including your own kitchen and bath, at all times—complete, self-contained independence.

Cons: Unless you tow a car (which in turn creates other inconveniences and expenses), or find other means of transportation, you have to travel everywhere in the RV. When the motorhome breaks down, you have to set up housekeeping on the side of the road, at the garage, or wherever the breakdown occurs. If you do tow a car, you have the hassle of unhooking and hooking up again whenever you need to use the car.

Down to Brass Tacks

Most RV manufacturers offer a large choice of layouts, and certain basic choices apply to both motorhomes and trailers. They include:

Built-in versus freestanding furniture. Until recently all furniture was built in by the RV manufacturer, but today you have a choice. Usually, freestanding pieces will be a sofa bed, swivel chairs in the living room, and separate dining chairs instead of a built-in dinette. Separate furniture may be more comfortable and stylish, but it means sacrificing the spacious storage bins that can be put under built-in sofas and dinettes. You may also tire of having to stow the dining room chairs so that they don't cause damage if you have to brake suddenly.

Bed size. All manufacturers offer a choice of double, queen, or bunk beds. King and full-size twin beds are harder to find.

Center versus side hall. In most layouts, you reach the bedroom through a center hall that also forms a dressing room/bath or through a side hall that goes past a separate bathroom. When you're shopping for a layout, think about traffic patterns, because in some you can't get from the kitchen to the bedroom if someone is showering or using the toilet.

Entry-door placement. Although some trailers have both front and rear doors, most RVs have just one entry, and you might give some thought to it, especially if you expect to be entertaining in your RV or if you have children who are constantly going in and out. In some motorhomes the only entry is through the cockpit (where the driver and front passenger sit), so that everyone has to maneuver around the passenger seat to enter the "living room." One of our friends said she hated a center entry that was directly opposite the bathroom. Some entry doors open into the kitchen, others into the living room or a hall.

This is another area where the choice for part-timers may not apply for fulltiming. The vacationer hops in and hits the road and wants easy access to the driver's seat. The fulltimer usually spends more time at "home" than at the wheel, so easy entry to the living quarters may count more than a convenient driver's door.

Windows versus cupboards. The bigger the window area in an RV, the less

The Winnebago Journey motorhome offers plenty of comfort inside, but you must either drive it everywhere you go or find another way to get around: towing a car or using bikes, motorcycles, or public transportation. (Winnebago)

Freestanding furniture now often replaces built–in. (Winnebago)

Most motorhomes have the living area just in back of the cockpit, then the kitchen and dining areas, then a hallway with bath and storage areas on one or both sides, with the bedroom in the rear. Bedroom lay–outs are available with queen or twin beds. (Winnebago)

wall space there is for cupboards, closets, medicine cabinet, and mirrors. And windows add to your heat gain (in hot climates) and loss (in cold climates).

Construction Standards

In addition to all the lifestyle, comfort, and decor questions you must ask when selecting an RV, you will also want to know that you are purchasing a well-constructed home. The RV industry, represented by the Recreational Vehicle Industry Association (RVIA), has its own standards, which assure quality and consistency among member manufacturers.

The RVIA bylaws require that its members certify that each RV they build complies with the American National Standard for Recreational Vehicles, the only nationally recognized consensus standard. Look for an RVIA seal affixed by the manufacturer near the door to the RV; it certifies that the unit complies with that standard and with the National Electrical Code.

RVIA inspectors make frequent, unannounced visits to manufacturers to monitor the manufacturing process and determine the level of compliance to the standard. A manufacturer who doesn't comply faces expulsion from the RVIA.

A full 95 percent of all RVs sold in the United States are built by RVIA members to RVIA standards. It pays to shop for a unit that bears this seal and to demand that repairs or replacements follow American National Standards Institute (ANSI; www.ansi.org) standards.

People Sizing

There's one last chore before making a final decision on an RV layout. Both you and your spouse or traveling companion should try sitting, standing, and lying anywhere in the RV where you'll be sitting, standing, or lying when you live aboard. You'll feel foolish in the showroom, but we urge you to sit on the toilet and close the door (is there enough clearance to do so comfortably?), lean over the bathroom sink as if brushing your teeth (do you have to bend nearly double?), take off your shoes and stand in the shower and/or sit in the bathtub (is each large enough for you?), and stand at the stove and kitchen sink (are they the right height for you?).

If it will be a part of your everyday life to turn a dinette or a sofa into a bed, go through the procedure. It may be more awkward than you realize, and the resulting

RVIA

Make sure you feel comfortable in your RV's layout. (Winnebago)

bed may have ridges and valleys in the worst places. Sit down at the dining table; is there room for table settings for two or maybe more?

Stretch out on the beds to see how long they are. Often beds appear to be standard sizes but are not. And some overhead bunks don't provide enough headroom for sitting up to read in bed.

Remember that these living quarters, as well as all the plumbing and wiring behind the scenes, have to be compatible with the needs of the vehicle. As a result, countertops may be higher or lower than in a house. The microwave oven may be too high for removing a hot, heavy casserole. Try and determine which differences you can live with, and which will drive you crazy.

While it's tempting to choose an RV based on its living comforts, don't forget the basic fact that it's a vehicle. Can you check the oil, batteries, and radiator cap without dismantling the living room, change a fan belt without taking the engine apart, or get at the generator to fuel and service it?

What's involved in filling the propane and water tanks, lighting any pilot lights, emptying sewage and gray water, stowing cords and hoses, flushing out systems, changing the oil, getting at spare tires, leveling the rig, managing the electrical system, and doing all the other routine maintenance required by a home on wheels?

Can you find room (and access to pipes and wires) to add items that you may consider essential, such as a drinking water filter, a generator, another air conditioner, additional lighting, a washer-dryer, an inverter to turn 12-volt juice into 110-volt power, more tankage (for fuel, water, and gray or black water), a dishwasher, or a trash compactor?

Only after these very important considerations are met can you start thinking about whether you want the sculptured carpet or the short shag, in beige or in robin's-egg blue.

About Custom Units

Almost any RV, even in lower price ranges, is made to order, so you'll probably have plenty of factory-installed options, ranging from color schemes to major structural changes. Unless you have experience in RV living, however, we recommend starting with a stock RV, new or used, to get a feel for the living patterns that will work best for you.

In a custom RV almost anything is possible. You can explore your options by talking to showroom salespeople, from manufacturers' brochures and Web sites, and by going to RV shows. That doesn't make it practical or wise. Exotic customizing—such as a darkroom, a sauna, or flocked scarlet wallpaper—adds to your costs and may reduce the resale value. So don't opt for nonstandard additions until you're sure they're right for you for the long haul.

Finding Your RV

Shopping for your RV is theoretically a worldwide pursuit, thanks to the Internet, and some fulltimers-to-be travel back and forth across the country looking for just the right rig. From the practical standpoint, it's best to start your search close to home. Look at as many RVs as possible—new and used, in the showroom and in the back lot. Even if you know you'll be buying a new unit, you can learn a lot by looking at used RVs, both at dealerships (where they're likely to be in top-notch condition) and through private owners (where you're more likely to see what a few years of wear and tear can do).

Even the largest showroom can't contain every model of every brand, so write and request brochures from any manufacturers listed in appendix 2 that make the type of RV you're interested in. Many manufacturers welcome your visit to the factory and will build to order if you're willing to pay the price. Top-of-the-line RVs, those in the $250,000-and-up class, are almost all built to order, rarely on speculation, so allow time for conferences, planning, and construction. Giant RV shows are held around the country, and they are a dazzling, shortcut way to see hundreds of RVs all at once. They fill entire stadiums, fairgrounds, and enormous exhibition halls. For a list of major shows, contact RVIA, Box 2999, Reston, VA 22090; www.rvia.org.

If you're looking for a used rig, try the Web sites www.RV-traders.com, www. buscentral.com, www.RV-links.com, www.RVnetlinx.com, and www.RVshownow. com. You'll also find lots of information and lists of used RVs for sale in magazines like _Trailer Life_ (best for travel trailers), _Motorhome Life_ (good for a wide range of motorhomes), and _Family Motor Coaching_ (best for top-of-the-line class A motorhomes). Large RV dealers are another excellent source; they usually have a good choice of sizes and models.

Negotiating is a skill honed through research. The more you know about the brand you want, the book value of the RV you're trading in, and about RVs in general, the better the deal you can make. Visit any dealer or show at least twice. The first time, hang out, look around, and have a good time. Listen. Look. Touch. But don't sign anything. The second time, after talking to a bank and working out some rough estimates of the monthly financing costs you can afford, you can start getting serious.

Financing Your RV

Dealer financing is the easiest way to finance an RV because the dealer has the best sources for RV-knowledgeable lenders. Dealers may also be more lenient about financing an older unit that a bank won't touch.

Your local bank, S&L, or credit union is another option; your financial institution will be familiar with you and your credit history.

An Internet search on the key words "RV loan" or "RV finance" will turn up other choices, but not all lenders are licensed in all states. Be wary of revealing too much personal information on the Internet without knowing where it's going to end up.

Most major banks will finance a new RV, or a used unit not more than 5 years old, for up to 15 years for up to 90 percent of its value. Finding bank financing for units older than 5 years is usually quite difficult.

EIGHT

Equipping
Your RV
Home
Your Way

Choosing the perfect RV is just the beginning of a long-term romance between you and the liveaboard life. Even if your RV is custom-built to your own design, it won't truly be a home until it is finished, furnished, and fine-tuned.

Fulltiming is a specialized lifestyle that requires specialized accessories. At first you may make do with paper plates and old army blankets, but you'll soon realize the importance of having the right sheets for making up odd-size bunks and the appropriate pots and pans for preparing whale-size meals in a minnow-size galley.

Remember, too, that unlike a house, a RV doesn't stay put. It accelerates, corners, maneuvers, and brakes to a stop. Every pound costs you fuel dollars; every ounce affects the way the RV handles on the highway. You have to add equipment sparingly and place it carefully; for example, heavy items such as canned goods or a microwave oven should be well balanced fore and aft and kept as low as possible.

Decor

The fun part is to work within existing decor to keep the RV interior as color coordinated, uncluttered, and spacious looking as it was in the showroom. If you have swatches of the existing upholstery and carpeting, visit a paint store to pick up a handful of free color sample cards in your RV's shades. Then tuck them in your wallet so they'll be handy as you shop for bedding, bathroom furnishings, throw rugs, tableware, and accessories.

Smart use of color and light can create moods, make small spaces seem larger, brighten dark corners, and mask soil and smudges. When window coverings match the walls and

55

area rugs match the flooring, they blend into seamless expanses that seem larger. Contrasting colors, on the other hand, chop up an area and make it appear smaller.

When you're choosing accents and accessories, think small. RV ceilings are low; use long, thin, vertical mirrors or wall hangings to make them seem higher. Walls and furniture are downsized, so don't overwhelm them with large accent pieces.

Use practical items that both fill the space and put it to good use. For example, a picture on the wall is merely decorative, whereas a clock, a barometer, a vase, a magazine shelf, or a sconce is useful as well. If you stuff throw pillows with extra bed pillows, puffy ski jackets, or your supply of knitting wool, you've also created extra storage.

Galleyware

Start with the bare-bones basics, then add to your galley gear as you develop your own RV cuisine routine. You may cook and eat much differently aboard than you did at home, perhaps eating in restaurants more frequently or grilling more.

When choosing cookware, bear in mind you don't need an entire set or a matched set. It's better to choose the best pot and skillet, casserole and baking pan for each purpose. The same goes for silverware, dishes, utensils, and cutlery. In RV living every inch counts.

Among items that we've found especially handy in the RV are a pressure cooker, because it saves time and fuel; nonstick skillets, which minimize cleanup; an electric hotplate for use indoors or out; a tri-level double boiler-steamer, because it lets you cook several items atop one burner; and a couple of heavy pots with heavy, tight-fitting lids. (When you must shuffle several pots among too few burners, thin pans with loose lids let too much heat escape. Here is one place where heavier is better.)

Microwave ovens are now standard equipment on almost all RVs. (Dometic Corporation)

For more about the RV galley, along with dozens of mouthwatering, roadworthy recipes, see Janet's *Cooking Aboard Your RV*, published by Ragged Mountain Press. To order a copy call 800-262-4729 or go to www.raggedmountainpress.com.

Bedding

Most RV manufacturers furnish the master bedroom with an innerspring mattress atop a solid wood platform. Unfortunately, innersprings are heavy and awkward to lift and handle. Opt instead for a good foam mattress, which will be more comfortable, lighter, and easier to move. Look for a featherweight, man-made polyfoam mattress or one of the high-tech "memory" foam units (try www.abed.com). Either will be easy to lift whenever you need to get at under-bed storage and easier to turn regularly to maintain firmness and freshness. Don't skimp on quality or thickness. Discuss the options with a mattress specialist, who will explain the many types and qualities of foam available.

Do you sleep with your feet in the far corners of the mattress? Probably not. If you round off the mattress corners at the foot of the bed, you'll gain more space for moving around the bedroom. Any custom mattress maker (look in the Yellow Pages, or see appendix 1) can whip out a mattress in the right size and shape.

If the bed in your rolling home is a standard twin, double, queen, or king, standard-size sheets and blankets are the best buys and come in the largest choice of colors. However, convertible and odd-size bunks, which are often used in RVs, present special problems. Standard bedding may be too narrow or too short. Worse still, some RV beds, especially convertibles, do not have a separate mattress that allows you to tuck sheets in. Unless you have a sleeping bag, you'll spend the night sliding around on loose sheets.

When a convertible RV bed has to be made up each night, and the bedding put away every morning, the job takes forever using conventional bedding. For these beds there are a number of choices. Most big camping supply stores offer a selection of single and double sleeping bags for all climates. You don't have to worry about tuck-in or overlap, and some come with removable sheets for easy laundering.

The more sophisticated sleeping sacks come in all sizes, from single to king, and have a light side for summer and a heavy side for winter camping. All of them can be rolled up in a few seconds in the morning and unrolled instantly at bedtime. Voilà! The bed is completely made up with sheets and blankets.

The bed in our RV is a standard-size double in what is called gaucho style. That is, it's a settee by day and a bed by night. It must be made up completely each evening, and all the bedding put away in the morning. (It's a nuisance, but it's a price we gladly pay for traveling lean.) If you have such a bed and want to make bed making easier without using a sleeping sack, use fitted sheets. You probably will not be able to find fitted *top* sheets for sale, however, so here's how to make your own:

Buy a matching set of sheets, one flat, one fitted. Cut both in half across the middle and sew one fitted half to each flat half, using a French or flat-felled seam and making pleats to take up the extra width of the top sheet. You now have two fitted top sheets. Add two matching fitted bottom sheets and whatever pillow cases or shams you need to complete the picture.

Inexpensive new "egg crate" mattress toppers do wonders in taming an RV bed that is too hard or lumpy. Because seams, cording, buttons, and crevices occur in many convertible beds, a thick and cushy mattress cover is a must.

Electronics

A TV screen is no substitute for a crackling campfire and the camaraderie of fellow campers, but there are times when the "tube" is a welcome companion. A VCR is also a must, especially if you spend a lot of time in areas where TV reception is scanty. You'll probably want a good stereo system, and most fulltimers subscribe to satellite TV. Services such as DirecTV or Dish Network start at about $30 a month, but you'll spend $50 monthly or more to get a wide range of sports, entertainment, and other special-interest channels plus major networks.

Other electronics to consider are: a good CB (Citizens Band) radio—CB has gone out of style with most drivers, but it is still used by truckers and RVers; a closed-circuit TV—on a large motorcoach, it increases visibility to the rear; and a computer set-up—for Internet access, navigation programs, and much more.

Many campgrounds now offer telephone and cable TV hookups at extra cost, sometimes by the night and sometimes only upon payment of an installation fee. For a free list of campgrounds that have modems available at campsites by the night, e-mail winfield3@aol.com. If you don't opt for satellite TV reception, you may want to add a rotating antenna with a control that can be operated from inside the RV.

Thanks to satellite reception, fulltimers can keep up with their favorite programs and teams everywhere they go. (Winnebago)

Flip–down television screens stow flat against the ceiling when not in use. (Rosen Products)

If you're doing extensive renovations aboard your RV, start planning your electronics early because wiring, antennas, cables, shielding, remote controls, user comfort, speakers, secure mounts, and ventilation all have to be planned before new paneling goes in. This is also a good time to add a sophisticated multifunction security system. Check with your dealer or a security company. See also chapter 24, Safety and Security.

For a Quieter Ride

In furnishing your RV, try to find ways to make the rig quieter on the road and at rest: opt for the thickest carpeting and padding and a minimum of vinyl flooring; choose fabric upholstery instead of plastic. Wherever possible, choose the softer or thicker or less brittle alternative:

■ Put coffee filters (or pot holders) between pots and pans to minimize clatter while underway; filters will also protect nonstick linings.

■ Use inexpensive carpet samples to line cupboards.

■ Cut the ribbed cuffs off worn-out socks to protect drinking glasses and glass bottles—or better yet, choose plastic containers and glasses.

■   Order a stovetop cover; it will quiet stove rattle and double as extra counter space.

■   Use cushioned drawer linings to keep kitchen utensils quieter. Knives should ride in their own holders, for their safety and yours.

■   If you carry any big, breakable items, like a bean pot or clay cooker, wrap them in bubble wrap.

■   If your bed has a wood headboard, replace it with fabric.

■   Cover a wall or refrigerator door with sheet cork; it will absorb sound and also turn the space into a bulletin board.

■   If you have accordion doors that clatter while underway, replace them with a sound-absorbent material.

■   Upholster your bathroom door on one or both sides with padded or quilted fabric.

Lighting

It's likely that you'll want to add a few interior lights to the RV, supplementing the basic system with lights that suit your individual needs—a night light near a child's bunk, reading lights over each pillow, mood lighting over the sofa, or a bright bulb over the table where you'll play cards into the wee hours. Visit a large RV store or consult an RV supply catalog to see what is available in light fixtures and in both 12- and 110-volt bulbs.

If you need new wiring to add lighting, you may have to call in an expert; however, much can be done with existing wiring. You might, for instance, change to a new-style fixture, substitute a warmer bulb for one that is too bright, put a double fixture in place of a single one, replace a short fixture with a longer one, or replace a light fixture with a wall plug or with track lighting—all with your present wiring. Just make sure you're not exceeding the capacity of each circuit.

Trash Storage

Suddenly one waste basket isn't enough. Most municipalities ask us to separate garbage from trash and to separate trash into numerous categories—five different types of plastic, colored glass, clear glass, newspapers, office paper, telephone books, steel cans, aluminum, hazardous waste, engine oil. And the RV dweller has the added complication of adjusting to rules that vary from place to place.

Unfortunately, RV manufacturers have lagged behind in the trend toward recycling and often provide barely enough room for a single trash container, let alone multiple recycling bins. So, to avoid the unpleasant task of sorting everything after it's been thrown together, most RVers compromise by making two or three compartments and separating the most important categories.

Other things you can do are minimize your use of disposables, put trash storage bins wherever you can (galley corners are often a good spot), and shop for containers that just fit the space(s) you've managed to find.

Trash compactors are available for RVs, but they are seldom standard equipment. If you camp in areas where strict separation is required, a compactor may be of little use anyway. Garbage disposals are even more uncommon in RVs as the increased volume complicates your gray-water issues.

"Basement" and "Attic"

Much of the sports equipment you stored at home in your basement, attic, or yard shed can go on the road with you and add to your fun. If you can find room for it inside, that's better for security and aerodynamics, but the RV offers plenty of spots where you can tack on extra equipment.

Tow a boat, carry an inflatable boat on the roof rack or in the "basement" storage areas underneath, or hang a folding boat on the side of the RV. Mount special racks in any suitable spot for skis, water skis, a canoe, golf clubs, tennis rackets, or fishing poles. Sturdy bike racks are available to mount on your RV or tow car. If you have toddlers, consider carrying a small inflatable swimming pool too. Add one or two roof pods, if necessary, to carry small items.

Modern RV awnings allow you to unfold a spacious front porch with the flick of a switch. Carry a couple of folding chairs in the basement or on the roof so that you can set up a patio wherever you go. The more you enjoy outdoor living, the more patio furniture you'll want to add—folding tray tables, a screen room, a gas grill, more chairs, strings of lights.

About Keepsakes

Keepsakes are a record of our lives, but in order to fit everything you'll really need into an RV, you'll undoubtedly have to reduce your possessions to the bare minimum, and leave behind most of your memorabilia

When you go on the road, one alternative is to get rid of everything. Another is to keep it all and warehouse it. A third and, we feel, more sensible option is to take only those keepsakes that mean the most to you and can be easily managed and enjoyed in your new home

If you have to take your family photos, make them wallet-size; or make a wall collage in a frame or on a cork board. Put your record collection on CDs. Replace your house plants with a bonsai or cactus garden or grow herbs, which will be useful in the kitchen as well as decorative. Take only one representative piece from your treasured collection, and remember to protect it from the bumps and rattles of traveling.

Storage Tips

■   Line closets with cedar; ready-made tongue-and-groove liner kits are sold in home improvement stores.

■   Use stuff bags; color coordinating them by their contents will help you find items more easily.

■   Buy the good-quality hangers; clothes swing constantly from road motion and thin or rough hangers will wear holes in them.

■   Buy travel versions of favorite board games; they have magnetic pieces that stay put.

Nine

Rest Insured

It can cost a king's ransom to replace your most basic necessities if you lose your household. If you ever have to start over, you'll need the hefty grubstake that good insurance can provide. And even if you never face a *total* wipeout, the proper insurance can help you avoid financial catastrophe.

Fulltimer Coverage

Imagine yourself in any of the following situations:

- Your cat scratches the child in the campsite next door, and the family demands that you pay the medical bills.
- You go on a business trip, and your suitcase is stolen at the airport.
- You're entertaining campground neighbors on your site's patio when your folding chair collapses under your guest.
- Your safe-deposit box is rifled in a major bank heist.
- Your sister and brother-in-law are storing your expensive Oriental rugs in their attic while you're on the road, and their house burns down.
- There's a fire in your RV, and your stamp collection, the family silver, and some expensive cameras are burned beyond recognition.

Your homeowner's insurance covers all this, right? Well, not necessarily. If you're no longer a homeowner, you can have the best RV insurance policy in the world and still not have all the coverage you used to take for granted.

As a fulltimer you need to insure the RV, its contents, and its liabilities. You also need a comprehensive personal liability (CPL) policy to cover such things as the cat scratch or the collapsed chair and floaters to cover those valuables that are carried aboard and those being stored elsewhere. We can't say it too often: When you're a fulltimer, you have special problems and needs that non-fulltimers often do not understand.

Even the special "personal effects endorsement" offered with some RV policies is designed more for part-timers, who can leave most valuable items at home, and still have homeowner's insurance, than for fulltimers, who carry all their belongings with them. The endorsement doesn't cover more than a small fraction of the value of expensive jewelry, paintings, silver, heirlooms, and keepsakes. You'll need special policies for each.

Before you move aboard, consult an insurance agent to review the coverage you have and find out what you'll need for the unique life you'll be taking up. Then make sure that the new policy is in effect before the old ones are cancelled to avoid even a moment's lapse in coverage.

If you're going to rent out your house while you're gone and plan to store some of your personal belongings there, cover them in your landlord policy. If you're simply going to leave your home intact and unoccupied, your existing coverage can continue as if you were a part-timer, but read the fine print in your policy: If the insurer can make a case for abandonment (e.g., uncollected newspapers or a neglected lawn), it could void some or all of your coverage.

If you tow a car or boat behind your motorhome, or if you tow a travel trailer with a car or truck, they will be insured separately. As a result, you'll need additional coverage for items you carry in the tow vehicle, such as shop tools or an outboard motor. Additional coverage may also be available through other sources. For example, a self-storage facility may offer (or even require you to buy) insurance for items you store there.

It's possible that your present underwriter can't offer the coverage you need simply because many insurance firms are unfamiliar with the fulltiming lifestyle and have no provisions for it in their policies. Even a specialist in RV insurance may require fulltimers to pay higher premiums than other RV owners because typical RVs are used only about fifty days per year. So even though you may spend weeks or months in one spot and face no more road hazards than the part-timer, you present a higher risk in terms of fire and other losses.

Here is our insurance advice for the fulltimer:

■   Use a camcorder, camera, and notebook to inventory your possessions and store the record somewhere other than in your RV (see Getting Paid, pages 64–65.)

■   If you need more coverage than the standard RV policy provides, get additional personal effects insurance. It costs about $18 per $1,000 in coverage. Update it as needed to keep up with inflation.

■   Valuables such as jewelry, guns, cameras, and collectibles should be covered by special floater policies. Again, you'll need a specialist in RV insurance because many companies won't write floaters unless they also write your homeowner's policy.

■   Towing a car behind a motorhome and using it for local errands may reduce your premiums. The reasoning is simple: When you're on the road in an $18,000 car instead of in a $180,000 motorhome less is at risk.

■ Don't lie about your state of residence or your fulltimer status. It could void your coverage.

■ Higher deductibles reduce premiums on collision and CPL insurance, but this is a "comfort level" decision. Most companies offer deductibles of $250, $500, $1,000, or higher. Ask for quotes and determine whether the savings will be meaningful.

Comparison shopping for bargain rates will be difficult because sources for full-timer coverage are limited. Even if you're not a joiner, it pays to join groups such as the Family Motor Coach Association or Good Sam just for the insurance benefits. Companies that specialize in RV insurance include American Modern Insurance Group, 800-759-9008, www.amig.com; Coach Net, 800-680-4554, www.coach-net.com; Conseco, 800-888-4918, www.conseco.com; Foremost Insurance, 800-325-1507, www.foremost.com; RV Alliance America (formerly Alexander & Alexander), 800-521-2942, www.rvaa.com; RV America Insurance, 800-266-9856, www.rvainsurance.com; and Specialized Insurance & Services, 800-360-5988.

Getting Paid

Once all the right insurance is in place, you must take the steps that will make it possible to collect on claims. You need a careful record of the inventory in your RV so you'll know exactly what is lost in a fire or what is missing after a burglary or a collision. Some underwriters will also want to see a bill of sale or a professional appraisal to document the worth of valuables covered under floater policies.

One way to take a household inventory is simply to start with pencil and paper and list everything aboard, plus what you paid for it, and when. An easier way would be to record the inventory on audiotape. Or use a camcorder or still camera to make a visual record. Remember that you're making a record, not a prize portrait. Go for completeness, closeups, and clarity. We prefer slides for this purpose because they take up very little space yet can be projected on a very large screen to magnify small details if necessary. CDs also provide compact storage; CD images can be enlarged and printed out when needed.

Make note of serial numbers, model numbers, and identifying features. Pan across the set of silverware, focus tight on marks or numbers, get a shot of your spouse wearing his or her expensive leather coat. Line up all the appliances, and do the same with items in every closet, drawer, and storage bin.

Don't underestimate the value of everyday items. A few pots can easily cost $200; a set of good cutlery can cost a fortune. Even a set of stainless steel flatware can cost hundreds of dollars, and a pair of men's canvas shoes can be $50 or more. So list *everything* that is part of your household—in, under, or atop the RV.

In the living room, for example, list the carpeting, curtains, drapes, wall hangings, books, records, CDs, plants and planters, musical instruments, and entertainment electronics.

In your porch or patio area you may have a grill, awning or folding umbrella, hoses, electrical cord and "pigtail" connectors, and folding chairs. In the kitchen you may have not just costly tableware, cookware, and appliances, but also food, cleaning supplies, curtains, and lighting fixtures.

In the bedroom don't forget books and tapes, the TV and VCR, expensive toiletries, clothing, and several hundred dollars in bedding (the mattress alone probably cost $300 to $800). You may think you don't have any expensive jewelry, but costume pieces add up too.

Your office may contain a computer, scanner, FAX, copier, cell phone, and other very expensive electronics, not to mention software and irreplaceable files.

Our bathroom is the size of a phone booth, but we counted up an impressive inventory in towels, the shower curtain, toiletries, electric razor, over-the-counter drugs, and prescription medications.

Don't forget to list items stored in the roof rack, bike racks, or "basement" storage areas—tools, spare parts, pet supplies, the folding shopping cart, luggage, out-of-season clothing, and holiday supplies you use only once a year.

Items that can be stolen easily, such as cameras and electronics, can be scribed in some hidden spot with your driver's license or social security number. While this identification may not help the authorities retrieve a lost item for you, it will prove that the item is yours if you do have a chance to claim it.

Consider getting a professional to appraise the valuables you carry aboard. Once the inventory is done, keep a copy with you and send others elsewhere for safekeeping. Update it regularly as you add new equipment or as the value of your jewelry increases. Review your insurance coverage regularly too. Many homeowner's policies increase coverage automatically with inflation; your RV policies probably don't have this feature.

Storing Valuables

If you want to leave some of your belongings in a safe-deposit box, think carefully about what to store and where to store it. It makes sense to have two or more signatories to the box—perhaps you, your spouse, and a close family member who could get into the box if you need something from it while you're on the go. If, however, the box is located in a state where all financial instruments are sealed when one signatory dies, you could lose access to your own safe-deposit box for weeks if your spouse or any other co-renter dies. Ask.

If you need to store things that are too large for a box, commercial vaults, not to be confused with self-storage facilities, can be found in large cities. They have more security, including fenced parking lots, closed-circuit surveillance, and guards. The cost is high, perhaps $2,000 a year or so for a vault about 3 by 4 by 2 feet, plus optional insurance. Ask your banker if he or she knows of a nearby vault service.

When choosing a vault, look into its security features, annual costs, and ease of access. Ask whether the facility is open all the time or just during business hours and whether you're allowed unlimited visits or just a certain number per year.

No security system is secure against all theft. No insurance can cover the total cost, heartbreak, and time lost if you suffer a complete loss of your rolling home and its contents. Still, you can ease the pain by setting up the right protections and insurances to make recovery as quick and complete as possible.

TEN

Managing Money on the Go

Imagine yourself a stranger everywhere you go, unable to walk into a bank where you're known, pay with a check at the supermarket or auto-parts store, or ask a friend to cash an out-of-town check for you. That's life on the go. The banking/credit/money transfer scene has undergone dizzying changes in the last few years. Such changes mean higher costs for banking services, easier access to your money at some times and outlandish hassles at others, and enormous penalties for mishaps such as a small overdraft.

Banking

First, forget all your old banking habits and shop ruthlessly for the best prices on the services you now need. When you're on the road you probably will do all your banking by mail or electronic transfer anyway, so there's no reason to stick with your old accounts or your neighborhood bank. In fact, the answer for you may not be a bank or savings and loan (S&L) institution at all; you may choose to open an account at a brokerage or credit union, to bank online, or to deal primarily in cash.

Look also at other options that make sense in your new circumstances, such as a senior citizen's account if you're 55 or older or a low-activity account, designed especially for people who write only a few checks each month.

When comparing such packages, weigh all the perks, such as free life insurance or a free credit card, against per-check charges, the cost of any extra services, penalties, interest rates, fees for allowing your balance to fall below a certain minimum, or charges for writing more than the allotted number of checks per month.

Beware, too, of inactivity fees. Believe it or not, banks commonly charge for the privilege of holding onto your money. Fulltimers who stay out of touch for months at a time, thinking their money is quietly earning interest, sometimes receive nasty surprises.

After you've narrowed the choice of accounts, take another keen look at the list of benefits. Some of them, such as a slick monthly magazine, an insurance policy that pays only if you're killed in a plane crash, or discounts on hotels, are of little or no value to the RV fulltimer.

Banking today is a giant shell game, constantly shifting, so it's no longer wise to park your money or your loyalties permanently. Keep abreast of costs and reshuffle the deck as necessary. (Beware, though, of penalties for closing an account too soon. Not to be confused with penalties for early withdrawal, these are fees banks charge to offset the inconvenience you cause if you close an account within, say, six months or a year after opening it. Such fees can be charged for *any* accounts, not just CDs.)

Now that you're fulltiming, you'll probably want to look for such account features as

■   The best checking account based on the way you'll use checks on the go. Charges vary wildly, so choosing the wrong package can be costly.

■   The best deal on electronic transfers. If you'll spend time in Canada, Mexico, or other countries, compare international transfer costs too. If you'll be banking online, look for the lowest fees and greatest convenience and security.

■   The best "extras" for your needs, such as a fee-free credit card, free traveler's checks, or low-cost overdraft protection.

■   Safety. It goes without saying that bank safety is a special concern these days. Even if all your money is in federally insured accounts, a bank failure might cause a delay in access to your funds or loss of interest, so it's best not to have all your nest eggs in the same banking basket.

Cashing Out

We had some rude shocks when we first went fulltiming. Instruments we thought were as good as cash turned out not to be. A Florida bank refused to honor the cashier's check we'd brought from our home bank; a discount store refused to take our traveler's checks for a basketload of supplies; a S&L balked at redeeming our savings bonds.

Here are some ways to get cash on the road.

Credit cards. With most major credit cards you can get cash at a bank or automated teller machine (ATM) and sometimes at other outlets as well. Some cards, such as Discover, also offer emergency hotline help for cash emergencies such as a highway breakdown. For a cash advance, you pay a transaction fee, which could be a percentage or a flat rate, plus applicable interest. Most cards charge interest on cash advances from the day of withdrawal even if you pay the bill each month and are not subject to other interest charges. See About Credit Cards, pages 70–72, for more on credit cards.

Debit cards. Major credit card companies (Visa, MasterCard) also issue debit cards, which automatically deduct funds from your savings or brokerage account.

You pay no interest because you're withdrawing your own money. However, there may be an annual fee and a charge for each transaction. Many banks also offer debit cards.

ATM cards. Usually issued free by your bank, an ATM card can be used to get cash automatically from your checking or savings account at any member bank, street kiosk, airport, supermarket, or mall. For the fulltimer, the best ATM card is the one belonging to the largest network, with the most outlets convenient to your travel route. Networks may be local, regional, or international.

When comparison shopping, ask about transaction fees, which may vary according to whether the ATM is located at a branch of your own bank, at a member bank, or at a commercial outlet. Take precautions when using an ATM, especially at isolated machines, and keep your personal identification number (PIN) in your head, not written down.

Traveler's checks. A traveler's check is more theft-proof than cash, but it won't be accepted by everyone every time. Traveler's checks are issued free with some savings accounts. Otherwise you'll pay about 1 percent. Even free checks cost you money, however, because money invested in traveler's checks is tied up and earns no interest.

When shopping for traveler's checks, ask exactly what you must do if they are lost or stolen. If you have to travel miles to report a theft or wait days for your money, you could be stranded. Replacement rules and times vary, and the process seldom is as quick and easy as you expect.

Read the fine print about your responsibility. If the company can prove that you were negligent in handling traveler's checks, they may refuse to pay. In one incident a few years ago, people were denied refunds for stolen traveler's checks because they had signed them at the issuing bank with erasable ballpoint pens. The thieves simply erased the signature and penned in a new one, then added a matching counter-signature.

Savings bonds. Series EE savings bonds, available for as little as $25 each ($50 maturity value), are as safe as traveler's checks, but they earn interest. At this writing the interest on savings bonds is 6.5 percent if the bonds are held to maturity—a better rate than is currently offered by money market funds or T-bills. Moreover, the interest is tax-deferred until you redeem the bonds. You might stock up on them during your last few years at work, then spend them on the go when you're in a lower tax bracket. For more information go to www.savingsbonds.gov.

The disadvantage of savings bonds is that they must be held for at least six months before you can redeem them, and they can be cashed only at savings institutions. That means you're out of luck on nights, weekends, and holidays, when thrifts are closed. Nor can you use them in other countries; savings bonds can't be cashed outside the United States, not even in branches of U.S. banks.

Bonds are no longer issued immediately. You must apply at your bank or S&L, and the bond arrives by mail from the Federal Reserve two or three weeks later.

After one southern S&L refused to cash bonds for us, we wrote the U.S. Treasury and were told that institutions that sell such bonds are _required_ to redeem them as long as you have adequate identification and do not ask for "unreasonable" amounts. Now we cash only a few hundred dollars at a time, offer a passport and a driver's license as ID, and stand up for our rights. If you meet all the rules and are still refused, report the institution to the U.S. Treasury, Savings Bonds Division, 1111 20th Street N.W., Washington, DC 20226.

Money by wire. Money sent via Western Union arrives across the country in as little as fifteen minutes, so it's instant cash in an emergency. It can also be used to send cash to Mexico or Canada (although international transfer takes longer).

Wire transfer is fast, but it's cumbersome and expensive. You can ask someone to go to a Western Union desk in person, with cash, or you can charge a transfer against a credit card. Costs range from about $15 to send $50–100 to $43 to send $400–$500. To claim your cash, you'll need ID, such as a driver's license. For information and locations, call 800-325-6000, or go to www.westernunion.com.

Wire transfers between banks usually cost a flat rate, so they are a better deal than Western Union if you're sending large amounts but less competitive for small amounts. Things can get sticky if you're not a depositor at one or both banks, but it's worth a try. You can also arrange a cash transfer via American Express.

Other methods. Here are ways to get cash in a real pinch:

■   Have someone send you a cashier's check via Express Mail or an overnight express service. You may have trouble cashing a cashier's check in a city where you have no account, but most banks are willing to accommodate you if you have good ID (such as a passport), and are willing to pay for a long-distance call to verify the check.

■   Have someone send you cash via registered mail. It takes longer than regular mail because it must be signed for by each person who handles it, but if cash must be mailed, this is the safest method.

■   Have someone send you a postal money order via a fast method such as Express Mail or FedEx. Money orders are inexpensive and safe. On the downside, post offices aren't open at night or on holidays, and a small post office may not have enough cash on hand to cash a large money order.

Hang Onto Your Cash

You'll have to get cash less often if you use checks and credit cards wherever possible. Our rule is to try personal checks first. They're *always* accepted for bills paid by mail, *usually* accepted for campground fees, prescriptions, and medical and dental charges, and *occasionally* accepted (but don't rely on it) for stamps and other postal supplies, flea-market buys, restaurant meals, groceries, auto parts, fuel, and purchases in variety stores.

When checks fail, we try a credit card *if* we can charge the item at no extra cost. Always ask about this, especially at fuel stations and small businesses; some merchants charge a premium price for credit card purchases. Some gas stations have three price structures, based on whether you pay by cash, their own credit card, and other credit cards. Small businesses might want an additional 4 percent or so to put your purchase on the plastic.

We're assuming that you prefer not to carry large amounts of money aboard. However, if you do feel more comfortable with a stash of cash, invest in a fireproof safe that can be mounted in a hidden spot in the most theft-proof, crash-proof manner you can devise (such as welding it to the RV frame).

Ironclad ID

If you find that your driver's license isn't enough identification, get a passport. We've always carried ours, and they have been a big help in establishing our identity in situations where a driver's license alone was getting us nowhere.

Good ID is crucial to the rootless wanderer, but it's important to safeguard personal information. Now that some states have passed laws prohibiting the practice, most merchants no longer ask for a credit card as additional ID for cashing a check. Be suspicious of anyone who asks for a credit card as ID, because it's of no use to an honest merchant. Unless you have used it to make a purchase, he cannot make a claim against your card even if you gave him a bum check.

Never reveal your calling card number, and never write down your PIN in the same place as the number.

Thieves can access your bank account if they can get the number. A signature isn't needed. Don't give your account number or PIN to anyone who calls you; don't use deposit slips to write grocery lists or as substitute business cards when you want to give your name and address to campground friends.

About Credit Cards

Even if you've never been a credit card user in the past, plastic can play an important role in maintaining your fulltiming life. But be aware that not all credit cards, not even all Visas or all MasterCards, are alike.

Interest rates differ among issuing banks and also according to limits set by state law. Some bank cards charge interest at a set rate, whereas others charge it at a variable rate tied to the Federal Reserve prime rate, which changes frequently.

Each month, *Kiplinger's* magazine publishes lists of the best credit card buys for those who carry a balance (i.e., pay interest) and those who don't. Get the latest issue. Annual fees range from zero to $50, and interest rates can go as high as 20 percent or more. Most lending institutions have a toll-free number, so you have nothing to lose by shopping around. Call for several credit applications, then read the fine print and apply only for the cards that will cost the least according to the way you will use them.

Below are some features to consider when selecting a credit card for fulltiming.

Cost of Using the Card

■ **Annual fees.** Fee-free cards are available; others cost $35 or more per year. Often, cards with the lowest annual fees charge the highest monthly interest. If you get a card that carries no annual fee and pay it off each month, you pay nothing for the convenience of having a credit card unless you incur transaction fees or penalties.

■ **Interest charges.** If you pay your credit card bill in full each month, it won't matter to you if interest rates are in the 18 percent bracket. If you get your mail regularly and pay bills by their due date, this convenient credit costs you nothing. Once you get sucked into the interest vortex, however, it isn't always easy to claw your way back out. When you carry a balance, interest rates begin at once with each purchase and are calculated on the average daily balance.

If your mail sometimes is delayed and you want to avoid getting caught with interest or late payment charges, work with a credit card company that allows you to pay the bill even if you don't receive it. To do this, keep track of all your credit purchases and send a check to pay the amount owed each month *before* the due date. Some companies aren't equipped to deal with your payment without all the data contained in the stub that comes with the bill, so ask first.

■ **Penalties.** In addition to interest, charges are made for late payments and for charging more than your limit. If your mail is often delayed, keep track of your account on paper so you don't incur these charges. Or track your account on your credit card company's Web site.

If you're dealing with a Visa or MasterCard debit card from your bank or broker, you're simply withdrawing your own money from your own account and are not subject to interest charges. Another plus is that you can have a very high spending ceiling, limited only by the size of your account. The disadvantage to these cards is that you get no "float;" as soon as the merchant reports the purchase, your account is charged. Brokerages may charge a fee of $25 to $35 per year for cards that are available from banks for nothing.

Kickbacks

With the popularity of the new "affinity" cards (Visa or MasterCards connected with another business or organization) have come all manner of paybacks connected with credit card use. Every time you use an affinity card there is a payoff to your favorite college, cause, or charity, or to you in the form of frequent-flyer miles or some other benefit. The Discover card, for example, pays you back a percentage of your purchases each year, in cash. The RV Real Value card, issued at Flying J Travel Plazas, is used like a MasterCard anywhere, and when you use it at Flying J locations, it results in discounts on gasoline, diesel, propane, and merchandise. All purchases add "RV Points," which are redeemable for meals at Flying J restaurants or for merchandise from the RV Real Value Club catalog.

All major credit card companies also offer prestige, or "gold" cards, which cost more per year but also offer higher kickbacks, benefits, or privileges.

Extras

With most major credit cards you can get a cash advance almost anywhere in the world. Compare bottom-line costs, including interest and transaction fees.

If you use credit cards for business expenses, consider designating one card for business purposes only. Business credit cards can offer services such as a monthly breakdown by type of expense or a yearly breakout of costs by category. This is a tremendous help with bookkeeping and taxes.

Another benefit offered automatically by some cards, and at additional cost by others, is warranty protection that insures you against loss or breakage of any purchase charged to that credit card.

Most cards also offer optional insurance against credit card theft or fraud and another insurance that pays your balance if you die or become disabled. Insurance that takes over payments is, of course, of little value to those who pay their balance in full every month.

Read the fine print in your card contract to acquaint yourself with your rights and obligations when your card is stolen or when you are charged for merchandise that you never received or that arrived in unsatisfactory condition. Sometimes you're protected only if the item was bought or ordered within, say, fifty miles of "home," which in your case may be a forwarding address in a state you never visit. If your card is stolen, report it immediately; it's likely that you won't be liable for charges even if you didn't buy the extra insurance.

Brokerages

Just as it may no longer make sense to stick with a hometown banker, it is wise to re-think your brokerage too. We were paying top commission rates to a "full-service" broker who was available to us only during Eastern-time business hours and who could only offer us a limited selection of funds. We switched to a 24-hour brokerage, and now we are able to trade via telephone at any hour. We also have a wider choice of funds, and we pay lower commissions.

If we choose, we can do the entire trade by touch-tone telephone or entirely on the Internet. To be honest, however, we're reluctant to use online trading because of security concerns. Each year in March, *Barron's* evaluates online brokers according to fees, ease of use, security, quality of research, and other factors.

Using online or discount brokerages may not be for everyone since it means doing more of your own research and relying less on calls from your broker to tell you about a new issue or suggesting that you bail out of Tanking Enterprises.

When shopping for a new brokerage, keep in mind that commissions vary greatly, as do services. Small traders generally pay higher fees than high rollers; the deepest discounters usually do not offer 24-hour service except through their Web sites. And while some mutual fund companies offer round-the-clock service and no commission (load), they deal only in their own family of funds and cannot sell you individual stocks. They may not offer any check-writing privileges and probably cannot offer a credit/debit card, as a brokerage can.

Additional Financial Finaglings

Other wealth. Two of the best "bank accounts" for fulltimers are cupboards filled with food and a stock of spare parts.

Power of attorney. Everyone today needs a will, a living will, and other legal documents, but the fulltimer has added reason for giving power of attorney to one or two trusted friends or relatives. When you're far from home, this person can act on your behalf in hundreds of useful ways. Discuss it with an attorney.

Joint bank account. An inexpensive way to empower a trusted friend or relative to act on your behalf is to open a joint bank account with him or her. In what we call the Friendly Account with Janet's mother, we keep a small balance that Mom can use to pay bills that come due when we can't be reached. She can draw on this account for family birthday gifts or funeral flowers and deposit checks that arrive when we are out of touch.

Joint accounts can, of course, present problems in cases of the inevitable deaths and taxes, so keep balances small and manageable. Be wary of sharing a safe-deposit box or bank account with a relative in a state where accounts are frozen and boxes sealed when one party dies. You could lose access to your valuables for weeks.

Other joint ownerships. Because so many of today's relationships are made up of people who are not married or otherwise legally related, lawyers keep busy untangling the many wrangles that result. Marriage is a legal contract, and as a spouse, relative, or legal heir you have certain rights that the law does not extend to your lover or best friend, no matter how strong and cherished the personal attachment between you, *unless you get it in writing*. Where rights and possessions are at stake between or among partners who have no legal relationship, see a lawyer now to avoid the possibility of bitter, costly, and perhaps futile battles later.

ELEVEN

Keeping in Touch

Mail on the Trail

Whether it's a letter from Aunt Hattie, a pension check, or a charge account bill, we all want our mail to reach us securely and quickly. On the other hand, we're also pursued by tons of junk mail that we *don't* want. It's tricky to keep the postal spigot running full force while filtering out as much unwanted mail as possible.

The more important the content and speed of your correspondence, the more you'll depend on mail, e-mail, FedEx, UPS, Express Mail, faxing, paging, and other special services. And that in turn can mean higher fulltiming costs.

The wireless revolution has impacted fulltiming so fully that you can be reached anywhere, any time, by anyone. A special training unit, www.rvcollege.com, has even sprung up for the purpose of training RVers about e-mail and the Internet.

As a fulltimer you will need to establish one permanent mailing address and a means for getting mail from it to you. If you'll be fulltiming for a long time, handling your mail will eventually become drudgery to anyone, no matter how willing and able, who does it for you. And when friends and family go on vacation, get sick, or have busy periods, your mail problems may take second place. This will not be the case if you use a professional forwarding service, nor will the forwarding service snoop into your personal affairs.

We, however, are lucky enough to have Janet's mother available to forward our mail. We can ask her to throw away the seed catalog but forward the L.L. Bean catalog and the alumni bulletin, to sieve out checks and deposit them for us, and to contact us immediately if she senses an emergency. When we are in other countries, where forwarding costs are very high, she throws away excess tonnage, trims borders off letters, and chooses which things to send via Priority Mail and which to send via the cheapest method.

The chief advantage of having a trusted family member handle your mail is that you can get completely customized service, always with your best interest in mind. Despite all their other advantages, none of the mail forwarding options listed below can think for you like Mom or Sis or good ole Charlie. However, since such people are rare, here are some other options.

Keeping Your Home Address

If you're going to be fulltiming for a year or less, you can continue to use your home address, even if someone else is living there. The U.S. Postal Service forwards all first-class mail free, directly from the post office, within the United States for one year. Non-first-class mail is forwarded free for up to sixty days. See your postmaster for details. (If yours is a small post office, send a cheery postcard or even a box of candy or some silly souvenir once in a while just to remind the hometown crew that they are appreciated.)

Forwarding from the United States to Mexico and Canada also is free, but you'll probably have to pay to receive the mail on the other end. Postal strikes in Canada have made things very inconvenient for us in the past, and mail to Mexico can be hit-or-miss, although some Mexican states are somewhat more reliable than others. Once you leave North America, mail forwarding becomes more complicated and expensive.

If you are using your home address, as described above, the U.S. Postal Service will continue to forward newspapers and magazines at your expense after the sixty-day limit has expired. You leave a check to cover costs, then send additional money as needed. The upside to all this is that the mail comes into the post office, gets a new label, and goes right back out the same day. With forwarding services, the delay could be several days; if it goes to a friend or relative, it could sit there for weeks.

The downside to this method is that after a year the post office will not continue to forward mail sent to your old address. If you're not home by then, you'll have to supply a new address.

There's also a chance that mail sent to your old home will go astray, and there are sure to be some snafus with mail labeled "Do Not Forward. Return to Sender." This invariably seems to happen with very important mail, such as a new credit card or a bill, and it may wander around for weeks before you receive it. If you're using this type of mail forwarding, you might try writing to your credit card company, for example, alerting it to the fact that this may happen. Then request that the company not change your permanent address unless notified by you to do so.

One more point about dealing with the postal service: your instructions must be in writing and signed. Laws requiring this are for your protection, so allow plenty of time for changing your forwarding address each time you move on.

Receiving Forwarded Mail

Half the battle is to get the mail headed your way, but more headaches await on the receiving end. Wherever possible, we prefer to have our mail go to a friend, relative, business associate, or other personal address or to General Delivery rather than to a campground we have never visited before.

Although most campgrounds are highly sensitive to the value of mail, we've been in some where all guest mail is thrown into a box for anyone to root through. If your travel plans change and you go elsewhere, it may sit there forever. If you do want a campground to safeguard your mail, it helps to write ahead to announce that you're on the way and to ask that your mail be held there until you arrive or send further instructions.

If you're using General Delivery, do some research in advance at www.usps.gov or 800-ASK-USPS (800-275-8777) so that you can have mail sent to the small town or branch post office most convenient to your campsite. If it goes to a large city, it ends up downtown at the main post office, where traffic is heavy and parking is impossible.

Mail sent care of General Delivery can be held for a limited time, usually ten to fifteen days, before the post office is required to send it back where it came from. So if you are delayed, notify the postmaster *in writing*. (Another advantage of dealing only with small post offices is that the personnel are friendlier, and they receive so little general-delivery mail that they are likely to remember your name and give you more personal service. In the few cases when we were delayed beyond the ten days, we've phoned ahead and assured the postmaster that written instructions were on the way. Each one bent the rules for us.)

In some small-town post offices we've been welcomed like old friends because our mail had been piling up and they were curious about us. As an added precaution, we usually send a postcard ahead to the postmaster, indicating cheerfully that we are on the way and asking that a lookout be kept for our mail.

Even after you and the mail both arrive, it's not over until the mail is safely in your hands. Take identification to the postal window; it may be required. Suspicious clerks don't want to give mail to the wrong people, and that's good. Also, it can help the clerk find your mail. If your name is a difficult one like *Groene*, pronounced *GRAYnee*, it isn't enough to ask for it verbally because it's filed under *GRO* but the clerk hears *GRAY*, or *Haney* or *Raney*.

We once checked into a resort to find that all our mail had just been sent back to our permanent address because a family named Greene had just checked out. Starving for mail, we felt as if a feast had been snatched from under our forks. After that, we started writing ahead to *any* address where we might be receiving mail.

Presenting your name in big, block letters is even more important in areas where another language is spoken. In Mexico the clerk may look for the Bennetts under V and the Yardleys under *LL*. In French Canada, when the O'Rourks request their mail, the clerk may look under *Au* or *Eau*. Write it down.

No matter how well you have covered all the bases, leave a forwarding address with each campground and post office before you move on. If you don't know where you're going next, leave your permanent address. If you don't, and if mail arrives after you've left, it will be returned to the sender.

One way to make sure you get all the mail that has been forwarded to any one address is to have your mail forwarder number the packets. Checking in by telephone, you can compare notes on how many packets were sent, and then you'll know when all of your mail has arrived.

Always keep in mind that FedEx, UPS, and other services cannot deliver to general-delivery or a post office box address. Because most mail-order merchandise is not sent through the mail, don't order anything unless you can supply a street address.

Some other tips:

■   If your mail forwarder knows where you are at the time any certified or registered mail arrives, he or she should give your address to the mail carrier. Once signed for, it is considered delivered, and it will have to be re-registered or certified to get the same protection when it is forwarded to you.

■   Make sure your mail forwarder uses enough postage. If it arrives marked "Postage Due" and the campground or other receiver refuses to take delivery, it could end up anywhere.

■   Although it's very tempting to arrange for mail to be waiting for you at General Delivery when you arrive, it's sometimes better to get there first and then decide on the best place to have the mail sent.

■   Rates keep changing, so we won't quote them here, but good values for small packets include Priority Mail, Express Mail via the post office, and Second-Day Air via a package delivery service. If you use one of the large mail forwarding services that deals daily with these services, you won't get hit with the additional pickup charge.

■   If you're in a desperate hurry for a delivery, decide on the best course of action for each situation. Special Delivery is no longer the only choice; according to our local postmaster, Express Mail is faster.

■   If the campground office is closed when the mail carrier delivers your special-delivery mail, it will go back to the post office, and a note will be left for you at the campground office. And if that little note goes astray, it may be days before you collect your mail. Certified and registered mail also goes back to the post office if there is no one to sign for it.

■   FedEx and UPS do not consider Saturday a working day, so weekend service costs a hefty premium. However, Saturday deliveries of Express Mail are standard. Two services are available: post office to post office, and post office to addressee. If you arrange by phone for someone to send you something via Express Mail, specify whether you want it to go to the post office or to a personal address. Another advantage of Express Mail is that it can go to a post office box; FedEx and UPS deliveries cannot.

■   Renting a post office box has many advantages for the fulltimer who stays in one general area. Mail waits safely in the box until it's convenient for you to collect it. Box access hours are usually much longer than post office window hours, sometimes even 24 hours a day, so you can pick up the mail at night or on weekends if you like. Private postal box services are also springing up around the country.

Forwarding Services

Many options are available, from very inexpensive mail forwarding services that are included in some camping club memberships to high-tech services that also offer voice mail and other advantages. Compare not just price but also speed and accessibility. Some services have toll-free telephone numbers and 24-hour service. With others, you can call only during business hours, on your quarter.

Things to consider include the following.

■   The option of discarding all mail of a certain class or rate (e.g., bulk rate).

■   Total costs, including monthly or annual fees, extra services such as voice mail, phone calls (if the service doesn't have a toll-free number), and any additional fees for forwarding certified mail or UPS deliveries.

■   How long the company has been in business and how many hours a day you can access a live person. Reliability and communication are crucial.

■   The total elapsed time between the time your mail is received by the service and when it reaches you. Does the service forward daily, weekly, or at their convenience? Does it send mail via first-class, Priority, or Express Mail? How fully can you fine-tune the service to your own needs? Can it handle mailings when you are out of the country?

■   Does the service have a street address that you can use for all legal purposes, including putting your children in school or getting a driver's license?

■   Postal stores are found nationwide, often in strip malls, but their use to full-timers is limited. You can rent a postal box for about $20 a month, and the postal store will forward your mail for a fee plus boxes or envelopes. Most, however, are at-tuned more to local traffic. They usually don't have a toll-free number, e-mail, or an answering machine that you can call outside of business hours.

American Home Base, Box 2430, Pensacola, FL 32513. American Home Base sends all your mail, including mail received that same day, once a week on whatever day you choose. The fee is $10 a month plus postage and a one-time startup fee. The company also provides fax service, voice mail, a toll-free number, and phone cards. Call 888-726-6245 or e-mail amhomebase@amhomebase.com.

DFB Enterprises, Box 161549, Fort Worth, TX 76161. DFB sends most mail out once a week, usually on Fridays. Fees are $20 to $28 monthly depending on how much mail you receive. You'll pay extra for special services and for boxes. The company can also pay your bills, handle your voice mail, and sort catalogs so you get only the ones you want. Call 800-525-2691 or e-mail flattop@ticnet.com.

Escapees Mail Service, 101 Rainbow Drive, Livingston, TX 77355. This service specializes in people who live full time in RVs and is among the most personalized available. The staff will even open mail and read it to you if you like and will send you a card to tell you if you don't have any mail. Yearly fees are $70–$100 plus postage, one-time enrollment, and membership. You can vote by absentee ballot, from this address, pay federal income taxes with no state taxes, get a Texas driver's license, and so on. The group also provides voice mail and phone cards. Call 800-231-9896 or e-mail mail.service@mail.escapees.com.

Family Motor Coach Association, 8291 Clough Pike, Cincinnati, OH 45244. FMCA membership, which offers mail forwarding on a schedule of the association's choosing, emergency message service, and other benefits, is $35 per year. Members must have motorhomes, not other types of RVs. Call 800-543-3622 or go to www.fmca.com.

Fast Forwarding, Box 917729, Longwood, FL 32791. For $140 a year this company forwards your mail as often as you like. You pay for postage and envelopes. They put their return address on all mail, a nice feature, which takes it back to your forwarder if it doesn't reach you. The company also has emergency messaging. Call 800-321-9905 or e-mail maillady@hotmail.com.

Mail Forwarding Services, Box 90, Jefferson, OR 97352. For $10 a month plus postage this company forwards your mail at most once a week. It accepts UPS packages at its street address, accepts COD parcels, and will fax important mail if you specify what to watch for. The company offers emergency service and a discount if you pay six or twelve months in advance. Call 800-452-2130 or e-mail mfs@dnc.net.

Rocky Mountain Homebase, Box A, Clifton, CO 81520. Rocky Mountain Homebase charges $200 a year plus postage to give you exactly the kind of service you want, sending the good stuff and shredding the rest. If you're looking for something special and it arrives, they'll e-mail you with the news. They work mornings only, but the toll-free number can take messages, including emergency messages. Call 800-872-3089 or e-mail griffinr@gj.net.

Travelers Remail Association, 6110 Pleasant Ridge Road, Arlington, TX 76016. This association also provides a state tax haven. Mailings are made almost every day, or less often if you like, for an annual fee of $50 plus postage and a handling fee equal to half the postage. Extra fees also apply for other services, such as same-day mailing. The message service and emergency locator service are included. You can tell them if you are looking for a special letter or don't want to get certain catalogs. Call 800-666-6710.

Other companies include *Mail Call USA*, 877-447-2758; *Our Mail Travel Service*, 800-723-0110; *Associated Mail and Business Services*, 888-706-0378; *Snowbird Mail & Message Service*, 800-800-0710; *Re-Mail Plus*, 800-221-9609, www.dnc.net.mfs; *Homebase Oregon*, 800-689-8923, homebase@oregoncoast.com; *Keep 'N Kontact*, 800-722-7468; *Mail Room Plus*, 800-435-9876; *Travelers Mail Express*, 800-843-7282; and *Alternative Resources*, 800-477-2664, www.alternativeresources.net.

Managing Mail

Once you have an address, the next step is to eliminate as much mail flow as possible. Arrange for automatic bank deposits of your checks, automatic investment, and automatic bill paying where feasible. Notify those correspondents you no longer care to hear from. One effective way to get off some mailing lists is to mark an envelope "Refused, Return to Sender," and give it back, unopened, to the mail carrier.

Get your name off junk-mail lists by writing Mail Preference Service, Direct Marketing Association, 11 W. 42nd Street, New York, NY 10163-3661 and Equifax Option, Box 740123, Atlanta, GA 30374-0123. Be sure to give your complete name and address. You may have to write more than once if you are listed under more than one name, and you'll probably have to write again later. Mailing lists multiply like rabbits.

When you order something by mail, note on the order blank: "Temporary address. Do not add to *any* mail list." If you underline the word any, it emphasizes that you don't want it on their list or on lists they sell to others.

Subscribe only to magazines you can't buy at a newsstand. Ask your broker how you can reduce mail poundage such as stock proxies and annual reports, perhaps by giving proxy power to someone else. Inquire about receiving electronic checking account statements.

Once you select an address, *carve it in stone*. Trust us on this one: once an address gets written down, mail goes there forever. It's impossible to keep all your friends and relatives, let alone businesses and banks, abreast of your ever-changing addresses, so don't even try. When Mom is handling our mail and people ask for a more up-to-date address than the one they have, she just says, "Oh, just send it here. The post office handles all that automatically," or, "They're on the go again. Send your letter here so I can send it via FedEx with their next mail packet." Commercial mail forwarding services can be more blunt. They will refuse to give your address to anyone without your authorization.

If you alternate between only two addresses per year, as many fulltimers do, have stationery printed with both addresses, like this:

Marilyn and Bob Bennett
May 1–October 1: P.O. Box 5555, Ogunquit, ME 55555
October 1–May 1: 10 N. 10th St., #345, Naples, FL 44444
mbbennett@emailservice.com

The Mail Order Maze

Ordering by mail has caused fulltimers more grief and relief than anything but the tire pump. Whether or not you've been a mail-order user before, you may have special need for it as a fulltimer.

If you have a credit card for no other reason, it can be a lifeline to Internet and telephone orders when you require one of the following.

- Emergency delivery of a hard-to-find spare part.
- Quick and efficient gift giving without having to wrap and mail a package.
- Exactly the right size, color, or quality in clothing, linens, and other supplies. By always dealing with the same catalog house or Web site, you are assured of consistency. For example, we know what size L.L. Bean hiking boots fit us and what shade of yellow towels from Penney's will match our bathroom. Ordering by mail also saves time and fuel.
- Tremendous choice. Even in a large store, you probably won't have the choice of items that you can find in one catalog or Web site. Despite the size and weight, we carry Penney's catalogs. We order from them constantly for ourselves and for gifts, and we use them as price guides when we're shopping for a big item, such as an appliance.
- Access to the specialty and oddball merchandise that is often needed in fulltiming. On the Web you can find anything, from a 12-volt VCR to an automatic pet feeder. Through specialty catalogs you can also find all the things you need for any hobby, no matter how exotic, from operating ham radios to raising hamsters.

Mail ordering also has its negatives, and they are worse for fulltimers. Here are some ways to cope.

- Most mail order firms do not deliver to post office boxes or General Delivery; you must provide a street address. Sometimes you can specify that an item be sent by mail or not at all, but don't count on it. Most mail order outfits simply aren't set up to use the mail.

■   Returns, follow-ups, credits, and warranty work get much more complicated when you're on the move. Sometimes it's better to deal with local merchants or national chains.

■   Shipping costs are increasing. You pay 10–20 percent for freight and handling. We once sent a check for a long list of items, most of which were out of stock. Although the company sent us a full refund for the merchandise that was not available, we ended up paying $4.50 in shipping and handling for the one $4 item we received. Now when we order several items from a company that charges a high minimum shipping cost, we write on the order, "Do not back order, or fill order partially. If you cannot fill the entire order, please cancel it and return my check."

■   Sales tax may be charged. Compare the bottom line.

■   Packages are not forwarded free of charge, which means a big increase in your shipping costs if an order doesn't arrive before you move on. You might state on each order something like, "If order cannot be shipped to arrive before [date], cancel order and refund my money by return mail." When ordering by phone, ask whether the item is in stock for immediate shipment.

Additional tips on coping with the mail order maze:

■   When you receive duplicate or unwanted catalogs, put them in the campground's literature-exchange bin. Someone else might need them.

■   Keep meticulous records of telephone and e-mail orders, including warranties, verbal promises made over the phone (get the name of the person), confirmation numbers, dates of all orders and correspondence, and every scrap of paper that comes with the merchandise. Exchanges usually can't be made without key reference numbers.

The Next Best Thing to Being There?

Although fulltimers come in all sizes, shapes, and ages and their incomes vary widely, all have similar contentments and complaints. Chief among their pleasures is the freedom to move on as they please. One of their most common gripes, on the other hand, is telephones. Here are some tips for telephoning on the go.

Using Your Phone Card

At this writing, phone card use remains problematic. Although laws are making it tougher for telephone companies to block your access to discount dialing via a toll-free number, we still encounter difficulties.

Your primary defense is to know the access numbers for your long distance company. If you simply dial "0" plus the phone number, following the instructions on the pay phone, the call will go through promptly, but you'll be billed by whatever carrier handled the call, sometimes at prices far higher than those charged by your chosen carrier.

If you get a lot of bills from telephone companies you've never heard of, call your primary carrier and ask how to access its service from wherever you are. And if you find that you can't reach that service, complain to the campground or other merchant whose pay phone you're using, as well as to the Federal Communications Commission, 1919 M Street N.W., Washington, DC 20554.

When you check into a campground that has telephone hookups, always ask for a full rundown of how charges are computed for the calls you make from your own campsite. There may be a flat, daily fee, or you may be charged by the call or by the minute.

Cell Phones

Cell phone prices and per-minute charges are going down, and coverage is now worldwide. There are few places on earth where you can't be reached by cell phone, fewer still where you can't use a satellite phone. Reception is clearer, faster, and more reliable, and additional features are as sophisticated as those you can get in hard-wired phones. They include CallTrace, Caller ID, Automatic Callback, Automatic Recall, Call Waiting, Call Forwarding, and much more. Read price lists carefully and compare costs. Communications are changing so rapidly that it's hard to keep up. Old-fashioned costs for roaming, busy signals, and unanswered calls are disappearing in favor of prepaid, disposable cell phones.

It pays to keep inquiring, shopping, and learning. Our mail from readers continues to tell us that AT&T's One Rate program is far and away the favorite with fulltimers.

Other Ways to Communicate

Don't assume that you have to run out and invest in a cell phone; you have many other choices, and our survey of fulltimers found that many manage without cell phones. Some campgrounds have landline telephone hookups, which allow you to make calls from the comfort of your living room. If you have a computer and modem, you can communicate worldwide over telephone lines by e-mail or fax.

Many fulltimers prefer less expensive, more relaxed options. You might, for example, have an answering machine hooked up somewhere and call in for messages when you get around to it. Some camping clubs and mail forwarding services (including all those mentioned in this chapter) offer message taking or voice messaging services. Telephone companies also offer complete voice mail services.

Modem Hookups

E-mail winfield3@aol.com for a list of RV parks that provide overnight phones and modem hookups at campsites. While more and more campgrounds are providing Internet access in some form, fulltimers still have to go out of their way to find at-site phone and modem hookups by the night. (For long-term site rentals you pay $50 or so to the telephone company to set up phone service.) Some campgrounds provide phone hookup free; some charge a nightly fee and/or a per-minute charge. The convenience of having a phone in the privacy of your RV is well worth an extra few dollars per night. If you can add to this list or comment on it, please e-mail Winfield Sterling at the address above, who does the list as a service to fellow RVers.

Licenses by Mail

Can't keep up with hunting, fishing, and driver's licenses when you are living in a dozen states each year? Go to www.fileamerica.com. In many states you can file online, and in others you can download the forms and mail them in.

The E-Mail Revolution

When we last surveyed readers of our fulltimers column in *Family Motor Coaching* magazine more than half were already online, and many others indicated that they planned to access the Internet or at least to use e-mail. However, some respondents made it obvious that they have no interest in joining the computer era, let alone using e-mail, the Internet, or electronic bill paying.

A few complained that since they'd been on e-mail their kids had stopped writing real letters and called less often. However, most like the speed and flexibility of free e-mail and the ability to get instant photos of the new baby or the puppy's latest antics.

Laptops and notebook computers take up little space and handheld devices even less, but you can manage with no computer at all by using the free computers at many libraries. Cyber cafés and many campgrounds, truck stops, airports, train and bus stations, and hotel business centers offer Internet access for a fee. Free e-mail is getting harder to find, but is still available at www.yahoo.com and www.hotmail.com.

If you don't want to go as far as getting a computer and modem, small e-messengers are a good compromise. A small, 6-by-3-inch device that sells for about $120 can handle your e-mail only. You call a toll-free number in the United States or Canada to send and receive as often as you like. Unlimited service costs $10–$20 monthly. Try PocketMail, 925-454-5066, www.pocketmail.com or MailStation, 408-776-3193, www.mailstation.com.

Even more powerful but more costly to buy and use are wireless handheld devices that can access the Internet, including e-mail; some also incorporate a telephone. At this writing the devices sell for $150–$400, with monthly services offered in the $40–$75 range. Wireless satellite telephone service costs about $170 monthly for 100 minutes, $1.49 for additional minutes, or $30 a month for access at $1.70 per minute. For more information, contact 877-SATPHONE or www.globalstarusa.com.

Features and availability are changing so rapidly that we can only suggest that when you're ready to shop for a wireless device, get the latest magazine devoted to that technology and do some Internet research.

TWELVE

Kids on Board

For years, families with children have lived and cruised full time in boats. For the children's education most of these families depended on mail-order schooling, which was an educational challenge as well as a major expense—for tuition, work materials, tutorial and grading services, and postage. By contrast, it used to be that most full-time RVers were senior citizens, usually empty nesters.

Suddenly everything changed, thanks largely to the Internet, which allows parents to home-school children anywhere, with a worldwide support system, and at little cost. With education problems out of the way, young parents can find countless ways to support a life of fulltiming. Some work as they travel—temping, Workamping, or telecommuting. Others travel unhindered, making a living online as consultants, writers, web designers, programmers, traders, and entrepreneurial innovators in fields that were unheard of a decade ago. Still others have a mobile business, such as evaluating campgrounds, selling RV awnings, or selling their arts and crafts at fairs and festivals.

It's still rare to find fulltimers with children, but their ranks are growing, not despite their children but because of them. One young couple wrote to us that they'd sold their business and hit the road with their toddler because they considered parenthood a sacred trust, one they couldn't turn over to a sitter, nanny, or daycare center. Many couples who want to experience both travel and full-time parenting find that RV living is the ideal way to have both.

Fulltiming with children, once you've solved the income problem, is much the same as parenting at home. You have to house, feed, and educate children and keep them safe. Safety precautions in an RV are much the same as those you observe in a house, with a few exceptions. First, RVs lurch, rock, and move. Seat belts are a must under way—always, no matter how short the trip, whether it's in a motorhome or the tow car. Nobody rides in a towed trailer; it's against the law.

Second, you're in unfamiliar surroundings much of the time, so it's important to review family safety and fire escape drills often and to write new rules as necessary in response to local conditions, such as urban settings, the waterfront, or hazards such as rattlesnakes or poisonous plants.

We've known fulltimers whose babies were born and reared on board. Children ages eight and over can be seasoned campers, able to make an important contribution to family safety as well as to do chores. As they're able, teach them campfire safety, how to recognize problems during a walk-around check prior to getting under way, how to stow gear for the road, and so on.

If you have children, we're assuming that you have chosen your RV with them in mind. Each child needs privacy, a place for naps and study, a place to play, and a share of the stowage area for his or her own toys and treasures, no matter how frivolous. We've seen children who were happy as clams in nothing more than a single, overhead bunk that served as bed, study, and play area, and others were lucky enough to have a separate room. Older children can have privacy in their own tent on your campsite (freestanding or a room that attaches to the RV) or in a cuddy cabin created by a camper shell in a tow vehicle.

Gordon Groene

There's an old saying in marinas that a boat is nothing more than substandard housing until it leaves the dock. The same can be said of your RV home. When you're on the go you and your family will have the outdoors and its wonders as part of your home.

Child Safety

Debra Smiley Holtzman, J.D., M.A., is a nationally recognized child safety expert and the author of the popular child safety book *The Panic-Proof Parent: Creating a Safe Lifestyle for Your Family* (McGraw-Hill/NTC). She gave us some specific recommendations for life on the go.

■ Check for hazards in every part of the RV from your child's perspective. Get down on your hands and knees and crawl around indoors and out. You'll be quite surprised about what you will find. Ask yourself what looks tempting and what is within reach. Check floors and carpets for buried dangers like pins or coins.

■ Make sure that all child safety devices are properly and carefully installed and are well maintained. Check them frequently. Remember, the use of a child safety device does not mean that the item is completely childproof. Proper supervision is always required.

■ Your RV should, of course, be equipped with safety devices appropriate to the child's age, and it should meet RVIA safety standards. Make sure you have all of the required safety equipment, such as a fully stocked first-aid kit, a fire blanket, fire extinguishers, fire escape routines and equipment (e.g., a break-out tool). Test the smoke alarms and carbon monoxide alarms and keep them properly maintained.

■ Install child gates if needed to keep a child out of the kitchen or bathroom. Keep constant eye contact and close supervision when children are around water. Hand over responsibility for the child just as naval officers hand over the helm. Know who is in charge so you won't suffer one of those "But I thought she was with you" tragedies. Sailors say *aye-aye* for good reason. When you or your spouse take over supervision of the child, or communicate some other important message, give or receive an answer.

■ Install latches and locks for drawers and cabinets. To prevent strangulation, keep window blind cords and other types of cords, ropes, or strings out of the reach of children. Don't let a child sleep near a window or drapery.

■ Keep all tools, batteries, and machinery locked and out of the reach of children. Lock and store poisonous materials, all sharp objects, and flammable materials, including matches, emergency flares, and lighters, out of the reach of children. (Older, responsible children should be taught the dangers and proper use of flares and other safety gear.)

■ Never store flammable materials near a heat source.

■ To prevent burns, use a spill-resistant mug for hot beverages. Do not hold or carry a child while holding hot foods or beverages. Use the back burners on the stove and turn pot handles toward the back of the stove. Keep all appliance cords from dangling over the edge of counters. (Children are naturally curious and may pull on cords, unintentionally pulling the appliance and its scalding contents on themselves. Placemats and tablecloths that a child could pull off the table shouldn't be used for hot food or beverages, which can cause serious burns.) Keep hot food and beverages, glassware, and knives away from the edge of counters and tables. Set the water heater to no higher than 120°F to reduce the chance of scalding. Supervision at bath time is important for the child's safety and to prevent water waste. If you use campground showers, be especially vigilant because the water heater may be set far higher than is safe.

- Keep children out of the galley when preparing meals.
- Cover all unused electrical outlets.
- Anchor furniture and safely secure objects that could fall on your children.
- Install toilet locks. Unlike an adult, a young child's weight is concentrated in the top half of the body. When they lean into a toilet bowl, they may lose their balance, fall forward and drown in as little as 1 inch of water.
- Make sure your child's crib meets current national safety standards and has not been recalled by the Consumer Product Safety Commission, 800-638-2772 or www.cpsc.gov.
- If firearms are kept in the RV, keep them locked, unloaded, and stored out of reach. Secure ammunition in a separate, locked location. For more on firearms, see chapter 24, Safety and Security.

We'll add child safety seats to this list of "musts." Virtually all states require some sort of safety restraint. For more information, see chapter 24, Safety and Security.

A few more safety tips: we like to use chemical light sticks (e.g., Cyalume or Orion light sticks) for cool, sparkproof emergency lighting. You might also install shockproof, 12-volt LED courtesy lights at strategic spots around the RV. It goes without saying that you'll teach children about the stranger danger, especially in a campground situation, where everyone is considered "family." Just as you wouldn't let children go alone to a rest room at a mall, don't let them go to the campground shower room alone.

Homeschooling

There is nothing new about raising children on the go or in areas where there are no schools. Children have been successfully nurtured and educated in wagon trains, whaling ships, remote ranches, gypsy caravans, and the Alaskan and Australian Outbacks. Worldwide, missionaries have raised their kids in the most isolated areas for centuries.

If you choose this option, be aware that homeschooling has become so popular that the establishment feels threatened. It is railed against by teachers' unions, most newspapers, and many politicians. No matter what your politics, you'll face hassles from a vocal antivoucher, antihomeschooling movement. When you become a homeschooler, you'll probably find yourself allied with some surprising bedfellows, from right-wing zealots to left-wing nuts. But most homeschool families are ordinary folks who, for a variety of reasons, opt out of public schools.

While it's still possible to get courses by mail order, it's essential that a computer and Internet access become part of your fulltiming life. Start with doing your own homework, hours of it. Do searches under "homeschool," "home school," "home schooling," and "homeschooling." You'll discover hundreds, even thousands of Web sites. All of them have to be evaluated for your own needs, the ages of your children, and the academic goals you have for them.

A search of www.homeschool.com alone turns up special sections for home-schoolers who are not affiliated with any religion or are Catholic, nondenominational Christian, Afro-centric, or Islamic, as well as for homeschoolers in dozens of other countries. If you're new to homeschooling, friendly old-timers will lead you through the basics. Online you'll find support groups, as well as long lists of support groups for each state. (If you're having problems with local truant officers, contact the Home School Legal Defense Association at www.hslda.org.) You'll find lessons, lesson plans, activities, clip art, professional tutors who work online, supply houses selling books and materials needed by homeschoolers, and groups that help parents with science or math. Art and music courses are available, as well as programs for foreign language study and gifted children, to name just a few. You'll also find accredited schools that offer online courses from kindergarten through college level. One of the largest and most respected homeschool programs for kindergarten through eighth grade is the Calvert School, 105 Tuscany Road, Baltimore MD 21210; 888-487-4652; www.calvertschool.org. Some schools deal with the student on more of a one-on-one basis, involving parents less than in a pure homeschool situation.

While the Internet is the most obvious source for today's homeschoolers, your homework should also include "hitting the books." Good choices to start with are Mary Griffith's *The Home Schooling Handbook* and *The Unschooling Handbook* (School Wise Press), and *The First Year of Homeschooling Your Child* by Linda Dobson (Prima Publishing). Other popular books, according to the July 9, 2001 issue of *Publisher's Weekly*, are *Beginner's Guide to Homeschooling* and *Growing Without Schooling* by Patrick Farenga (Holt Associates), *Pre-Hysteric Parenting* by H. Norman Wright Cook (Cook Communications), and *Homeschooling* by Debra Bell (Thomas Nelson).

For children in kindergarten through sixth grade, *Publisher's Weekly* singles out *Getty-DuBay Italic Handwriting Series* (Continuing Education Press), the Young Patriots Series (Patria Press), *Geology Crafts for Kids* by Alan Anderson (Sterling), and the For Kids series (Chicago Review Press). For homeschooling teenagers, try the best-selling *Teenage Liberation Handbook: How to Quit School and Get a Real Life and Education* by Grace Llewellyn (Lowry House).

Online you'll find family newsletters published by individual homeschoolers who relate their own experiences, share holiday ideas, or offer to be pen pals. One written by and for fulltimers with children is www.familiesontheroad.com. Finding local homeschool groups in your travels is especially useful if you want to get in on field trips, museum visits, sports, proms, and the many other activities that homeschool families organize to keep their children socialized and active.

If, however, you find yourself on the road so much that you can't plug into local groups, use the Internet to find other mobile families with kids of your kids' ages and arrange to meet in spots where the children can play together. Between get-togethers they can keep in touch by e-mail. We've met families who purposely planned their itineraries to mesh with those of other families from time to time. They all traveled at their own pace to their own choice of places, yet met up often enough, usually for a special festival or event, that the children had lifelong friendships. We've also known families whose children kept in touch by ham radio, a hobby and very useful skill for fulltimers.

In campgrounds you'll find a built-in social life that includes swimming, hay rides,

RVIA photo archives

square dancing, game rooms, and much more for all ages. Join camping clubs that focus on family activities. Network with other RVing families. Visit Granny and Grandpa for a week at a time without having to sleep on the sofa. Visit Huntsville or Cape Canaveral to attend Space Camp as a family. Camp near Colonial Williamsburg while you all take courses in the minuet, weaving, or candle making. Attend an Indian pow-wow so your kids can play with Native American kids. Camp in Quebec and let them learn French from local kids.

You'll soon see how laughable it is for the antihomeschool forces to argue that your children will grow up to be elite, alienated, antisocial snobs. The world of homeschooling is as alive, nurturing, positive, fulfilling, mobile, and viable as fulltiming itself.

If you're still fulltiming after your kids get their high school diplomas, and you want to continue their (or your own) education, once again, you'll find many options online: California Virtual Campus, www.cvc.edu, offers more than 2,000 online courses; you can get a bachelor's degree from Indiana University (www.indiana.edu); study medicine, midwifery, or engineering with the University of Pennsylvania (www.upenn.edu); the University of Wisconsin (www.uwex.edu) offers more than 150 online courses. Western Governors University (www.wgu.edu) even gives college credits for life experience.

Other Alternatives

We've met only one couple over the years who sent their child to boarding school, but that's one choice for fulltimers, especially if your child needs special education or you want him or her to attend military or prep school. Another is to stay in one spot during the school year and travel during all vacations and holidays. A third, especially if you plan to fulltime for only a year or two, is to arrange for your hometown school system to supply lessons based on your children's familiar curriculum and teachers. Not every school will allow it, but it's worth a try.

Over the years we have met many families who lived on the go. Some of the kids are now parents themselves. There may have been failures among them, but we never met one. In every case that we observed in which a homeschooled child went back to conventional school, he or she shot to the head of the class. Never have we met such responsible, smart, resourceful kids. If you think fulltiming with kids is for you, you won't get an argument from us.

THIRTEEN

The Fulltimer's Pets

Before including a dog, cat, or other pet in your fulltiming family, consider the joys and penalties. The dangers and disruptions are so many that friends of ours chose an extreme solution and had their beloved, 18-year-old cat put to sleep rather than subject him to the rigorous roadway life.

Pets, for all their winning ways, mean more expense, more problems finding and keeping campsites, more potential for wrangles with camping neighbors, and lots more time spent on pet care than ever before. Pets get carsick, scared, thrown around in panic stops, hurt in accidents, and killed along the roadside. They get bored, bitten by bugs, thirsty, hungry, and restless when they can't run free. We've heard countless horror stories about innocent pets involved in highway accidents and about owners who delayed their trips for days because the cat disappeared or whose budgets were strained by unexpected veterinary bills when the dog needed an operation. An RVer in Alaska lost her little poodle to an eagle that swooped down and grasped the dog in its talons so quickly that the owner had no chance to save it.

Pet ownership isn't to be taken lightly, especially when you live on the go.

Many campgrounds won't admit pets at all. Those that do admit them have strict rules. Even then, you may have problems if the dog barks when you're not aboard or if the cat squirts on the neighbor's tires.

Do you really want a pet on board? If the answer is a thoughtful, loving, and selfless yes, here are some ways to make fulltiming fairer to both you and your pet(s).

Preventive Medicine

Well before leaving, see your hometown vet and make sure your pet's shots, tags, and all necessary certificates and documents are up to date. Carry these papers as carefully as cash. They'll be vital if your pet bites someone, if you cross national borders (and sometimes state), or if the animal becomes ill and needs treatment by a vet who hasn't seen it before. Most kennels require these papers, and they sometimes require extra shots before boarding a pet.

Explain your travel plans to the vet and ask if the areas you'll be visiting present any special hazards for your pet. Heartworm prevention is needed almost everywhere, and you may need to alter the pill schedule. Histoplasmosis is endemic in parts of the United States and Canada. Lyme disease and Rocky Mountain spotted fever are regional, tick-borne ailments to which pets are susceptible. Your vet knows what dangers await where.

If new immunizations are needed, have them done well enough in advance that the pet can recover if it has an adverse reaction and fully develop an immunity.

Carry ample supplies of vitamins and medications. If your pet gets carsick, it will probably adjust eventually; in the meantime a tranquilizer or a motion sickness pill might help.

If your pet hasn't already been spayed or neutered, have it done before you go. The vet can explain the many advantages to the animal's health and welfare.

RVIA photo archives

Guarding against Loss

Buy or make a pet ID tag on which you can change your address each time you move to a new campsite. You could use a capsule-type ID or a luggage tag that opens so you can change the message often. In it, place a note with your campground address, the dates of your stay, and a third-party contact if you have one. A regular ID containing your "home" address is of little value because it could take days to get word to you even if your pet is found a block away from your campsite.

If you're a dog owner, consider joining the National Dog Registry, P.O. Box 116, Woodstock, NY 12498; 800-NDR-DOGS (800-637-3647); www.natldogregistry. com. Have your local vet tattoo each of your dogs with your social security number (tattoo costs vary according to locality). For a one-time fee of $38, which covers all your dogs, the registry supplies a medallion, which explains how to call the registry via a toll-free number, that can be attached to your dog's collar. If your dog is lost, you call the registry and report where you are and how to reach you. Anyone finding the dog will see the medallion, look for the tattoo, and call the registry, which then reunites you and your dog. The registry claims a 98 percent recovery rate.

Safety and Comfort

Equipment that will make the trip safer and more pleasant for you and your pet may be found in pet and camping supply stores; on Web sites, including www. PetTribune.com and www.doggonenl.com; and in specialty catalogs. You can get a spacious carrier for small pets that is soft sided and easy to store, and it rolls like a carry-on suitcase. For information see www.rollerpet.com.

If your RV floors are cold, get a 12-volt heated pet bed. You'll find such things as portable kennels that fold up when not in use, folding fencing, and special leashes and swivels that allow the pet to be staked out in the most comfortable corner of your campsite. Also available are poop scoopers, leakproof or automatic feeders and watering bowls (although your pet may be reassured by old, familiar bowls, at least at first), and nonskid place mats, which protect the RV floor as the pet eats or drinks.

It's also a good idea to keep a pet life vest on board if you like waterfront camping or if you will be doing any boating. Dogs and cats can swim, but they can't get back aboard a boat, climb the side of a pool, or hoist themselves out of a canal. If a pet goes overboard, say experts at Ralston-Purina, a life vest will allow you to lift it by the harness; lifting it by the collar could injure it. And don't, says Ralston-Purina, take a pet whitewater rafting. In the case of an upset it may not be able to swim to safety.

If you're really serious about pets, get a towable kennel trailer. Designed for hunters, these trailers provide a cozy home for the dog(s) underway and at rest, as well as storage room for equipment and shotguns.

On the Road

People are protected by seat belts, but in an abrupt stop or accident a loose pet becomes a projectile. The pet could be hurt and so could you if you're the first thing it hurls into. Find a safe place for it to ride, install a divider in your vehicle, or keep the pet in a travel cage that is safely anchored. With a Sherpa Pet Carrier system, the pet is safely latched in. Call 800-743-7723 or go to www.sherpapet.com.

Pets need plenty of fresh air, but don't let a dog hang its head out a window; flying debris could damage its eyes. Also, never leave a pet alone in a vehicle, not even on a cloudy day. It's thoughtless, risky to the pet, and illegal in some municipalities. After only a brief time in an overheated car or camper an animal will die. Not only will you lose a cherished pet but you might be prosecuted, fined, and perhaps even jailed for animal abuse.

When driving, stop often and give the pet a brisk walk and a drink of water. Always leash the animal before opening the car or RV door because even well-trained animals sometimes run when frightened or confused. The chances of recovering a pet that bolts away from a rest stop along a busy interstate are not good. Don't risk losing yours.

If your pet is a caged bird, gerbil, or hamster, it too needs special care in the full-timing life. Movable objects such as swings and toys should be taken out of the cage. Road motion could make them swing hard enough to injure the pet.

Don't let a bird ride on your shoulder or fly free in the RV. It could escape or, worse still, be smashed against the windshield in a collision. Carry the cage in a safe spot that has gentle air flow and is out of direct sun.

When you are underway, don't leave water in the cage. Spills make for a damp cage where harmful organisms can grow. Instead, provide juicy fruits and vegetables. Then make sure to offer plenty of fresh water as soon as you park.

Pet Life on the Go

A good guidebook will enable you to find campgrounds that admit dogs and cats. Even so, it's best to call ahead to confirm that your pet will be allowed, and under what circumstances. Sometimes "pets allowed" means that your dog can be housed in the campground kennel, free or at extra cost, but will not be allowed to stay in your RV.

Some Internet sites to try for pet-friendly campgrounds and advice on traveling with pets are www.petswelcome.com/milkbone/campmap.html, www.recreation.gov/advsindex.cfm (select "pets"), www.camping.about.com/cs/campgrounds/, www.rvadvice.com/pets, and www.traveldog.com. If you search on "pets" and "campgrounds," you'll get a list of thousands of related sites.

Most state and national parks (but not all—call ahead) allow campers to bring pets if they are kept on a 6-foot leash. You and the pet will be evicted if the pet disturbs other campers or any of the park's plants or wildlife, and what constitutes a disturbance can vary. If the dog so much as startles a squirrel, or the cat jumps at a bird, the ranger might call it a crime against the native wildlife and send you all packing. Private campgrounds can be more lenient, especially if previous campers and their pets were on their best behavior. If former guests allowed their dogs to bark annoyingly or make messes or washed them in the public bathrooms, you're sure to find a "No Pets" sign at the campground entrance.

Campground living means close quarters, and tempers can fray. We once parked next to an RV in which a big dog began barking the moment its owners left for the day's fishing and didn't stop until they returned. When the owners were home, the dog didn't make a sound. Annoyed as we were, we didn't blame the poor dog. Left alone and surrounded by strange sounds, it was probably baffled and frustrated. Because of these thoughtless pet owners, that campground no longer allows pets.

If you're fulltiming with pets, be meticulous about their manners. It isn't enough to bury the dog's droppings; especially in parks, you should bag their droppings and pack them out for proper disposal. Be careful too about where the dog and cat piddle. If a pet wets on the neighbor's wheels, it's offensive to the other camper and highly corrosive to the metal.

Leave the pet alone as little as possible, and not at all if it barks while you're gone. Never bathe a dog in the campground showers, pool, or beach. Take it to a professional groomer.

Cats can suffer liver damage from DEET (N,N-diethyl-meta-toluamide), an ingredient in some insect sprays, so be cautious when using tick repellents. Check all pets often for ticks, and if a pet seems sick, take it to a vet. It might have a tick-borne disease that could affect you next. Early treatment is important because relapses can occur after the pet appears to have recovered. Ticks also can cause pet paralysis.

All pets are potential targets for thieves, so fulltimers should be aware of the dangers. Rare cats and dogs or valuable birds are easy targets; some thieves specialize in feisty dogs, entering them in illegal dogfights. There is also said to be a criminal traffic in stolen pets, which are sold to laboratories for experimentation. On the road, just as at home, safeguard the family pet.

Housekeeping Problems

Four-footed friends track in sand and mud, so vacuum frequently and use a carpet deodorizer. Change kitty litter more often than ever before. Be meticulous about airing and frequent floor cleaning and carpet shampooing because in the small area of your RV home odors can build up more quickly than you realize. Your guests will notice even if you don't.

Use tick and flea control medication (available from your vet). You can also start fighting fleas before you move into the RV. Spray everything well with a flea treatment that kills fleas in adult, larvae, and egg form. (Some powders and sprays kill only adult fleas.) Follow directions carefully; incorrect use wastes money, reduces effectiveness, and can endanger your family or the pet. You may need to respray weekly, monthly, or only after two or three months. Some products have residual power for months; using them more often than needed won't help.

If you're moving out of the RV for any period, make sure your flea control program is up to date. Fleas spend most of their lives in the carpet, furniture, or floorboards and jump onto the animal only long enough for a hearty meal. If you and the pet move out for a few weeks, you need a product that will go on killing new fleas as they hatch.

FOURTEEN

Driving
the Big
Ones

I'd love to have the biggest motorhome I can afford, but driving one scares me." It's a common fear.

If all your driving experiences have been in cars, we have reassuring news for you. High off the road in a big motorhome, you can see farther ahead and behind than in a car, so you're better able to slow down for trouble ahead, change lanes, and otherwise keep control. People see *you* better too. It's less likely that someone will pull out of a side street in front of you.

Of course, larger units are more difficult to maneuver in a tight, defensive driving situation. They take longer to stop and longer to get up to speed. And if you have to pull off the road to let an emergency vehicle past, it might take some time to find a spot large enough.

Clearance

Learn the height of your motorhome in exact feet and inches and make a label to stick on the dashboard so you or other drivers will never be in doubt. Underpasses, bridges, and fuel station canopies are usually marked, so you won't have to guess, but in some other places, such as fast-food drive-up windows, you can't be sure. One old trick is to mount a whip antenna on the front bumper, to the exact height of the tallest point in your rig. If it hits, you can back away before scraping off the air conditioner.

If you're about to start towing a big trailer for the first time, get a feel for your new

Equip your car with the big mirrors needed for towing. They'll improve your visibility, but be aware they also increase the width of your vehicle. (Gordon Groene)

width by mounting towing mirrors on your car (some states don't permit this). You'll discover that if something this wide will fit on the road without knocking all the mail-boxes off their posts, then the vehicle behind you will fit too, whether it's 30 feet long or 300.

You now know that you can tow anything of a given width down the interstate forever. Problems arise only if you want to turn a corner or back up.

Steering

The steering geometry of every rig is different, depending on length, overhang, and po-sitioning of the wheels. And because you can't see what the outside rear corner is do-ing in a turn, you have to learn to guess where it will be. A good way to get the feel of steering is to borrow a small trailer, such as a utility trailer, and practice in a wide-open place such as the far corner of a parking lot. Get used to making the trailer do what you want it to.

If you continually get confused backing up a trailer, here's a tip from truckers: Hold your hand on the wheel at six o'clock; the trailer will head in the direction you move your hand.

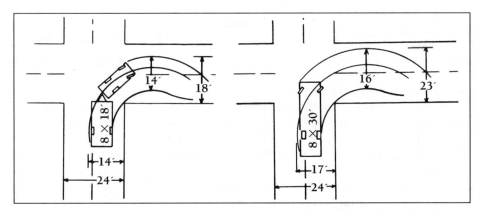

Practice driving in uncrowded places until you know exactly where all the corners of your RV will end up when you make a turn.

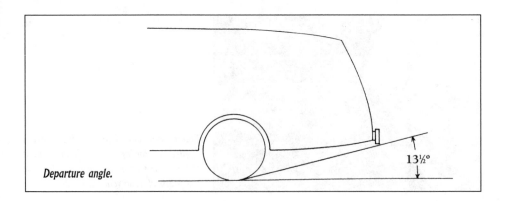

Departure angle.

13½°

Later, set up pylons or plastic trash cans and practice backing, parking, and maneuvering with your RV trailer. Set up a typical highway corner and keep practicing until you know just how wide you must swing to clear the corner with the rear wheels.

The other problem with vehicles that have long overhangs is the departure angle, the angle between the road and an imaginary line from the rear wheel up toward the rear bumper, clearing the lowest point in sight. In other words, you want to be able to judge whether a ramp angles up too sharply. Otherwise, you'll scrape something that's covered with dollar signs—usually a gas tank or plumbing fitting. Some vehicles have protection built in; on others a heavy steel roller can be added. Otherwise, you must defend yourself with a knowledge of your departure angle and drive so that you never exceed it.

Courtesy

Extra courtesy gains full-time RV drivers a safety edge and helps keep other drivers from seeing us as "those blankety-blank old road hogs." If your rig is big and cumbersome, always notice when you're holding up the parade. If a line forms behind us, we pull off the road and watch the world go by. Courtesy is always appreciated, and there is a selfish motive: In a panic stop you'll have fewer vehicles to pile into you.

In the Campground

Many times we've seen an RV driver make a braying ass of himself by loudly chewing out a copilot for "letting" him back into an overhead branch, a sand trap, or a chuck hole. Tell it to the marines. As driver-captain of this land yacht, you're in charge. Anything that goes wrong is *your* fault.

A Boeing 747 can be parked on a pinpoint at the airport without a word, so there is no reason why fulltimer teams can't develop clear hand signals that allow them to communicate in complete silence. When you're shouting to be heard over the noise of the RV engine, you only call attention to yourself as you miss the hitch for the forty-fifth time.

As we said, you the driver are responsible for whatever happens, so don't just blunder anywhere your partner points. Before attacking the campsite, both of you should get out of the RV and look things over carefully. Note the location of the hookups in relation to your outlets. Discuss any special problems, such as low-hang-

Hand signals are a big help when parking. (Gordon Groene)

ing branches, a sharp tree stump that could damage a tire, or a struggling seedling you want to avoid.

The sidekick's job is to stay within sight of the driver, either directly or in the mirror or rear-view television. Hand signals can indicate right or left, point to the sewer outlet, or show that you have "this far" to go. Tell the copilot exactly where you want to stop, so the signal will be given when you reach the right spot.

During parking the sidekick can also monitor such things as whether the backup and brake lights are working. As the tires turn slowly, look for cuts or breaks. Note any fluid leaks or bearing squeals.

Campers are nice folks who want to help, especially if you're alone. But don't let an offer of assistance turn your attempt to park into a shouting match in which you find yourself letting someone tell you where you can put your own RV. Get out of the RV and take all the time you need to walk around the campsite, decide where you want to go, and tell the neighbor what kind of signals to use.

Driving a big RV is a new and different skill, and more than a pushbutton pushover. Still, it's a skill that can be learned and enjoyed with confidence and safety. Go ahead. Drive yourself happy.

The Rental Car Puzzle

We have already discussed the pluses and minuses of having a big tow car and a travel trailer, a motorhome towing a car, or a single-vehicle operation. The big drawback to having only one set of wheels is that it's expensive and cumbersome to take a big RV everywhere you need to go.

Alternatives to using a big RV to do small errands include renting or carrying bicycles or motorbikes, walking, or taking public transportation. Just for fun, because the idea is so radical to Americans who are accustomed to having a car, compare the cost of owning and towing a car with the cost of renting a car, say once a week to do all the nuisance errands—shopping, the post office, and so on. Add up what it will cost you to own, insure, tow, and maintain a car, then call around to see what is available on rentals. Costs vary around the country, but even in expensive areas, you can usually get a weekend or rent-a-wreck special.

Here are some tips on car rental.

■   Cars are usually available in six classes, ranging from economy to luxury. In between are the compacts, mid-size, full-size 2-door, and full-size 4-door. Usually we get an economy for zipping around on errands; we rent larger cars if we need them for business or major hauling.

■   Pricing is a giant shell game, made more complicated by all the discounts, frequent-flyer bonuses, weekend specials, coupons, and other gimmicks that differ from company to company. Although we qualify for various discounts through half a dozen organizations we belong to, we can usually do as well or better without them because so many restrictions apply. Don't lose sight of the bottom line.

■   If you're price shopping underway, your best bet is to go to an airport during off-peak hours and counter-hop to comparison shop. Free telephones at airports connect you with firms that don't have counter space at the airport but are often cheaper. We've almost always been able to get to an airport and shop for a good rental easily, without reservations. You may strike out, though, during a big convention or bowl game that ties a city in knots. If you have the time, try shopping the growing number of travel sites on the Internet.

Some other points about car rental:

■ Special models are available at major rental outfits for the hearing impaired, for drivers who need hand controls, and for skiers who want tire chains and a ski rack.

■ Understand exactly what your existing RV insurance covers. You may not need the optional (and very high priced) coverage offered by the rental company. Add-on insurance is one of the biggest expenses in car rental, so be alert for alternatives. Some rental companies now include it; sometimes it's included automatically if you charge the rental on certain credit cards.

■ Always ask about special promotions. You may save a bundle by taking the car on a weekend, midweek, off-season, or for a specified block of time.

■ Fill the gas tank just before you return the car. If the rental firm fills it for you the per-gallon price will be much higher.

■ If you are a permanent or seasonal resident of a campground, see if there's enough interest to get a community car. Enlist an attorney and accountant to work out the legal and financial details.

■ If you make reservations by phone, get a confirmation number.

■ Check into used-car rentals (Ugly Duckling, Rent a Dent), but again, look at the bottom line, including insurance.

■ When renting from local companies with rock-bottom prices, ask what support they offer if you break down out of town. The national chains have nationwide support; with the independents you may be on your own.

■ Before taking off, walk all around the car checking for damage or missing pieces and report them then, in writing. That's your only defense if you're later accused of causing the damage.

■ If you want a one-way rental, check into "drop" charges. They vary widely among companies.

Should You Lease a Car?

When Bob and Mary went fulltiming, they knew they wanted to tow a car behind their big motorhome, but they didn't want to dump a big down payment, followed by high monthly payments, into the car they had in mind. They'd just sold their home and furniture and were liquid, footloose, and fancy free.

They had a cash buyer for their old car, one that wasn't suited for the fulltiming life they planned, and they didn't like the idea of putting all that money back into another car. It was beginning to feel good to have it as part of their nest egg.

So they leased a car.

Once a rarity, leased cars are now driven by more than a million people, and leasing seems to be catching on. On the plus side, there may be no down payment. If you were going to ante up, say, a $2,500 down payment on a new car, you could invest the money instead. Instead of tying money up in a car, you could have it in the bank, in bonds, or in T-bills, earning interest and available for emergencies. Meanwhile, you pay only a manageable, monthly lease fee. If you use the car as a business deduction, the advantages of leasing are even clearer (ask your certified public accountant).

However, there is a dark side to leasing, one that spells Buyer Beware. One pitfall is hidden charges. Some lease contracts start out at a temptingly low monthly rate but balloon after a certain date. Read the fine print in your contract.

Bob and Mary's story could end happily or on a sour note, depending on several factors, including luck. Most leases don't include repairs. If the car is a lemon, they'll have to pay all the maintenance bills on top of their monthly lease payments.

If their plans or goals change, and they want to turn the car in before the completion of their contract, there is a big penalty. And if they turn it in in bad condition or with high mileage, they'll be charged for repairs or a per-mile overage fee.

Some leases leave you, at the end of your obligation, with the car worth "fair market value" *as determined by the leasing company*. After four years, when Bob and Mary's lease ends, the residual value of the car will be X percent of the sticker price, and their contract says that they can buy it for that if they choose. Percentages and lease times vary, but Bob and Mary's contract stated a figure rather than a vague "fair market" value.

RV Driving Tips

A long-haul truck driver we know suggests trying the following big-rig tricks, along with any new ones you can dream up to add to your visibility, predictability, and safety. For example:

- In hilly country where there are passing lanes, plan ahead to get into the slow lane *before* someone comes up on your right side.
- "Get a run at" hills, making sure that you have a good head of steam before starting up the hill.
- On multilane highways pick the lane that is moving at the speed most comfortable for you so you don't impede others.
- Magnify all your best driving manners—turn signals, stop signals, headlight dimming, and a flick of the headlights to show truckers that they have passed you safely.
- When passing another vehicle, don't pull back into the lane until you're a good distance ahead; you should see both headlights in your right (flat, not convex) mirror.
- Mount a convex spot mirror on both sides of your vehicle.
- In mountainous country, downshift to hold down speed on downgrades to prevent brake failure.
- Leave a minimum three-second "cushion" between you and the vehicle in front. How fast you can stop in three seconds depends on your speed, your brakes, and the road conditions.

The other precaution Bob and Mary took was to talk to their insurance company. In many cases insurance for a leased car covers just the cost of the car, not the monthly payments. If it's totaled or stolen, you have to continue paying off the lease even if your insurance pays far less than what you still owe on the car.

In reading the original contract, Mary spotted a provision for some fancy add-on fees for paperwork and nonsense and got them deleted from the final draft. And Bob noticed that there was a mileage limit that he felt was too low, so he had it hiked in the final contract. They have been smart on another score. They know that no matter how rough the sledding in the future in doing repairs or meeting their rental payments, it's their baby.

Although some used-car agencies run ads offering to take a leased car off your back, subleasing is contrary to the contract, and it is a felony in some states.

Just as you look at much more than the sticker price when you're buying a car, you need to look beyond the monthly payments when leasing. The deal could be a dream or a nightmare.

FIFTEEN

Mini-
Hobbies
for Your
Mini-Home

Most of us need absorbing, rewarding pastimes to enliven our "off-duty" hours. Hobbies are even more vital to fulltimers, who may have to pass rainy days and long evenings in areas where they have no friends, no TV reception, and no local entertainments. No one wants to be cooped up in a box that measures 8 by 25 or 30 feet with nothing to do and no room to do it in.

Here are ways to miniaturize your present hobbies and suggestions for new hobbies that might suit your skills and interests.

Radio

Although the CB craze is not what it once was, these radios still play an important role among people who make the highways their home—truckers, emergency services personnel, traveling salespeople, and RV fulltimers. With a CB you can make friends, ask directions, find out where to get the best buys on fuel on the road ahead, and learn how to get around traffic tie-ups and detours.

A CB is essential when you're traveling with another RV or in a caravan. For the greatest convenience, you'll need a CB in the cockpit and another in your living quarters.

Other radios that make for interesting hobbies are VHF, which requires a special license and will give you a window on the boating and fishing world; scanners, which allow you to eavesdrop on emergency channels; and radios that receive aircraft frequencies, which allow you to listen to activity in control towers.

Ham radio is to CB what caviar is to sardines. The equipment isn't inexpensive, and

104

you must invest hours of study to get even the most basic license. You'll also need room aboard for your equipment, plus a good source of power and an efficient antenna.

In return for this investment you will have a fascinating hobby for the entire family. It's not uncommon for husband, wife, and older children all to get ham licenses. Through ham you can converse with people all over the world, talk to your friends and relatives via phone patches, help out during disasters when other communications are down, and join "nets" that keep you in touch with people who share your interests in almost any field. And if you plug into the local ham club when you're in a new community, you will have an instant circle of buddies.

For information on becoming a ham contact the ARRL (American Radio Relay League), 225 Main Street, Newington, CT 06111; 860-594-0200, www.arrl.org.

Sewing and Crafts

Many of us would be lost without a sewing machine, not just for the love of making clothes but because sewing and mending save money (and can be used to *make* money if you're good). In an RV there are three important rules for successful sewing:

■ Keep the machine in a place where it won't break loose on curves or in panic stops—it's heavy.

■ Allow extra space for patterns, notions, and work in progress, but try to finish one project before starting the next. Carrying tons of bargain fabric on the road costs fuel dollars.

■ Get yourself a roomy cutting table. I found an inexpensive folding cardboard table-topper in a fabric store. It stows under the mattress and provides a smooth, clean surface atop the dinette table or the campsite picnic table. More compact sewing hobbies include quilt piecing, lap quilting, knitting, macramé, needlepoint, embroidery, crewel, and huck weaving. If space is tight, rediscover these traditional favorites.

Hang Out at the Library

As busy as most fulltimers are, there are days when you're at loose ends. You're a stranger in town, without friends, and it's the off-season, so the campground is deserted. You're tired of malls, and movies cost too much.

The library is one place that brings both of us unending entertainment and learning even though we have very different abilities and interests—and it's free.

We find libraries in towns of every size. Now we schedule at least one day a month for a library stop and usually end up going back for more. We can easily spend all day there, taking a lunch break in the parking lot in our RV.

It's true that as a stranger passing through town you probably cannot get a library card or borrow books. But if you think libraries are nothing more than literary takeouts, it's time to get reacquainted.

We have found libraries offering everything from language lessons to lectures, from free movie classics to classes on local history or wildflowers. Most libraries have story sessions for children. Some have displays or small museums, extensive collections of recordings, listening booths, VCRs, and tapes. Many have computers, some with Internet access. There's almost always a coin-operated copy machine, coin phones, a pleasant reading room with comfortable chairs, and other reading areas where you can sit at tables or desks and make notes. Most reference rooms also have special sections for books on regional and local topics covering everything from history to folklore, city directories to the most recent Yellow Pages.

Librarians—who are worth their weight in platinum—have helped us find everything from out-of-town phone numbers, to lists of little-known sites we wanted to visit, to an address we needed to order a spare part for an old outboard.

Book Swaps

Some campgrounds have their own "libraries"—book swap boxes or shelves. If you find yourself at one that doesn't, urge the manager to start one. All it takes is a clean cardboard box, a couple of books as "seed money," and a sign inviting campers to "Take One, Leave One; Honor System." In most cases the box will soon brim with excellent reading because many people will leave more than they take.

Five books we consider essential for the RV life are Charles Kuralt's *On the Road with Charles Kuralt* and *A Life on the Road*, William Least Heat-Moon's *Blue Highways*, John Steinbeck's *Travels with Charley*, and Bill Graves's *On the Back Roads: Discovering Small Towns of America*.

Discover the Ag Center

While the library is the heart of a community's cultural life, the office of the County Agricultural Extension is the core of its natural life. When you're on the go and need to know how to deal with specific local fruits, vegetables, fish, or game or hazards such as poisonous plants, it is here you'll find expert help.

Workshops

The secret to success in any workshop hobby is having the right equipment, the raw materials, and a place to use them. We met one van-dwelling hobbyist who towed a travel trailer that housed a complete workshop with a workbench and plenty of drawers and pigeonholes.

Just as the RV galley is a specialized work area that should be furnished with the right stuff rather than kitchen castoffs, the workshop should be equipped so that every inch and every ounce do yeoman duty. It may pay to bite the bullet and buy new tools that are appropriate for the RV life.

Dremel makes a complete line of serious small benchtop tools and accessories. You can carry a Dremel drill press, router attachment, scroll saw/disc sander, vise with swivel head, table saw, and enough accessories to build an ark, all in the trunk of a car. For the address of your nearest dealer, contact www.dremel.com.

Other trusted names include Skil, known for its circular saws and now a line of full-size benchtop tools, Stanley, Black & Decker, and Craftsman, with its international Sears network of spares and support.

One of the most effective mini-workshops we've ever seen was a suitcase-size kit designed by a man whose hobby was clock repair. Opened, it formed a lighted work shelf. Closed, it corralled a creditable collection of tiny replacement parts.

We met a fisherman, a retired Air Force colonel, who had a compact workshop he used to make lures and other custom fishing gear for himself and to sell. On sunny days he set up his gear on the picnic table at his campsite. He continued to work as he jawboned with anyone who stopped by and inevitably made several sales into the bargain.

Miniature projects that fit well (and often sell well) in the fulltiming life include dollhouse furniture, toys, jewelry, model planes or boats, and wooden nameplates made with a router.

Gardening

Among ex-fulltimers one of the most commonly expressed reasons for settling down again is, "We missed our garden." However, gardening can be a portable hobby. We met one family who had two dozen pots of herbs, which they set in dishpans and carried in their shower while underway. When they parked, they would move the plants to a sunny spot. They always had plenty of fresh parsley, basil, cress, and the like.

Small gardening projects include bonsai, which requires artistry and skill, or sprouting edible seeds, such as mung beans, alfalfa, and wheat, which even a child can do. Trade plants and cuttings with like-minded fulltimers. You can even make pin money by starting house plants and selling them at flea markets.

One of our most enjoyable summers was spent in a North Carolina campground where campers were invited to work in the communal garden. By the time we moved on in the fall, we'd eaten our fill of fresh produce and canned much more.

If you own your own campsite, you can landscape it. Or if the grounds of the campground need to be kept up, you may be able to trade your gardening talents for some free rent.

Gordon Groene

Treasure Hunting

This one is addictive. You live on a hopeful high, believing that the Big Find is just around the corner. Every treasure hunter on the beach has a story about finding a handful of coins or a valuable ring, and treasure hunters occasionally find ancient Spanish coins on Florida beaches after heavy storms.

We met one couple who found a BB-size gold bead near an old Indian mound and a 17th-century brass candlestick at low tide outside an old fort. On the site of a long-abandoned village in Vermont we found part of an old cookstove, a large silver spoon (in two pieces), and a 1910 revolver that had rusted into a solid mass.

As a practical tool, a small metal detector will help you find small screws or other tiny metal parts if you lose them in the grass while working on the RV. The more you spend, the more sophisticated a metal detector you can buy. The cheapest models "see" any metal, so a lot of time is wasted in digging up aluminum cans and other junk, but even these are useful and fun.

One warning: it's illegal to use, or to have in your possession, a metal detector in a national park or at a national historic site. When in such areas, remove the batteries and otherwise render a metal detector inoperable. In any case, it's just good citizenship never to detect or dig in a site archaeologists may want to excavate someday.

Square Dancing, Line Dancing, and Clogging

Group dancing continues to be a national craze, especially among campers. Once you learn the steps and lingo, you'll fit in wherever you go. It's an international language spoken in campgrounds everywhere. Chances are that there's a dance at least once a week at almost any destination campground you visit, and you'll find countless hoe-downs in camps and in towns as you travel.

Volunteer Work

If you've been active all your life in church and charity work, fulltiming presents special problems because you're a stranger everywhere you go. That will change quickly once you check in with the local volunteer bureau, a church of your own denomination, Habitat for Humanity, Meals on Wheels, or other services. Even if you can spare only a few hours a week and will be in town for only a month, there is work for you.

If you have a special skill, such as teaching literacy via the Laubach method or transcribing for the blind, or have always worked with a national group such as the Red Cross, contact national headquarters before you leave and ask how you can keep active in your field as you travel.

If you have a talent that would entertain elderly shut-ins, volunteer in nursing homes as you travel. You might give a lecture–slide show on your travels, call a square dance, tell tall tales, or play an instrument.

For those of us who are never in one spot long enough for any kind of volunteerism, one-on-one projects can give you a sense of useful purpose. We keep a list of homebound friends of friends and relatives of relatives, and we send them a constant barrage of mail as we travel. We rarely get mail in return from these folks, usually because they are too ill to write, but the payback comes from imagining their happiness when they get an upbeat message on a picture postcard from a faraway place.

SIXTEEN

Home, Sweet Campground

The more we travel, the more amazed we are at the variety of campsites in this great land of ours. You can still find a cozy nook without hookups or facilities of any kind in a Corps of Engineers area for free. And you can pay $40 a night or more to loll in Lucullan luxury in a resort that has a health club, sauna, golf course, stocked fishing lake, full-time social director, and fireworks on Saturday night.

We've tried them all, and we love them all—even the grubby campsite next to the railroad track if it's close to our business or sightseeing goal for the day. If you're like us, you'll choose different campsites for different reasons: wilderness sites for solitude, resorts for the social whirl; the campground closest to the theme park, the overnight stop handiest to the highway; the site with the best view of shuttle launches or the one closest to the beach.

Finding a Campsite

For advance planning we rely on our Kampgrounds of America (KOA) Directory and the indispensable guides published by Woodall or Wheeler Publications, available at bookstores and camping gear suppliers. Although they aren't published for every state, superb guides far more comprehensive than the catalog-type guides are published by Foghorn Outdoors (www.foghorn.com) under such titles as *Florida Camping*. For suggested routes and campgrounds read our *Great Eastern RV Trips* or Jan Bannan's *Great Western RV Trips*, both published by Ragged Mountain Press (call 800-262-4729 or go to www.raggedmountainpress.com).

109

If we are on the road and only searching for an overnight stop, we rely on highway signs. Some of our happiest camping experiences have been serendipitous, the result of simply jumping off the road to look over a campground because we saw a sign.

Off-season, it is seldom difficult to find a site. During high season, however, it's wise to call ahead for reservations. In winter, when many campgrounds are closed, especially in cold climates, advance planning and reservations are also advisable. If you need special facilities or have a pet, calling ahead is always a must.

We also stop at almost every highway welcome station we come to—not the tourist traps that want to sell something in exchange for advice but those run by local, regional, county, state, or provincial agencies. Here, we stock up on free maps, campground directories, and brochures describing state or regional attractions. Often operated by cheerful and knowledgeable volunteers, welcome stations have provided some of the best advice we have received in our travels.

Lists of state campgrounds are available free from each state's tourism office. For a list of state, city, and regional sources of tourist information go to the Web site of the Travel Industry Association of America, www.tia.org.

For information about camping in national parks and federal lands contact:

Bureau of Land Management, Recreation Sites Information, Public Affairs Office, Department of the Interior, 1849 C Street N.W., Washington, DC 20240; 202-452-5125; www.recreation.gov.

National Park Service, 1849 C Street N.W., Washington, DC 20240. For reservations call 800-365-CAMP or go to http://reservations.nps.gov.

National Recreation Reservation Service, www.reserveusa.com, is a computerized reservation service for lands managed by the National Forest Service and the Army Corps of Engineers. You can also call 877-444-6777.

National Wildlife Refuges, U.S. Fish and Wildlife Service Public Affairs, Arlington, VA 22203; 800-344-WILD; http://refuges.fws.gov.

Cutting the Cost of Full-time Camping

When you're a part-timer, nightly camping fees seem like a bargain compared with staying in hotels. But to the fulltimer, $25 a night adds up to $750 a month, a sum that in some parts of the country will still get you a smart, spacious, two-bedroom, two-bath apartment big enough to hold your RV four times over. Even if you average only $15 per night for camping, that is $5,475 per year.

Here are some ways to chop the cost of nightly camping.

Anchoring out is our term for parking anywhere that it is permitted and reasonably safe. No hookups are provided. A guide titled *Travel Centers & Truck Stops*, published by Exit Source, is available through bookstores, at large truck stops, or by calling 800-494-5566. National chains that permit free overnight parking are Flying J truck stops and Wal-Mart stores (although some communities have cracked down on the practice). The price you pay for some of this free parking may be the all-night din and odor of diesel trucks starting and parking, neighbors only a breath away, and a complete lack of scenery. On the plus side, truck stops are located on major routes and have fuel and restaurants. And at Wal-Mart Super Centers you can do all your shopping. If you're a members of the Elks Club, you can usually park for free in the clubhouse parking lot.

In California a special program called Enroute Camping allows free parking in the daytime parking lots of state parks, with the payment of the basic camping fee, from sunset until early the next morning. No hookups are provided, so only self-contained rigs are welcome. On the minus side, state parks are seldom on the major highways. So even though the scenery may be better than at a truck stop, if you are in a hurry and only want a place to sleep, a state park may not be worth the detour.

Join a membership campground chain. As a member of a nationwide chain, you'll pay only a few dollars per night to stay at any member campground. Investigate the deal carefully because an initial investment of $1,500 to $7,500 is required, yearly fees run about $450, and many restrictions apply.

State camping permits. It may pay to establish legal residence in a state that gives its residents a break on camping fees—especially if you buy a yearly permit, are a senior citizen, or both. Most states also have a special discount for people who are handicapped.

Golden Eagle Passport. Anyone over the age of 62 can receive a free passport good for a 50 percent discount on camping fees on public lands. You can stay only fourteen days in any one site, and your site probably won't include a sewer hookup. Golden Access Passports, also good for a 50 percent discount, are available to the handicapped of any age.

Own your own campsite. We've seen mobile home lots for as little as $6,000 and condo campsites with pool and other facilities for $35,000 and up. You'll pay your own utilities and taxes plus, in a condo park, a monthly maintenance fee. Resale value will be a question mark, depending on what happens to real estate prices in the future. Another choice is to buy country acreage that is zoned for mobile homes, put in your own well and septic tank, and come and go as you like.

Monthly or seasonal rates. Monthly and seasonal rates vary greatly from one part of the country to another depending on the season, electricity costs, and taxes, but we found most campground owners eager to sell monthly or seasonal deals—unlike government parks, which limit your stay to two weeks or so. Some campground landlords want to look you over before quoting their most enticing long-term rates. Because the big discount might also involve a lease or a nonrefundable advance payment, a trial period is in your best interest as well as the landlord's. Be aware that in most states, state sales tax is charged on nightly campground rentals. However, on a longer contract, usually a minimum of six months, you're considered a permanent tenant, and sales taxes don't apply. That's a savings of 6–10 percent.

Other freebies. Because our motorhome is only 21 feet long, we fit in metered parking spots, so we often park on the street or in parking lots at trade shows. We have also spent a lot of time in friends' driveways or backyards. Working as we go, stopping here to do a lecture and there to do a writing assignment, we ask if we can plug in—or at least park—for the night at our business destination. Most business parking lots have 24-hour security, and although they are sometimes noisy, it's more than worth it because we're already "there" when we wake up in the morning. We avoid supermarket lots and overnight rest areas for security reasons. (We keep on the go all the time, so we've never been hassled by police or angry neighbors. Since we're just there for one or two nights, nobody gets nervous about our becoming permanent squatters.)

Private deals. If you intend to spend every summer for the rest of your life at Camp Lazydaze on Lake Fishalot, you can approach the owner about a twenty-year lease, a lifetime deal, or some other mutual commitment. With the help of a lawyer, you and a campground owner can work out an agreement that is fair and binding.

Trade-offs. Work in a campground in exchange for a free site. If you work the right deal, you'll do a fair amount of work, have a fair amount of free time, and spend nothing for camping. We have also traded a month's camping for specific tasks, such as taking photographs for a brochure. Barter any of your marketable skills—carpentry, gardening, electrical repair, painting. If you need work as well as a free campsite, subscribe to *Workamper News*, 201 Hiram Road, Springs, AR 72543; 800-446-5637; info@workamper.com; www.workamper.com.

Camping Clubs

Look into camping club membership even if you don't consider yourself a joiner; the benefits are more than social. With membership you may get discounts, mail forwarding, emergency road service or medical evacuation, a monthly magazine, group insurance rates, message service, and much more. Dues are modest, usually $35–$50 per year.

Brand-name camping clubs. Contact the manufacturer of your RV and ask how to join an owners' group. Most major brands, from Avion and Alpenite to Shasta and Winnebago, have such clubs. A list of names and contacts is available from RVIA, P.O. Box 2999, Reston, VA 22090; www.rvia.org.

Escapee Club. This organization of fulltimers has its own co-op campgrounds. Contact them c/o Kay Peterson, Rt. 5, Box 310, Livingston, TX 77351; 409-327-8873; www.escapees.com.

The Family Motor Coach Association. The FMCA membership numbers about 120,000 motorhome owners. Chapters are divided not just according to geographic area but also according to special interests—fulltimers, single-handers, musicians, Elks, the disabled, hams, treasure hunters, members of Coast to Coast Resorts or Thousand Trails Resorts, golfers, and a long list of brand-name camper chapters, including three for GMC owners—one for owners in general, one for GMC preservationists, and one for owners of GMC bus campers. To join a chapter, and you probably will want to join more than one, you must first join the national FMCA. Contact them at 8291 Clough Pike, Cincinnati, OH 45244; 800-543-3622 or 513-474-3622; www.fmca.com.

Family Campers & RVers offers group campouts, programs, education, emergency road service, message service, and many more benefits. Call 800-245-9755.

Good Sam Club. More than a million campers belong to this international club, which has 2,200 chapters throughout the United States, Canada, and Europe. There are also special-interest chapters for square dancers, ham radio operators, singles, the deaf, U.S. Marines, and computer owners. Contact them at 2575 Vista del Mar Drive, Ventura, CA 93001; 800-234-3450; www.goodsamclub.com.

Handicapped Travel Club Inc. For a membership application, send a #9 or #10 self-addressed, stamped envelope to 5929 Ourway, Citrus Heights, CA 95610 or go to www.dbyeaw.com.htc.

Loners on Wheels. Singles travel together for fun and mutual help. For information, contact P.O. Box 1600-WB, Cape Giradeau, MO 63702; 888-569-4478; www.lonersonwheels.com.

RV Elderhostels are offered throughout the country by Hostelling International, 80 Boylston Street, Boston, MA 02116; 617-426-7788; www.hiayh.org. They are educational projects like other Elderhostels except that you live and travel in your RV. Some cover a region; others involve lengthy trips.

For additional networking, log on to www.rv.net for forums, chats, buying and selling, information, and campground listings.

Camping Resorts

Camping resorts, usually open year-round, offer both indoor and outdoor activities, including swimming, fishing, health club, tennis, golf, and more. Most offer memberships; most also accommodate nonmembers. Some are local. Others are national chains, including:

Coast to Coast Resorts, 64 Inverness Drive East, Englewood, CO 80112; 800-538-8136 or 303-728-2267; www.coastresorts.com. **Thousand Trails/NACO,** 15375 S.E. 10th Place, Bellevue, WA 98007; 800-288-7245; www.thousandtrails.com. Campground membership resales can be arranged through **Campground Membership Outlet,** 800-272-0401, www.membershipresale.com. With membership in the **United RV Campers Club,** at $15.75 monthly, you can camp in member campgrounds for $5 nightly. Call 800-521-6978 or go to www.unitedrvcampers.com.

Campground Chains

Destiny RV Resorts are found in seven areas. Call 800-RV-DESTINY, or go to destinyrv.com.

Kampgrounds of America (KOA), Box 30558, Billings, MT 59114; www.koa.com. Write for information, or pick up a free directory at any member campground.

Yogi Bear's Jellystone Park Camp-Resorts, also **Safari Resorts,** 6201 Kellogg Avenue, Cincinnati, OH 45230; 800-558-2954; www.campjellystone.com.

SEVENTEEN

Put the RV in ConseRVation

Being homeless, rootless, and routeless is not without its culture shocks. One of the blows to the ego is that some people look down on RV campers as gas hogs, nature tramplers, and the all-time chief polluters of the outdoor world. You can expect some dirty looks on the highway and a few nasty cracks from tent campers and backpackers.

We know what it is to be on both sides of the finger pointing. During the ten years we lived on the go full time the RV was our summer home. In winter we lived aboard a sailboat, using only the free energy supplied by the wind. One year our fuel consumption for the entire season was the twelve gallons we used to recharge the batteries once a week.

We sailors called powerboats "stinkpots" and looked at them much as canvas campers looked at us and our RV in summer. It was silly, but it did help us laugh at ourselves when we were looked down upon by campers who thought they were more "pure" because they were backpacking, biking, or canoeing.

Fulltimers can only hope to make others understand and see the good in us, but we *can* recognize the good in ourselves and go on truckin' without apology, knowing that our lifestyle is conservation at its best.

Look at it this way: Back in what we now call "real life" we lived in a huge, drafty, older home that had a furnace the size of Rhode Island and a bathtub that held as much hot water as the YMCA pool. Our internal-combustion inventory included two cars plus a fume-belching arsenal of yard care equipment. We lived in the Midwest, where temperature extremes forced us to run either the furnace or the air-conditioning almost every day. Winter days were so short that the lights went on at 3:00 P.M. and sometimes burned throughout the dark day.

We exchanged all that space and energy dependence for tiny living quarters that follow the seasons. The RV furnace is seldom lit, and we rarely turn on the lights during the day. When we *do* run the heat or air-conditioning, it's for an entire home that has less cubic footage than *one bedroom* in the average house.

The consumer needs of most RVs are minuscule compared with those of even the smallest homes. A typical RV water heater holds 6 gallons or less. The largest RV refrigerators (and few of us have the largest) measure only about 10 cubic feet—the size of the smallest home refrigerators. Most of our entertainment electronics work on 12-volt power, which we supply ourselves by charging our batteries while underway.

We RVers are abstemious with water, not just because we have to fill our own water tanks but because we have to *empty* our wastewater tanks. Homeowners may let a faucet drip for a few days until it's convenient to fix it. Not so in the RV, where every drop wasted is a drop closer to an empty tank!

RV owners can't let the faucet run until the water is cold because we know that our tanks have only 50–100 gallons in reserve. And if we let it run until it's hot before stepping into the shower, it never takes more than a pint or two because the pipe run is so short.

Our toilets flush for a week on the amount of water used in a water-saver household toilet in a day. Few fulltimers have automatic dishwashers, disposals, or trash compactors. Those electric servants that we do have, from power tools to the vacuum cleaner to kitchen appliances, are chosen for their light weight, small size, and energy efficiency in ways that most house dwellers never think about. We know the cost of energy because we pay for it day in and day out at the fuel pump, at the campground, in charging the battery, and in running a generator.

Fulltimers develop a sharp eye for value, long wear, compactness, and versatility in everything we buy, from clothes to tools. When we say we are self-contained, we mean that we can take care of ourselves when necessary without hookups. When you're making your own electricity, running your own waterworks, and operating your own sewer system, you gain a conservationist perspective the hard way.

It's because they are self-contained that many RV fulltimers are thoughtful enough to stay out of state and national parks and off the highways during busy holiday weekends, when vacationers need the roads and tenters must have the toilet and shower facilities that campgrounds provide.

It's true that RV travel requires plenty of fuel, but who says a fulltimer has to be on the road every day or even every week? Most fulltimers have to budget for fuel more carefully than other travelers because they are fully or partially retired and living on a limited income.

We know people who think nothing of commuting 60 miles per day to work, driving 50 miles to see a movie, and covering a couple hundred miles sightseeing over a weekend. And most families these days drive their children anywhere that is more than half a block away. Fulltimers, by contrast, use more gallons per mile but make every mile count for something.

The fulltimer thinks twice before unhooking and stowing all the umbilicals and wrestling the rig out of a campsite. Errands are lumped together; trips are planned carefully. Once at a destination, a fulltimer can settle down for a while, make friends, and savor the local scene for a week, a month, or a season—unlike the rushed vacationer who pulls up stakes every day.

Simply put, some people use more fuel than others, and living in an RV doesn't necessarily make one a fuel glutton. This isn't the place to go into a discussion of big RVs versus small, or gasoline versus diesel. Our point is that no matter how efficient the RV, the fulltimer uses it with the utmost conservation in mind because it wasn't bought to be a station wagon or a sports car. It is, above all else, a *home*.

What You Can Do

Now that you're committed to fulltiming and have made the wide world your home, you have more reason than anyone else to do your part to save the earth. Here are some conservation points that apply specifically to the fulltimer way of life.

Prevent Sun Damage and Heat Gain

■   Get insulated window coverings that keep out the cold or hot sun. Any good custom drapery maker can design attractive curtains with double or triple linings. If possible, buy an RV with double-glazed windows. When replacing skylights, opt for double-glazed types. Have solar film professionally installed (do-it-yourself installations are usually doomed to failure) on at least some windows.

■   Check regularly for air leaks and caulk them. In an RV they're rare compared with the many gaps found in a house, but some voids may be found around the furnace, the refrigerator, or other through-the-wall installations.

■   Get awnings for the side, for individual windows, and to shade the side of the RV over the refrigerator coils. Make, or have made, a cover for the windshield. You might even order two, one in a dark fabric to absorb heat on cold days and another in white for use in hot climates. Park in the shade in hot climates, in the sun when it's cold.

Gordon Groene

Camping World

■ ·Get a high-quality, heavy-duty cover for your spare tire, not just a thin cover with a cute logo on it. Sun fade is as destructive to tires as road wear. When you're parked, use sun shades on all the tires.

■ Use polishes with ultraviolet inhibitors. Don't wash the RV in the sun. It's not good for the paint, and more water will be lost through evaporation. (Observe campground rules; washing RVs may be prohibited, or it may be permitted only in certain areas or during specified hours.)

Going Solar

Although solar energy hasn't yet become practical for most households, it makes special sense in the RV life because you can use it to charge batteries, and batteries run RV lights, television, radio, and much more. Add solar panels to the roof as you can afford them.

■ An excellent resource is *RVer's Guide to Solar and Inverter Power*, available from RV Solar Electric. For information about solar panels and other solar accessories, contact them at 14415 N. 73rd Street, Scottsdale, AZ 85260; 800-999-8520; www. RVSolarElectric.com. See appendix 1, Useful Addresses, for more solar resources.

■ Consider getting one of the portable solar water heaters sold by camping or boating suppliers. One brand, Sun Shower, is a complete unit, including water bag and shower spray. If you devise a permanent hanger for it in your shower stall, you can hang it outdoors to allow the sun to heat the water, then bring it inside for use in the comfort and privacy of your own bathroom.

The more solar panels you can add to your RV, the more independent you'll be. (Kyocera America Inc. and RV Solar Electric)

■ Another good solar accessory is an overhead hatch with a solar-powered exhaust fan. It fits into standard-size hatch openings and is easy to install.

Outside the RV

Fulltimers have storage problems that other RV campers don't have. It's bad enough that the living quarters are stuffed and overloaded, but in addition, each time you step on the gas pedal, fuel must be used to get all that inertia rolling.

■ Try to keep the exterior as sleek and uncluttered as the designer intended. When possessions start spilling over from inside the RV to the roof, sides, or front bumper, you're adding both dead weight *and* aerodynamic drag. Carrying things on the front bumper may also interfere with air flow to the radiator.

■ If you must add exterior storage, keep it as aerodynamically clean as possible. You can tell just by looking at them that some roof pods, side mirrors, awning containers, and air conditioners will cut through the air better than others. Depending on the configuration of your rig, an aftermarket fairing (you've seen them on eighteen-wheelers) may be available to channel air flow more advantageously.

Consumables and Recycling

Most of us have been recycling for years, but new habits have to be learned on the road because each campground and community has its own rules. In one town you may be asked to separate only a few categories, such as aluminum, newspaper, and clear glass; in another you might have to separate just trash and garbage; and the next may have elaborate sorting rules involving different types of plastics, different papers, clear and colored glass, and separating aluminum foil from aluminum cans.

■   In those campgrounds where everything goes into the same bin, you can still maintain your own voluntary recycling program for at least some items. Crushed aluminum and steel cans take up little space or weight and can travel with you until you find a recycling center.

■   Water is another resource that most of us learn to use and reuse. Instead of letting a faucet run until the water is hot, catch the surplus in a pitcher and use it to water plants or rinse sprouts. Instead of draining a big pot of spaghetti, save the hot water for washing dishes. If you're rinsing dishes, save the clean, slightly soapy water and do a batch of hand laundry or wash the dog.

■   In the coin laundry, use cold water whenever possible. Clean the dryer filter before every use. Use concentrated detergents and measure out only as much as the manufacturer recommends.

Extend storage space with a box that bolts to the trailer tongue. (Camping World)

Waste storage is often inadequate on RVs. Devise ways to separate and store trash for recycling. (Rutt Custom Kitchens)

■   During droughts in some areas, campgrounds ask that gray water be emptied onto nearby trees. Otherwise, dispose of this water only in designated places. It's illegal to discharge it on the ground in most states. Don't use formaldehyde in black water tanks; buy only the new, biodegradable toilet chemicals. Although water conservation is considered a virtue, when the ratio of solids to liquids is too great, it can create a problem in your own black water tank and even greater problems in campgrounds that have septic tanks. Unless water is in short supply, flush tanks generously. Mucky buildup can also interfere with probes that tell you the level in the tanks. To clean them, empty the tank, add clean water and a half cup of liquid laundry detergent (dishwashing detergent is too sudsy) and drive for a while, then empty the tanks. Retreatment may be necessary.

■   Used engine oil and all other automotive chemicals, dead batteries, and worn-out tires and tubes must be disposed of according to state or local law. If you've picked up a heavy load of road salt, be careful where you wash the RV. Salty runoff can damage plants.

The Campfire

Although most fulltimer RVs have a gas stove with oven and perhaps a microwave, most of us still enjoy campfires as part of the camping experience. Observe local fire laws and be aware that they can change from day to day based on the weather conditions.

■   Learn to start wood fires with tinder and kindling rather than chemicals. If you gather wood for cooking, always use dead wood already on the ground—never cut tree limbs (even from dead trees) for fires. You can usually buy wood at campgrounds.

■   When you have a wood fire, try to use an established fire site instead of starting a new one. Don't add anything except clean burnables and well-seasoned wood. Packaging that contains metal or plastic pollutes the air and leaves junk in the fire pit. Always make sure you've doused the fire completely before leaving the fire site unattended.

■   If you cook with charcoal, use an electric starter and/or bellows rather than chemical starters and dispose of the ash according to campground rules. Remember that charcoal can look cold even when it's scorching hot; keep children away from it and make sure the coals are cold before leaving them.

■   To minimize charcoal use, carry a gas grill that hooks up to your main propane tank. Or bring your portable electric grill outdoors.

Additional Environmental Tips

■   Don't feed wildlife or try to tame it. If you have a pet, remember that you and the pet are the outsiders in parks and other wildlife refuges. If you find injured wildlife or young that appear to be abandoned in a state park or other government-managed area, call a ranger. It's probably illegal to interfere, no matter how much you want to help.

■   Invest in rechargeable batteries and a charger. Disposable batteries are expensive and contribute toxins to landfills.

■   Don't pick any plants except where allowed, and then don't take more than your share.

■   Take care not to damage trees and bushes at campsites. Don't hammer nails into trees to hang clotheslines or hammocks. And don't tie anything to them either, because even the smallest abrasions can create voids where bugs or disease can get a foothold.

■   Carry a screw-type stake and put the dog's chain through that rather than around a tree or shrub. Shop for the kind of chain that is enclosed in a plastic sleeve.

■   Don't add to erosion problems by driving on fragile beaches, shoulders, deserts, or fields.

■   Don't pick sea oats or other natural dune protectors.

■   Consider adding a screen room to provide both shade and bug protection without chemical sprays.

■   Instead of towing a car or a boat or hanging bicycles or motorbikes on the RV, consider renting what you need, when and where you need it. Club Nautico is a nationwide organization in which members get a big discount on boat rentals everywhere they go. Contact them at 800-BOAT-RENT or www.clubnautico.com. Most tourist areas have bikes or mopeds for rent; they may be available right at the campground.

■   Rediscover public transportation. Ask at the campground what is available. In many areas, free shuttles run between campgrounds and major attractions or shopping areas. In others, city bus stops are only a short walk away from the campgrounds. You save fuel, tolls, and parking fees and make friends during the ride.

■   Save fuel by starting each city visit with a guided tour. When we want to see a tourist area thoroughly, we first take a guided tour, such as the Conch Train in Key West, one of Boston's tourist trolleys, or a Grey Line tour. Instead of touring with one eye on traffic and another on the map, we can relax and see the sights while an experienced narrator regales us with local yarns. Then when we do take off on our own, we have a better idea of how the streets lie and how traffic flows.

■   Disposing of unneeded prescription medications? Don't flush them if the campground has a septic system—they could kill helpful bacteria.

■   If you break a mercury thermometer, carefully collect the bits by using a toothpick to push them into a glass bottle. Then cap it and turn it in at a hazardous waste facility. Don't vacuum it, or the vacuum cleaner will be permanently contaminated. Get a digital thermometer that doesn't contain mercury.

■ Line closets with cedar and/or use one of the new, natural citrus fresheners. Mothballs contain naphthalene, which you don't want venting into your living quarters. If you do use mothballs, seal clothes in tightly lidded containers.

■ Don't use formaldehyde mildew-cides either. Depend instead on frequent airing and washing of stored fabrics.

■ Don't buy clothes that need dry cleaning.

■ Buy food, shampoo, and cleaning products in bulk when possible and repackage them in reusable containers. Foods, however, should be stored only in food-quality plastics—not soap dispensers or garbage bags.

■ Don't use a disposable product if it's available in reusable form. The list includes disposable razors, emery boards rather than a nail file, disposable pens (buy a refillable ball point or a fountain pen), and paper products for the kitchen.

■ Don't use merchants' paper or plastic bags. Take your own canvas carry bags when doing any shopping. You'll not only cut down on disposables, you'll find endless uses for these bags in the RV life—and their hefty web handles make them far easier to carry than paper or plastic sacks.

■ Good arguments can be made both for and against disposable diapers. If you use cloth diapers, or any other contaminated items that need special laundry treatment, ask at a medical supplier for the hospital-type plastic laundry bags that dissolve in hot water. Once put into these bags, laundry does not have to be handled again. It goes into a washer, bag and all. Use very hot water (both to dissolve the bag and to sanitize the wash) and effective disinfectants that will decontaminate the wash and the washer.

■ Report illegal dumpers, poachers, and polluters. Most states have a toll-free wildlife hotline that you can use to blow the whistle on illegal hunting, trapping, or fishing, as well as wildlife abuse of any kind.

■ Join adopt-a-beach, adopt-a-highway, and other cleanup programs.

■ Volunteer for a season as an unpaid worker in a state or national park. You'll be rewarded with a free campsite as well as with new friends and a feeling of real accomplishment.

■ Don't get so caught up in recycling that you lose sight of the fact that you shouldn't have bought the item in the first place. Mix your own drinks using powders or concentrates, and you'll have no cans and bottles to store, transport, and recycle. Buy fresh fruits and vegetables, and you'll have no cans to squash, no cardboard packaging to burn, no plastics to recycle.

■ Buy good wood-and-fabric folding chairs. Repaint them as needed and sew up new canvas seats and backs as the old ones wear out. They'll outlast plastic and aluminum chairs by decades.

■ Keep all the RV's filters clean. An air conditioner with a clogged filter has to work harder. A vacuum cleaner with a full bag has to work longer. A stove exhaust with a greasy filter uses just as much energy to move half as much air.

■ Don't hold up the parade. RVs are not as responsive and speedy as cars, and much of the resentment against them comes from drivers who are in a hurry. Try not to drive during rush hours or holiday weekends. If a line of traffic piles up behind you, pull over and let them pass. They'll appreciate it, and you're less likely to get involved in a rear-ender or a pileup.

■   Rediscover the old ways. Our grandparents knew how to reverse a collar to double the wear, let hems up and down as fashions changed, re-sole shoes and boots, turn dress scraps into baby clothes and scraps from baby clothes into quilt pieces. There was little waste, few disposables, and no landfill crisis in those days.

EIGHTEEN

Portable
Professions

I f you're independently wealthy, or retired with enough income to bankroll your fulltiming life, you can skip this chapter. Most of the rest of us face one of the following scenarios:

■ Fully in the work force, not yet eligible for a pension or social security; looking for a way to stay on the road while making enough money to live on, build for the future, and eventually retire.

■ Fully in the work force in a profession that requires such frequent moves that it's more economical to live in a portable home.

■ Retired or disabled, but with only a bare-bones income; in need of supplemental income for now and something to put away for the future.

■ Young but temporarily retired, on sabbatical from a job you'll return to after fulfilling your fulltiming dream; or seeking an occasional job that will enable you to keep up with your fast-changing field.

■ Sick of your present career and eager to start one that involves full-time travel.

■ You want to travel with your children while they're still young. You will have to educate as you go, and work along the way to support your family.

Once almost unheard of, midlife career changes are now commonplace. Some changes are gentle ones, such as leaving a corporate career as an engineer and forming your own engineering consulting firm. Others are very difficult, involving years of additional education or other new training.

If you want or need serious career opportunities, they are available to fulltimers. And there are not-so-serious work opportunities out there for those whose only aim is to keep on truckin'.

Here are some avenues to consider.

Workamping

Theirs is the happiest of stories: Greg and Debbie Robus realized their own dream and then began devoting their lives to helping others do the same. Both have college degrees, Greg in parks administration and Debbie in elementary education. Working as a park ranger for the Corps of Engineers, Greg began to see a need for linking up fulltimers who needed extra income with parks and other employers who needed dependable, but not necessarily year-round, workers.

Debbie, a kindergarten teacher, had experimented with newsletter publication in the field of needlework, her hobby. So the couple sold everything they owned, bought a computer, moved to a farm in Arkansas, and founded *Workamper News.*

The bimonthly *Workamper News* offers free classified ads of up to 100 words to employers who can offer jobs to RVers. A typical ad might read: "Wanted: Neat, semi-retired couple to work in small, family campground May–September. Free campsite with hookups, and small salary."

Ads offer full-time, seasonal, part-time, or temporary jobs that are ideal for those fulltimers who want to stay free but who need the occasional boost to the bank account. Some ads are invitations for bids to work for a government park, usually at $40 to $60 a day. Others offer jobs in marinas, guest ranches, farms, orchards, mobile home parks, RV parks, gift shops, theme parks, and resorts. One ad is from a company that needs experienced RV drivers to work for movie companies.

No matter what your talents or background, *Workamper News* may list just the job you need. A couple who were living in a 13-foot trailer landed jobs at Silver Dollar City, a theme park in Missouri, and lived a fairy-tale life in calico and buckskin. They were soon able to afford a more spacious RV and lived happily ever after.

Professional musicians sing the song of the open road, often playing in RV parks or to church groups. A licensed nurse and her husband, a Mr. Fix-It who carries all his own tools, find work as they travel the country where and when they please, using *Workamper News* as a resource.

Workamper News also prints ads for volunteer positions that offer no payment but do provide a free campsite with utilities. While most of the jobs assume that readers are fulltimers who will bring their own housing with them, some employers offer a cabin or apartment.

In addition to the free ads, the Robuses publish paid ads from both job seekers and employers, and they also offer a referral service. Workampers, as these members of the fulltimer family call themselves, fill out a resume and job preference form. For a modest fee, it is kept on file, matched up with employers in each field and geographic area, and mailed or e-mailed out by the Robuses to prospective employers.

Greg and Debbie are kept busy reading their fan mail from happy campers who are able to stay solvent thanks to Workamping and from delighted employers who find

Workampers reliable, industrious, and highly qualified (often because they were formerly successful in business or the military).

The salary range for most Workamper positions in 2001 was $8–$12 per hour, including the value of a free or discounted campsite. To compute the full value of your compensation, add up the value of your benefits and divide by the number of hours you work. If you contract to work 20 hours per week, and a $320-a-month campsite with hookups is part of the deal, the campsite is worth $4 per hour. Negotiate for the rest depending on your skills, job description, and other benefits. Then get it in writing, for your benefit and for that of the employer.

Workamper News subscriptions are $18 for one year and $33 for two, plus additional postage for Canada, Mexico, or overseas mailing. A sample, 3-issue subscription is $12.75. For information contact *Workamper News,* 201 Hiram Road, HCR 34 Box 125, Heber Springs, AR 72543; info@workamper.com; www.workamper.com.

Working the Internet

The work-at-home movement is hot and getting hotter thanks to the World Wide Web. Thousands of professions can go on the road with you: creating specialty software, international commodity trading, consulting, publishing, online tutoring, and much more. If you have a background in law, medicine, or some other specialty and/or a wide network of industry contacts, it will be a snap to shift into self-employment via the Internet or by telecommuting to a real job.

The onboard computer center of one computer operator serves as a mobile school where she trains others. She runs ads offering to make her RV/office available to businesspeople who need computer training, refresher courses, or software installed.

While it's possible to make a good living on the Internet, no matter where you park, be aware that millions of hopefuls are being led astray today by the same work-at-home schemes that were once advertised in magazines. Each day's e-mail brings us "spam" sent by people who buy lists of e-mail addresses and then spend a lot of time composing a campaign to sell us something. We erase them all without reading them, but we can tell from the subject lines that most of them have to do with products or services that are not of the remotest interest to us. Probably most of these hopefuls soon give up in despair, but endless waves of new victims continue to buy those lists.

Nor can you rely on a Web site as a way to make your fortune by selling a service or product. As consumers as well as writers, we are constantly besieged with e-mail pleas to visit some Web site or other. The race for eyeballs is beyond desperate. Chances are, you won't get enough hits on a Web site to support yourself even if you spend a fortune on paid links, advertising, and promotion. A Web site can be an essential sales tool, but it's only one of many tools you'll need to make a living on the Internet.

The Internet is no more a route to easy, work-at-home money than stuffing envelopes was a generation ago. You still need a product or skill that others are willing to pay for, hard work, and tireless follow-through. To get started, evaluate your skills and think about how they could support you. Do you have a product or service to sell? If yes, what do you know about selling in general? Or selling online? How will you stand out in the crowd? Who is your target audience? How will you reach them?

In addition to spending time on the Internet looking for ideas, information, and resources, try *Spare Time* magazine (5810 W. Oklahoma Avenue, Milwaukee, WI; 414-

543-8110; www.spare-time.com), a good general magazine for entrepreneurs. Also check out the latest computer publications; you'll need to keep up with both the technology of the Web and the latest news in your own trade. At bookstores, browse some books in the area you're interested in. In print and online, make sure your sources are credible; if something sounds too good to be true, it usually is.

A rule of thumb we tell people who are interested in our field, freelance writing, is to hang onto their day job until their "spare time" work is bringing in either half the income they need or they have saved enough to support themselves for six months—or both.

Arts and Crafts

Create items at your leisure and sell them at flea markets and craft fairs as you travel. Or if you'd rather not deal directly with the public, visit boutiques as you travel and ask if they'd like to sell your wares. Ski shops, for instance, may take sweaters on consignment, and larger shops may contract with you to knit for them.

Consignment, of course, has its pitfalls, especially if you leave your products behind and are miles away when a merchant goes out of business, declares bankruptcy, or otherwise goes south with your goods or money. Diversify, and deal only with established, reputable outfits. Among them, if the quality of your work justifies it, are museum gift shops and nonprofit craft stores operated to benefit artisans.

Your success might be in anything from country crafts to custom Christmas ornaments. But in the crafts field, as in so many others, having the talent to make the crafts is just the beginning. You must also be a savvy, persistent salesperson and a self-starter who can keep turning out the work on a regular schedule. Keep in mind that public taste can be fickle, so it's best to find products that both sell well and suit your talents, interests, equipment, and work space.

Writing

To anyone in the creative arts, fulltiming can be the best of all muses. It certainly was for the best-selling romance writer Janet Dailey, who launched her career from a travel trailer, where she wrote a novel set in each state in the country. Fulltiming can also, however, be a tremendous hurdle for the hungry writer.

Writing and photography supported our ten years of fulltiming and have continued to provide us income and adventure now that we are part-timers again. But before you rush out to follow our lead, let us clear up some popular misconceptions about freelancing.

Many people imagine they'll have such an exciting life as fulltimers that *National Geographic* will beat a path to their door or that they'll write the Great American Novel while gazing out over the passing panorama. Countless times, people have told us, "Oh, the stories I could write if I had time," or "I could write a book about my adventures." It might come as a surprise to those folks to discover that fulltiming itself will not magically turn them into writers.

Writing for a living is not something you do when you "have time." It's a demanding discipline that you work at, just as others work at dentistry, truck driving, or selling cars. Writing the material is only half the battle. You also have to market it.

Unlike handicrafts, which can be sold at flea markets and art shows, articles, books, plays, and poems have to be sold to publishers. This can be done in one of two ways:

You can market the material yourself by mail and e-mail, which is cumbersome and expensive, or you can send it to an agent, who will market it for you.

Unless you're already a highly successful author, no agent will take you on a commission basis, so forget that option unless you're prepared to pay handsomely for reading fees, critiques, and other services that rarely lead to literary success. You'll probably have to paddle your own canoe, at least in the beginning.

If you're already a selling writer, fulltiming will open some doors and shut a few windows. If you're not already writing, don't take off in your RV expecting to become a writer instantly. Even if you begin writing at once, which is unlikely because you'll have so many other things to do, and even if you start selling those writings immediately, which is even more unlikely, it will take months for the cash flow to begin.

Although the hows of freelance writing could fill an entire book, here are some basic tips.

■ **Set a daily writing goal.** Treat it like a business, and work regular hours. Invest in all the materials needed to put out a professional-looking product. At a minimum you'll need a word processor with a letter-quality printer, business stationery, and an e-mail address. If you can manage a telephone or other communication service (answering service or electronic mailbox), so much the better. Because we sell story-photo packages, and more and more editors now want photos sent electronically, a scanner is also a must for us.

■ **Buy a copy of *Writer's Market*,** published annually by Writer's Digest. You can also purchase it in electronic form at www.writersmarket.com. Study it to learn what markets are most suitable for the kinds of material you write.

■ **Write consistently and persistently.** This means turning out finished writings, as well as sending out regular proposals and query letters in search of assignments. By being a part of the literary marketplace day in and day out, even if all your efforts are rejected, you'll learn more about the writing business than you can by taking a course or attending a writers' conference or seminar.

■ **Find your own niche.** Editors are eager for pieces from writers who know their subject inside out, and you'll stand taller in a crowded marketplace if you can focus on a speciality. A food writer, for example, might be an expert in wines or, even more narrowly, in Napa Valley vintages. Travel writers might specialize in RV travel but will do even better by specializing further in RV skiing, RV travel with children, environmentally sound travel, or scuba diving. Outdoor writers can gain special notice as experts in ecology, whitetail rabbit hunting, bass fishing, or global warming. Fiction writers might specialize in short stories, mysteries, formula romance, religious books, children's literature, and so on.

If you have questions about making a living in freelance writing, contact us at www.GordonandJanetGroene.com.

Photography

Almost everything said above about freelance writing can also apply to freelance photography. Invest in good equipment (cameras, lenses, lighting) and presentation tools. Work hard, specialize, and market aggressively.

Because you live on the go, you'll be less able to get bread-and-butter work such as weddings or industrial brochures, but you'll be free to roam and snap anything that catches your eye.

As a freelance photographer, you can sell your work by mail and e-mail to magazines, calendar or postcard manufacturers, and greeting card companies. Or send all your work to a stock agency. If you can find an agency to accept your work, all you have to do is take the pictures and send them in. They'll do all the marketing and send you regular checks. While literary commissions run 10–15 percent, stock agencies take a larger cut; however, they may sell the same photo over and over, sending you a check for each placement. If you prefer to sell directly to the public, have your best shots made into prints. Then package them attractively, matted or framed, and offer them at arts and crafts shows.

Photographer's Market, another Writers Digest publication, is an excellent guide to the how, where, ethics, and business practices of selling your pictures. Technological changes have hit photographers hard because so many free images are available on the Internet. Find your niche, protect your intellectual rights, and keep up with the changing times by joining a professional organization such as the American Society of Magazine Photographers (www.asmp.org).

Publishing

At least two fulltimer couples publish travel newsletters on the go reporting on their RV adventures. If you have a specialty, you can make even more money by publishing a niche newsletter. (You can publish hard copy or via e-mail, or give readers a choice of hard copy for one price and e-mail for a lower price.) It needn't be related to RVs or even to travel. It could be anything from diesel engine repair to pet psychology to vegetarian cooking. A Florida woman founded a newsletter about exotic tropical edibles. A Maine homemaker began publishing a tightwad's newsletter, telling how she and her husband raise six kids on a shoestring. She was featured on network television shows, and subscriptions poured in. A new mother started a newsletter on nursing and parlayed it into a business empire.

The first thing to decide on is the subject of your newsletter; find out whether other newsletters are already available on the topic (and possibly free on the Internet). Be forewarned that the RV field is already very crowded. You'll have to come up with a new idea and do it better than anyone else.

The better your credentials and the narrower the focus, the more money you can charge for a few pages of truly meaty material. Subscribers pay as much as $100 to $300 per year for insider newsletters written by experts. One of our fulltiming friends specializes in a very obscure aspect of the stock market. He has only a few subscribers, but they each pay $500 annually for his monthly newsletter.

Another success story is the Ohio couple who fulltimed for three years with the sponsorship of their bank. Their newsletter reported on upbeat stories they encountered on their travels and had universal appeal. Their bank provided the newsletter free of charge on their Web site as a public relations tool.

Two good guides to publishing newsletters are *Starting and Running a Successful Newsletter or Magazine* by Cheryl Woodard (Nolo Press) and *Home-Based Newsletter Publishing* by William J. Bond (McGraw-Hill Professional Publishing).

Newsletters usually don't carry ads—all the income derives from subscriptions—although many newsletter publishers increase their profits by offering extra services or products. A microwave newsletter publisher, for example, also offers hard-to-find microwave cookware. A newsletter about Chinese cooking sells hard-to-find ingredients.

If you do sell a product through your newsletter, you don't have to warehouse, pack, and ship the merchandise. Find a supplier who will drop-ship. You process the orders, subtracting your cut from the check you send the shipper.

Temping

Usually, in exchange for temporary employment fulltimers settle for lower wages, few or no benefits, and little chance of advancement. Most are underemployed. A former plant manager might accept work as the weekend manager of a small campground; a one-time executive secretary, as a typist or receptionist; a former nursing supervisor, as an on-call R.N. Yet everyone wins—the fulltimer because he or she is free to move on with no hard feelings when the season ends, and the employer because no long-term commitment had to be made.

Nationwide temporary help agencies such as Kelly, Granny Nannies, and Manpower, or medical agencies such as Medical Personnel Pool, can allow you to pursue your profession and still stay on the go. We once knew a couple who worked for the same nationwide chain for years, staying in one place only long enough to build up their savings and then moving on until it was time to feed the kitty again.

Temping on the Road

Milt and Annie and their three children, ages 6, 8, and 12, are currently on the road in the West and Southeast. Milt took a year's leave of absence from his job; Annie's leave of absence is open-ended. They rented out their house for a year; the rent has been enough to cover taxes and minor repairs on the house.

To meet expenses, Milt gets temporary work as an electrician on construction jobs, and Annie makes some money with her online newsletter. So far, they haven't had to use any of their savings. Soon they have some decisions to make—whether to extend Milt's leave and the house rental or make a more permanent break. As Annie says, "It's one thing to make enough for a comfortable life on the road, but we have only one shot at parenthood, careers, and financial independence for our senior years, so it's only natural to have doubts. Giving up Milt's job security is a big step, and I can't tell you at this point what we'll decide to do."

The best feature of temping is that it is just that—temporary. You can work a couple of days here, a few weeks there, and move on without being branded a "job hopper." The employer usually loves the no-future, no-promises arrangement as much as you do.

Meanwhile, you're building up a work record, and in some cases seniority and other benefits (such as group health insurance), with a national firm that can put you to work in dozens of cities. Your record is faxed or e-mailed from one branch to the next, so no time is wasted on repeated applications and checking of references.

If you have an easily marketed skill, such as word processing, medical or legal clerking, inventory-taking, computers, or accounting, look into opportunities in temping.

Put Your RV to Work

Through the years, we've met countless couples who lived on boats full time before moving ashore and becoming RV fulltimers. Rose and Harry Willington were in the business of yacht chartering for twenty-five years before they went ashore at Pompano Beach, bought a 34-foot motorhome, and began chartering it as a land yacht.

The Willingtons chartered only by day. They picked up customers, served breakfast and lunch on the go, and delivered guests to their destination. If the trip was for more than one day, they took the passengers to a hotel each night. The service was so popular with business travelers, entertainers, and groups of couples who wanted a carefree golfing or tennis weekend with a designated driver, we wonder why more people don't go into the land yacht charter business.

If you want to use your RV for hire, make sure your insurance coverage allows for whatever business you're in, and get a chauffeur's license if it's required by the state or municipality.

Another way to use your RV as a working vehicle is to lead RV caravans. Or use it as a demonstrator/showroom for a camping-related product, such as awnings.

Your RV might also be turned to some specialty use. A photographer who specializes in shooting yacht races, for instance, put a complete photo lab aboard his RV and makes his prints and CDs on the spot. An accomplished kayaker guides whitewater trips by day and retires to his RV at night. A veterinarian makes house calls in her RV; so does a visiting nurse.

NINETEEN

The Mysteries of Mobile Medicine

The possibility of getting sick in a strange town sometimes becomes a reality. In a lifestyle filled with wonders and rewards, illness is one unpleasantness that must be planned for.

During our ten homeless years we had the usual routine care plus one hospital emergency and a couple of painful ailments that needed immediate attention, such as swimmer's ear and tooth emergencies. The important point is that we survived them all even though we were in places where we didn't know anyone, and we emerged each time with a heightened sense of affection, gratitude, and respect for our compatriots.

The American health care system is currently in turmoil and transition, and it's our guess that medical care will continue to be a financial problem for fulltimers, no matter what politicians do about it. So our first recommendation is to get health insurance now and hang onto it. If you develop a chronic problem, such as diabetes or high blood pressure, it may be impossible to get coverage later unless you can get into a group plan through an employer or an organization for the self-employed.

You have two other choices, unless you're old enough for Medicare:

■ Self-insure. Either pay medical costs out of your pocket or compromise by taking a policy with a very high deductible, say, $2,500 or $5,000, in which case you are not insured against minor ills yet protected, at minimum price, against being wiped out by a catastrophic health problem. They're complicated, but medical savings accounts (MSAs) are also available through your financial advisor.

■ Have no assets. Hope to receive free medical care if you become ill—an alternative many of us would prefer to avoid.

Before You Go

Once you're on the go full-time, you'll be responsible for your own health care in ways you probably never thought of before. When you have regular checkups from the same doctors, you can depend on them to note trends, dates of operations and treatments, names of drugs, allergies, worrisome changes, gains, and losses. However, when your yearly checkup is done by a different physician each time, only _you_ can tell whether your blood pressure is up, your weight down, or your mole larger.

Before leaving your hometown, make sure your shots, including a tetanus shot, are up to date, and get a written record to keep with you always. World Health Organization shot record cards are recognized worldwide and are a good way to keep track, especially if you will be traveling outside North America.

Your physician might also recommend that you get elective surgery out of the way and have some baseline tests, such as a blood profile or mammogram. We carry these records with us, plus the names of our prescription drugs. Know the generic and brand names, along with the dosage. Every doctor you see in the future will want to know.

When having a prescription filled, we always ask the pharmacist for the "Patient Information" sheet, which may not be put into the package unless you request it. Laymen don't always understand all the language in a P.I., but it's an invaluable record. During subsequent treatment for an illness, or even years later, this information can be vital.

Keep a medical diary so you'll have all available information in one place. Note ailments, dates, symptoms, insurance policy numbers, and the names, addresses, and telephone numbers of doctors, clinics, and hospitals where you've been treated.

Have a living will made listing your wishes concerning heroic measures, and keep a copy handy. Send other copies to next of kin. If you do not want to be kept alive by artificial means, you and your family may need all the legal ammunition you can muster, because the laws vary from state to state.

The more you know about what's happening to you, and what is being done to you by health care professionals who are strangers to you, the better. Many fulltimers invest in medical reference books such as the _Merck Manual_ or the _Physicians Desk Reference_. Browse at bookstores or on the Internet and choose a good first-aid manual.

The Internet can be an invaluable tool, but be sure any medical advice you get online is from reputable sources. Choose Web sites of known universities, clinics, and foundations. Online support groups can be useful sources for information on new research, exchanging experiences, and comfort and sympathy.

Ask your doctor for advice on putting together a complete first-aid kit. Learn the Heimlich maneuver and take a CPR course. As you travel, keep an eye peeled for free medical services in malls and hospitals. You might find free screenings for diabetes and blood pressure, mammograms, some eye tests, and even condom giveaways. If you are an honorably discharged veteran, you can get treatment at VA clinics. You don't have to have a service-connected disability. The paperwork takes ages, however, so get it in place before you need it.

Emergency Air Travel

Bill and Marilyn were in California when they received word via their message service that Bill's father had had a heart attack in Ohio and was not expected to live. Sue and her husband, fulltiming in Mexico for the winter, learned during a routine call home to Michigan that Sue's sister had been hospitalized after an accident at work. Sue's young nieces would be put into a foster home unless Sue could get home immediately to care for them. We were fulltiming in Fort Lauderdale when word came that Mom had pneumonia in Albany. Unless Janet could get there at once to give her home nursing care, she'd have to be hospitalized.

There are times when an emergency is too immediate for you to get there by RV and one or more family members has to leave the RV at a distant spot and fly home. Airline fares have been a turbulent, confusing shell game in recent years, but a recent wrinkle, "bereavement" or "compassion" fares, gives travelers a break on last-minute ticket purchases. However, these fares, like everyday fares, are a puzzle because rules vary from airline to airline.

If you have to fly home because of a family emergency, your best contact will be a sympathetic ticket agent. Call the airline's toll-free number, state your problem, and terminate the call if you don't get a caring response. These agents have far more flexibility than they let on; the next person who answers the phone may give you a better break. Better still, go to the airport and try several ticket agents. We have had little luck with the Internet in special situations, but that avenue is also worth a try if you have time.

Here are some things you should know about bereavement fares.

The emergency. Not all airlines offer compassion fares. Among those that do, different yardsticks are applied. Death of a family member is considered an emergency by all airlines, but in the case of Mom's pneumonia or Sue's trip home to take care of her sister's children the decision may be up to the telephone reservation agent or the agent behind the counter at the airport. In borderline cases ask to talk to a supervisor; underlings may not have authority to grant special exemptions.

Documentation. Airlines have been the victims of fraudulent sob stories, so they may require you to present a letter from a doctor, a copy of a death certificate, or written confirmation from a funeral home. Others may ask only for the name of the doctor, the funeral home, or the hospital. Provide as much information as possible.

Consanguinity. "Family" usually means a spouse or a close blood relative. Compassion fares may not apply in the case of the death of a cousin, uncle, or in-law. If possible, shop around. Some airlines have an ironclad policy defining which relationships are "close" and which do not qualify. Some make decisions on a case-by-case basis.

Restrictions. Make sure you understand whether the bereavement ticket is fully flexible / refundable, nonflexible / nonrefundable, or carries some possibilities for alteration. For instance, although you want to get there as soon as possible, you may not want to commit to a return date because you don't know how long it will take to settle the estate, nurse Mom back to health, or see Dad through a crisis.

Some airlines will waive advance-purchase requirements in an emergency but will impose the same restrictions as apply to Supersaver tickets (e.g., you have to stay over a Saturday night or fly only Sunday through Thursday). Although it's hard to think or care about the return trip before you go, try to allow for some flexibility on that end.

Senior citizens. Many airlines offer books of four tickets that are good for domestic flights from anywhere to anywhere at very low prices. Such tickets carry their own restrictions concerning advance reservations or blackout dates but are an excellent buy. Sometimes, especially in an emergency, you can fly standby without advance reservations. If you're over 55, ask whether you can get a discount. Different age limits apply depending on the airline, but 62 is the most common threshold.

The senior citizen deal may be better than bereavement fare. And most airlines allow each senior to take a companion of any age at the senior citizen rate. If you have frequent flyer miles, they too might be a quicker, cheaper route to an emergency flight.

Money angles. As already mentioned, fulltimers should carry at least one credit card for emergencies. Virtually all airlines accept major credit cards, traveler's checks, and cash; rarely can you use a personal check. Some airlines require you to pay the full tariff up front and then will refund the bereavement discount after you've sent in the required documentation. Some airlines do not refund this discount in cash, but only in the form of a voucher that can be used on a future ticket.

Bereavement fares are usually not the cheapest way to fly. Fully

(continued on page 136)

(continued from page 135)
restricted, nonrefundable tickets purchased well in advance are usually cheaper, but who can predict an emergency in advance? When one strikes, there is a good chance that you can get a break of 30–35 percent over regular coach fares.

Tell the airlines your story fully and honestly. Shop around if possible. Play by the rules, and be patient with those who are trying to help. When you need to get somewhere in the fastest way possible, compassion fares can help take some of the financial sting out of a personal loss.

Finding a Doctor

Because some physicians accept no new patients, or charge a huge premium for taking the medical history of a first-time patient, the fulltimer can have difficulty finding care. One answer is to get on the CB radio and ask the location of the nearest walk-in medical facility. These freestanding clinics are ideal for minor emergencies or a one-time visit.

If the community has a doctor referral service, call it and explain your special needs, including your transportation situation. If you're driving a large motorhome, you need a doctor whose office offers suitable parking. Big-city offices in downtown skyscrapers aren't your cup of tea.

Although life on the go creates certain medical care problems, it also has advantages. If you need a specialist, simply drive your entire household to the Mayo Clinic, or Houston, or Memphis, or wherever you can get the best care.

Special Insurance

An air evacuation insurance policy is offered by Medical Air Services Association. It covers you anywhere in the United States, Canada, Mexico, and the Caribbean for an emergency flight home if you're injured or become ill. Ask about group coverage, which may be available through a camping group. Call 800-643-9023 for information. Some insurance companies also arrange to drive your RV for you if you and your spouse have to be rushed home by air.

Fitness and the Fulltimer

One of the biggest frustrations in fulltiming is that there isn't room to swing a cat in an RV, let alone fling yourself around in a strenuous exercise program. One of the best exercises is brisk walking, but if you prefer a more serious program, you can:

■   Seek out campgrounds that have fitness directors, programs, and/or exercise equipment. Many camping resorts and destination campgrounds do.

■   Join a YW/YMCA. As a member of one Y, you will often be welcome to use the services of another one at discounted prices. Look into short-term programs too. Aerobics and other fitness classes often are available to nonmembers at reasonable prices.

■ Join a large, nationwide health club that has locations in many cities, then plan your travels so you'll always be near one. The advantage of national membership is that each of the club's individual facilities will share the same philosophy and type of equipment, so you'll get continuity of training no matter where you are.

■ Many hotels and resorts have fitness centers that can be used for an hourly fee.

■ The easiest solution is to work out your own fitness protocol using equipment you can carry on board. All you need for the best exercise of all, a power walk, is a good pair of walking shoes.

Dental Care

Prevention and education are the keys to carefree fulltiming, especially where your teeth are concerned.

Get your dental house in order at least six months before you set out fulltiming, advises Dale D. Batten, D.M.D., who practices in Deland, Florida. If you've neglected your teeth, consult a dentist as early as possible, as much as a year before your target getaway date, because you may need extensive work not just on your teeth but also on your gums, which may require a long-term course of action, Dr. Batten warns. "This is a tourist area, so I often see one-time patients who are just passing through town, as well as fulltimers who arrange to come to Deland for their regular checkups," he says. "If you've been an active patient, the only extra steps I'd take before you leave would be to take care of those teeth I'd been watching—those with minor fracture lines, for example. And I'd recommend that any teeth with large restorations or cracks receive full coverage cast restoration to add strength. Once you're on the road, you want to avoid trouble before it starts."

During your last visit to your hometown dentist, ask for a duplicate set of X-rays and a written report indicating what care you've been receiving and any special quirks or trouble spots. Ask your dentist what first-aid supplies are recommended, such as an over-the-counter, topical anesthetic gel to ease the discomfort of ulcers or other soft-tissue lesions.

If you use any special implements for oral cleaning and care, or require adaptive equipment because you are handicapped, get extras before you go because it may be difficult to find replacements later. Dr. Batten also recommends stocking up on any prescription mouth rinses or fluoride gels you are using. "It takes up very little space to carry a year's supply, so buy before you go, because sometimes prescriptions aren't honored across state lines," he recommends.

You might also ask your dentist to show you how to fix your dislocated jaw if you're subject to recurrent dislocations. It's a simple first-aid technique that could come in handy when you're far from professional help.

Once you're on the road, continue with regular checkups, usually every six months unless you require more frequent cleanings or checks. Batten suggests two ways to find the best dentists when you're in a new area.

One way is to call several specialists—orthodontists, endodontists, periodontists—and ask who they recommend for general dentistry. Each will probably give you three names, and when the same name pops up more than once, you'll know you've found a dentist who is well respected in the profession. Or contact the Academy of General

Dentistry and ask for membership services. They'll give you the names of three member dentists in the area you're visiting. Contact them at 211 E. Chicago Avenue, Chicago, IL 60611; 312-440-4300, 888-AGD-DENT (888-243-3368); www.agd.org.

What about advertising in the Yellow Pages, or the referral services advertised on television? Some "referral" services are simply an advertising co-op paid for by dentists who are trying to drum up business. Referrals are made only to dentists who have paid to be listed. You may get a better profile by calling a county dental society. Some use a comprehensive database to find exactly the dentist you want according to education, years in practice, location, and even marital status. If there is a dental school in the area, you might try asking there for a recommendation. While university dental schools do capable, highly supervised work at bargain prices, it's very slow going. Also, universities prefer to work on local people, whose dental history they can track for a sustained period.

Each time you see a dentist during your travels, ask for duplicates of X-rays and a memo outlining what care was given and any other information the dentist might like to convey to the colleague who will see you next. Although some dentists charge extra for this added service or for a first-time visit, we found that most dentists, especially in tourist areas, were understanding of the fulltimer's situation and did not take advantage of it.

Dental First Aid

Dentistry is not a do-it-yourself skill, but there are some things you should know, do, and avoid. "If a crown falls off, the first thing you want to do is to retrieve it," Dr. Batten says. "Second, replace it temporarily with denture adhesive or petroleum jelly. Don't use an over-the-counter dental adhesive, because it's probable that you'll seal the crown incorrectly. That makes it harder for the dentist to get it off again to do a proper repair, and it can lead to other problems, such as jaw pain."

When a tooth is sensitive to heat or altitude, Batten says, the nerve is probably involved, and you should seek professional help as soon as possible because it can become very painful very quickly. Cold sensitivity should be checked out, but it probably isn't as immediate a problem. You might also carry a wax-type repair to place over a broken tooth, or a tooth that has lost its filling, just to protect the jagged edge until you can get to a dentist.

Some such products contain a medication that helps soothe pain. "The object is to keep the air out and to keep sharp edges from cutting your cheek or tongue," says Batten. "But just because it feels better, don't delay getting help. A permanent repair must be made before bigger problems result. Keep fillings, crowns, or tooth fragments if possible. The dentist may want to see or repair them."

What not to do? Don't press an aspirin into the painful area. That's an old-fashioned remedy that can cause severe burns to the surrounding soft issue. Remember that aspirin is a strong acid; it is not meant to be used in concentration.

Some additional tips on preventive care and dental first aid:

■ Always wear a seat belt. When playing sports, wear suitable protective safety gear.

■ If you wear braces, carry orthodontic wax to place over any rough or broken wires to protect the cheeks and tongue until a repair can be made. If you don't have wax, try a cotton ball.

■   If a tooth is knocked out, pick it up by the crown, not the roots, rinse it very gently, and replace it in the socket. Get help as soon as possible. In the case of a young child, who might swallow the tooth, take it with you in milk, water, or a damp towel. The quicker you get help, the better the chance that the tooth can be saved. If you can get to a dentist in a half-hour or less, there's a 90 percent chance that it can be reimplanted successfully.

■   If a tooth breaks, save the parts and get to a dentist as soon as possible.

■   If the jaw is broken, immobilize it with a bandana or gauze and get to a hospital emergency room. You know it's broken if there is pain and you can't move it, or if your teeth won't mesh right.

If You Wear Dentures

Sundru Moodley, president of the All Denture Clinic in Denver, Colorado, suggests additional equipment to carry if all or some of your teeth are false. "Any do-it-yourself denture repair work is only a temporary measure," he says, "but there are steps you can take to resolve an immediate problem."

Moodley suggests carrying baking soda and a soft toothbrush for cleaning, a fast-setting glue, paste, or powdered denture adhesive, an emery board, and a second set of dentures, either duplicates or your old set.

"Bones change shape and structure with time," says Moodley, so your dentures may not fit as comfortably as they once did. Use denture adhesives to create a more comfortable fit if dentures are loose.

If a tooth breaks off the denture, replace it using the glue according to the manufacturer's directions. Don't put the plate back into your mouth until the glue is completely dry.

A broken denture can be repaired by applying the glue to one surface and putting the pieces together. After the glue dries, use an emery board to remove rough edges that could irritate the mouth. If you have to replace a broken denture, and you wear both upper and lower plates, replace both. "Dentures are made as a set," Moodley says, "and it's best to keep them together."

TWENTY

Housecleaning on Wheels

Your rolling home looks like a home, feels like a home, *is* your home. Yet you can't clean it like a house because RV construction differs from house construction in important ways. One reason is economic, to give you the most living space for the money. Another is that to save weight on the road, manufacturers use lightweight plastics and composites that won't stand up like the hardwoods and bricks that are put into a house.

Information: Your Primary Cleaning Aid

The most important aid in caring for your RV is the owner's manual packet. You should have received multiple manuals covering the vehicle, each system, and every appliance. Read them carefully. They're full of surprises about things to do, avoid, add, and omit.

If any manuals are missing, nag the dealer or manufacturer until you get every document due you, including warranties for the RV itself and for each separate item that is guaranteed. If possible, also get the manufacturer to give you use and care information for the carpeting, upholstery, surfacings, and other original equipment.

If you bought a used RV, track down as many instruction books and owner's manuals as possible. Write the factory, the chassis manufacturer, makers and suppliers for systems and appliances (stove, refrigerator), and perhaps the original dealer. A club for owners of your brand of RV might be a useful resource. As a last resort, write to the "Letters to the Editor" sections of RV magazines requesting input from owners of RVs like yours.

This sounds like a lot of work, but the earlier you gather this information, the better. As companies and components come and go, it becomes harder and harder to find cleaning recommendations and replacement parts, part numbers, repair information for older units, and routine maintenance needs such as gaskets or O-rings.

RV Cleaning Products

While they may cost a bit more than their household counterparts, RV products are almost always the wisest choice because they are uniquely formulated for RV materials, soils, uses, and abuses.

Before using any cleaner, make sure it's safe to use in or around an RV. Household window cleaners could harm nonglass RV windows; household cleansers can ruin the RV's plastic surfaces; and ordinary cleaners and coatings don't usually contain the ultraviolet filters that are put into RV products to protect against sun damage. Put the wrong chemicals in your RV toilet, and you can wreck an entire campground's septic system.

Among the strict no-no's are drain cleaners (which could damage valves and umbilical hoses), powdered sink cleanser (which can abrade away a gelcoat or plastic surface in seconds), and flammable cleaners (you probably have an open flame burning in the gas refrigerator or water heater).

One exception is the very harsh detergent sold for use in dishwashers. It's not suitable for hand dishwashing, but carry some aboard anyway. A soak in very hot water and dishwasher detergent is the best way to get stains and odors out of galley plastics.

Product Tips

■ Start with the mildest cleaner possible, then get tougher as necessary.

■ For overhead cleaning, such as light fixtures and ceilings, try a waterless hand cleaner. It will cling rather than dripping back in your face, and it's gentle enough for the most tender surface (including your skin). It's especially effective in cleaning around the exhaust hood over the stove. Rub it in with your hands until grease dissolves. These cleaners are formulated to work at body temperature.

■ In the galley and head, clean with baking soda. It's safe to use on the cutting board and other galley surfaces and deodorizes, neutralizes, and sanitizes without leaving a gritty residue.

■ When you're on short water rations and can't spare the gallons of running water it takes to flush away soaps and cleansers, be very sparing with cleaning products. The chemical residues they leave could be more dangerous than the dirt they displace.

■ Black streaks are a special problem for RVers. Exposed to road film, bugs, tar, and wind-driven dirt and sand, then drenched with rain, which reacts with both the pollutants and the RV's finish, the RV becomes streaked with mineral stains that can't be removed with ordinary cleaners. Look for products that will remove these streaks but are safe to use on RVs.

Plumbing

RV plumbing is very different from the septic or sewer system you had at home. "RVs are not houses. They are constructed of vastly different materials and are generally exposed to much more extreme external exposure," says Jeff Tieger of Star brite, which makes cleaning and maintenance products formulated for the specific needs of the rolling home.

"Typically, formaldehyde-based holding tank chemicals are used to treat waste," Tieger says, "but they are poisoning, staining, and unfriendly to the environment. Many dump stations will not accept formaldehyde-treated waste because of these problems. Star brite utilizes much better technology in its Instant Fresh Toilet Treatment. This product contains quaternary ammonium compounds that are very effective at breaking down waste, preventing gassing, and stopping odors. Yet they are non-staining and biodegradable."

Read your owner's manual. Some RV toilets need no chemicals at all; biological breakdown occurs normally, and odors are carried away through a correctly installed vent system. If you have an odor problem, it could be a leaky seal, inadequate venting, or odors from the campground sewer, and no chemical additions can improve matters.

Carpeting

Carpeting is a major cleaning problem because it takes so much wear and abuse. And if your galley area is carpeted, that abuse can reach the absurd. Once when we forgot to lock the refrigerator door, we lurched around a corner and watched a dozen eggs fall out and break on the galley carpet. Another time, it was a pot of beef stew.

To clean up after a carpet mishap, first scrape gently to lift as much goo as possible from the surface. The more you rub, the more you work the mess into the fiber. Avoid adding water, since that will dilute and spread the stain. After picking up as much as possible, press on the stain with thick bunches of paper towels. The more stain you can wick up into them, the less you'll be scrubbing back into the carpet. Blot slowly and with as much force as possible. Don't rub! If the spill is very wet, such as milk or juice, weigh down layers of paper towels with stacks of books and then give the natural wicking process time to work, replacing the paper towels often. Once actual cleaning begins, don't overwet the carpeting and dry it as quickly and thoroughly as possible. Most RV flooring is interior plywood, which can rot or delaminate if soaked.

Vacuum as often as possible, using a "real" vacuum cleaner, preferably one with a beater bar. Underpowered car vacs aren't strong enough. Once or twice a year have the carpet professionally cleaned and treated with Scotchgard. Baking soda is an effective natural carpet deodorizer. Sprinkle it on the carpet and let it stand about thirty minutes; then vacuum.

Closets and Their Contents

About once a year, during housecleaning, turn everything out of your clothes storage locker and clean the locker itself with a strong mildew-cide bathroom cleaner. Then dry it thoroughly with a hair dryer before refilling it with clean, well-aired clothes. If it's lined with cedar, skip the scrubbing but give the walls, ceiling, and floor a good vacuuming.

Storing Out-of-Season Clothes

It's important that fabric items be clean before they are stored. Soil and stains, even those that are virtually invisible before you pack clothes away, can take on a life of their own in storage. Once set, they're almost impossible to remove.

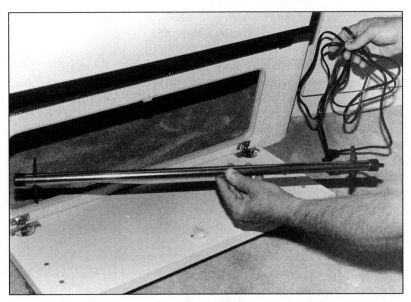

Golden Rod closet heaters are electrically heated bars that emit a constant glow of heat and reduce or eliminate mildew in small, enclosed areas. See appendix I, Useful Addresses, for contact information. (Buenger Enterprises)

Rotate all clothing and linens as much as possible. If there are some items that are rarely used, take them out for a sunny airing and a good inspection every few months. We've found mold on leather shoes and boots, mildew on a dress suit that hadn't been worn in some months, and moth damage on a wool coat.

When we wear any item, even for a short time, we wash it or have it dry-cleaned before banishing it to long-term storage. Man-made materials seem to have a special affinity for soil and need frequent washing. I'd never pack away anything that had been worn against the skin for even a few minutes.

If you swim in salt water, rinse your suit well in freshwater, hang it on the line until it feels dry, and then put it away. Otherwise, salt crystals that remain in the fabric will draw moisture out of the air and keep the fabric and everything around it damp. The same goes for beach towels or anything else that has been in or near salt water. Chlorine left in swimsuits can continue to degrade the fabric too, so before storing swimsuits, rinse them in several changes of water, and then dry thoroughly.

Rain gear should be completely dry before it is put away or it will rot. If we do have to bring a wet umbrella or raincoat inside, it goes back outside for a complete rinsing, drying, and airing as soon as the sun comes out.

Shops and catalogs that specialize in closet accessories sell a variety of cedar shavings, closet linings, and sachets. If your RV didn't come with a cedar-lined closet, as many do, it's easy to add this lining yourself. In a home-improvement store we found thin cedar planks that can be cut to fit and used to line any closet or locker. They are a fragrant way to protect woolens and to sweeten shoe lockers.

We've found that if we treat leather shoes with a natural wax, they become moldy faster. We've had better luck with silicone protectants, which also waterproof shoes and boots.

We store off-season clothes in as many separate containers as possible, even though these in turn may all be crammed into the same big locker. This way, it's easier to retrieve just the ski jackets, or only our wet suits, without pawing through the entire bin.

By putting things in their own boxes or bags, we're also able to give them whatever special treatment is best—woolens are sealed into bags with cedar, summer lingerie is sealed in a bag with sachet, leather shoes and hiking boots are given a coat of leather protector, swim fins and rubber boots are given a generous dusting of talcum before they're put away.

Our few dressy outfits are not banished to some deep locker but are put in their own clothes bags in the closet. They hang there ready and wrinkle free, but protected from everyday handling and jostling in the closet.

Do you have special table linens aboard that you use only a few times a year? After they are washed and dried, starched and ironed, warm them in the oven at about 120°F and then seal in plastic bags while they're still warm. They'll stay sweet and dry until the next time you need them.

Laundry

We'll assume here that you'll be doing most of your laundry yourself, in coin-operated machines. Another choice is to do the wash by hand, which we've done when in remote areas, using an inflatable swimming pool and a toilet plunger. Many RVers also put the laundry, water, and soap into a plastic garbage can with a lock-on lid and let it slosh clean on the highway. A third choice is to use full-service commercial laundries or the wash-and-fold service offered by some coin laundries.

Or, you can try machines that combine a washer and dryer in one unit. One source is Splendide (www.splendide.com). The best thing about having your own machine is that you can wash any time, anywhere you can get water and electricity, in your own washer. On the other hand, such units can do only small loads at a time, are useless when you don't have full hookups, and don't have all the features and settings found on full-size automatics. Only you can decide whether the convenience will be worth the cost, space, and weight of installing one aboard.

Of all the appliances we miss when we're on the go, the washer and dryer are at the top of the list. Yet coin laundries have their good points. You can use as many machines as needed, doing multiple loads in no more time than it takes for one. Better self-service laundries are air-conditioned, clean, spacious, and cheerful and have generous tables where the wash can be sorted and folded. They're great places to meet local folks, and the best ones have such extras as vending machines, television, and libraries.

Here are some coin laundry tips we learned the hard way.

■   Don't put clothes into any washer or dryer without first checking the machine, with a small flashlight if necessary. We have found a long list of horrors, including mess from diapers, goo from melted crayons or rubber pants, and rust spots or burrs on the metal drum that would tear clothes to shreds.

■ If the dryer has a lint filter, clean it.

■ Keep a generous cache of coins on hand; you may not be able to get change when you need it. Depending on the dryer, fuel, weather, and how well the washers wring out the water, it could take twice as many coins to dry the load as you expected.

■ Never wash an expensive piece in a machine you haven't used before. We've encountered washers that delivered hot water when the "cold" button was pressed, dryers that went directly into meltdown even on the gentle cycle, and washers that were not capable of spin-drying a heavy item such as a blanket or bedspread.

■ Bring a couple of Clorox bathroom wet wipes to clean and sanitize the table you'll use to fold your clean clothes.

■ Discover a product called Dye Magnet. Sold in supermarket laundry departments for about $5, it is a washcloth-size fabric that allows you to mix colors and whites without fear of staining. It can be reused many times.

■ Don't leave clothes unattended. An impatient customer waiting for a machine could empty the washer or dryer and dump your things in a wrinkly pile. A well-intentioned friend could put them in the dryer, but at the wrong setting. At worst, they could be stolen.

The Mending Basket

In addition to the basic supplies you'll need for emergency mending jobs, have a supply of shirt buttons that install without sewing and a large selection of heat-fusible materials to be used for mending and patching. They include iron-on jeans patches, sock patches, cut-your-own patches in all colors, knee patches, and even iron-in replacement pants pockets. To repair a hem, place a strip of heat-fusible tape in the fold and iron until it melts.

Speaking of ironing, we carry a travel iron that has a built-in water reservoir for steam ironing. Although small ironing boards are available, we do all our touch-up ironing on the galley counter, on a folded bath towel. Spray-on wrinkle removers are available, but we haven't found one that is 100 percent effective.

■ Few RVs have clothes hampers, so be sure to allot a large, well-ventilated space for laundry storage as you move aboard. We sort clothes as we use them, using separate laundry bags for whites, colors, and items that will need special treatment (heavy-duty cycle, hand washable, stain treatment, etc.).

■ Buy laundry bags or make your own from sturdy muslin or light canvas. Before leaving for the laundry, measure detergent, and powdered bleach if needed, into each bag. Dump the contents into the washer, then throw in the bag. After drying and folding, use the clean bags to carry the wash back to the RV.

Prevention

To help keep sand and mud out of the RV, add as many dirt-stoppers as possible. You might, for example, glue a layer of plastic turf doormat material to the RV steps. If you need an additional outside step, use an upturned milk crate, which will allow dirt to fall through. Carry one or two doormats to place outside the RV. Better still, leave shoes at the door, Japanese style.

Carpeting, upholstery, and other interior surfaces should be protected from sun fading. You might want to add solar-insulated curtains or have a solar coating professionally applied to the windows. Avoid do-it-yourself solar films, which can cloud, bubble, and peel.

Inside the RV as well as outside, continually fight dirt, chafe, corrosion, crazing, and rust by using the best cleaners, coatings, and protectants. The payback will be longer wear and a better price at resale time.

Twenty-One

Tools
for the
Fulltimer

R V vacationers can often wait until they get home to their workshops, floor jacks, and big toolboxes to do routine maintenance, upgrades, additions, and all but emergency repairs. Fulltimers, by contrast, have to deal with maintenance day by day, with tools that must be carried, hired, or borrowed.

Even if you are a savvy mechanic and can do all your own repairs, you simply can't carry all the tools you'd like to have. Tools are bulky and heavy; you have to be realistic about space and weight.

Yet even if you can't or won't do your own work, you should carry *some* tools, because it's likely that your rig requires some unique or little-used implements that not every mechanic or RV shop will have. We put together a basic kit in a plastic fishing tackle box so that the tools we need most often are handy and portable. It weighs less than 10 pounds and is easy to carry around the RV for every job from tightening battery cables to fixing door locks.

Here's what our basic tool kit includes.

■ Slot-head and Phillips-head screwdrivers, as well as whatever drivers you need to fit clinch-head screws and any other oddball screws in your RV. Screwdrivers also double as pry bars.
■ Pliers. We prefer Channellocks because they serve as both pliers and pipe wrench; also needle-nose pliers.
■ A side cutter

- An 8-inch crescent wrench
- A small brad hammer
- Various punches and nail sets
- Three grades of rat-tail files
- A couple of bastard files
- The smaller wrenches from a set of open end and box wrenches

While it would be nice to have additional tools so that you could fix everything from burned engine bearings to the kitchen sink, it usually isn't practical. So let's start with the possible.

Plumbing. For plastic plumbing you'll need a hacksaw, a file or a sharp knife for deburring, a can of PVC cement, and a grasping tool (such as the Channellocks) for work on threaded PVC fittings. A short-handled plumber's helper is light to carry and will solve most sink blockage problems. For copper and brass plumbing, carry a tubing cutter, a flaring tool, and a selection of connectors in the sizes you're most likely to need.

Carpentry. If you'll be doing any remodeling, you'll need more than these basic woodworking tools, but for basic repairs and replacement jobs, start with a hacksaw, which is the lightest and most versatile saw. If you need something faster, add a keyhole saw or a saber saw. An electric or eggbeater hand drill with a selection of bits up to ¼ inch will be useful. So will an adjustable hole saw. For smoothing equipment, include a plane, files, and sandpaper.

A supply of two-part epoxy glue can mend almost anything. We carry a couple of stamped metal, spring-loaded, clothespin-type clamps. Of all the clamps available, these weigh the least and yet exert a steady force for glue jobs.

Sewing. In addition to the usual mending supplies, bring heavy-duty needles and thread and an upholstery needle for first aid to cushion covers, curtains, and awnings.

Electrical. Take a combination wire cutter and stripper, a crimping tool, crimp terminals and connectors, and testing equipment such as a multimeter. A pencil-type soldering iron weighs only a few ounces and is handy for small electrical repairs.

Engine and drive train. First, read through all the manuals that came with your RV to find out whether any special tools are recommended. Almost every rig needs something odd, such as a special wrench to remove wheel hub nuts or a unique tool to remove an injector from a diesel engine. Even if you don't know how to use such tools, it's wise to have them aboard because a hired mechanic may not have them. A nut splitter is handy for exhaust work, and we also carry a pulley puller.

You probably also need a special tool for adjusting ignition timing. For oil changes, carry a strap wrench to use in removing the old oil filter.

Somewhere, you should also have the larger half (up to 1 inch) from the set of open end and box wrenches mentioned above and a spark plug wrench and/or injector tool. If you have to do a major engine job, you can usually buy an inexpensive piston ring expander and valve-turning tools as needed rather than carrying them around. Work on our RV often requires a torque wrench, so we find it worthwhile to carry one.

Tools for an automatic transmission are too specialized for most of us to carry, but with the tools already listed you can change the transmission oil and adjust the bands.

If yours is a manual transmission, check to see whether you need special wrenches for the oil plugs.

You can change your universal joints with basic tools, but to grease universals you'll need a special non-high-pressure grease gun. Don't let anyone grease yours with a gas station–type pressure gun—it'll blow out the seals.

Wheels and tires. It's likely that the equipment for wheel changing came with your RV, but you may prefer to invest in a heavier-duty, better-quality jack. A good hydraulic jack weighs more, but it's worth every ounce.

Try to remove a lug nut with the lug wrench provided by your RV manufacturer. If it bends, throw it away and buy a heavy-duty, commercial-grade, X-style lug wrench. If you'll be overhauling your brakes, the tools already named will do the job. For drum-type brakes it's handy to have the special spring remover/installer sold in automobile parts stores.

Spare Parts Are Important Too

To keep up and running you need not just tools but spare parts. Again, you have to make painful decisions about what to take and what to leave behind. But keep in mind that the more offbeat your RV and its equipment, the harder and more expensive it becomes to find replacement parts in an emergency.

First on the list of spares you *must* have, even if you can't install them yourself, are fan belts. We once drove a friend all over town trying to find a fan belt to fit one of the most common cars in the country. Double-check the fan belt sizes you need and get one in each size.

If you carry a portable air compressor, you can top off your tires—and fill the air mattress and inflatable boat, too. (Sears)

If any nonstandard equipment was installed when your RV was customized, you may need sizes other than those listed in the original owner's manual.

Here are some other items to consider carrying:

For the engine. Take spare radiator hoses, especially if yours are an unusual molded design. They'll keep a long time if you keep them clean and in a dark place, so the investment made today will pay off tomorrow. Carry a few extra hose clamps in appropriate sizes. We think it's well worth it to buy the best all-stainless clamps. (Beware: Some stainless steel hose clamps have steel screws.)

Spares for your cooling system should include at least one complete set of radiator hoses and a spare water pump, especially if you'll be in areas where you can't buy them readily. (Heater hoses and any other straight pieces of hose usually can be found anywhere, so you don't need a supply of those.)

Many of the new fuel pumps aren't made to be repaired, but if you have an older pump that requires periodic overhauls, carry an overhaul kit. We also like to carry an extra fuel filter element or two. If we pick up a bad load of fuel and clog one filter, we have a second filter to snare the next slug of crud that comes through the line.

Carry a spare ignition module. These "little black boxes" give no advance warning of failure, but when one goes, you're dead in the water. This is another item you can buy at a discount auto parts store for about half what you'd pay for a dealer-installed part. So, since Groene's Law states that the more desperate you are, the more difficult it will be to find the right-size module, this is one spare part to have aboard at all times.

Carry at least enough of your brand of oil to do routine topping off, and preferably enough for an oil change. When you see oil filters on sale, put one in stock. Have at least one spare spark plug; they can fail or break. If your engine is a diesel, it's good insurance to have a spare injector on board. One other spare to consider carrying is a universal joint, since you'll be stranded without one. They're fairly easy to change.

Chassis and drive. In hot climates, brake fluid is lost through evaporation, so carry extras of your brand so you can top off the reservoir. Our lives depend on our brakes. That's why we'd rather add fluid from our own clean, sealed can than from the derelict pail of fluid found sloshing around at gas stations.

Tires. It's vital to have a spare tire, and if your tires are not all alike, you should have one in each size. If tires match, rotate them once in a while so that they will wear evenly. Spare tires should be covered at all times. We found that plastic covers disintegrated after a year or so, so we had a sturdier one made from waterproof canvas sewn with heavy-duty Dacron (not cotton) thread. Such a cover costs more but wears years longer.

Living quarters. Unless you want to go to a motel every time something is out of whack, it's wise to have enough spares to keep your "house" up and running too. Carry some spare washers if your faucets use them, brass B-nuts for the plumbing (they crack), and an extra sewage valve. If you need a spare, it might be hard to find one in your size when you need it.

We buy 12-volt light bulbs by the case, not just for economy but also because the box provides the safest way to pack them. You'll soon know which bulbs you need most often.

Also carry fuses in every size needed for both your 12-volt and "house" systems, spare key(s)—somewhere where you can get at them in a pinch—and a spare cartridge for the water filter. It's bulky, but it weighs very little.

One of the best things about fulltiming is a feeling of independence on an endless highway. But you'll be independent only as long as the RV remains mobile. Broken down, both your home and your wheels are at the mercy of whatever help you can get. If you have the right tools and spares, you'll have a better chance of coming through a breakdown with a faster getaway and a fatter wallet.

Twenty-Two

Your RV's Engine and Drive Train

When things break down after a certain number of miles, make a note to expect the same failure after the same interval. If you were wrong and the initial breakdown was just a fluke, fine. But stresses are stresses, and components are components. The better you know your RV, the more you can predict and prevent problems.

The Engine

Probably the most expensive single item in your rolling home is the engine. Whether the engine is in the tow car, the pickup truck, or the motorhome, you want to protect this investment and ensure the utmost dependability. A breakdown on the road, besides being dangerous and troublesome, is extraordinarily expensive in an RV because towing charges are high *and* you have to pay lodging bills if your RV becomes uninhabitable.

Your most important aids are your driver's manual, any workshop manuals you can obtain from the chassis manufacturer, and perhaps other commercial manuals, such as those published by Clymer or Chilton, for your make of power plant. The more nonstandard your vehicle, the more important these manuals become; even if you don't do your own maintenance, a professional mechanic will need them for reference.

Most breakdowns forecast their approach loud and clear if only you know what to look and listen for. Often, if you pay attention, you can head off the posse at the pass. If possible, make replacements and repairs as soon as you notice a problem; that way you can have more control over the situation. You'll be able to choose a time and a suitable spot to work. To save money, pick up replacement parts at an auto-parts discount store.

A word of caution: When working with flammables such as gasoline, diesel, propane, and lighter fluid, never forget that your RV has many sources of ignition, including burners or pilot lights in the water heater, the refrigerator, the stove, and the oven.

Carry a complete set of fan belts. Even if you can't change them yourself, you'll always have the proper size with you. If one breaks on the road, you can soon be up and running, even if a mechanic has to come out to do the work. Otherwise you have to be towed in and pay top dollar for the fan belt—if the garage *has* the right size belt—as well as the asking price for towing and labor.

Cooling System

Most failures in the cooling system give ample warning: rusted and weakening hose clamps, deteriorated or soft hoses, slight leakage at connections, unusual noise, or weeping around the water pump. All these signs point to future problems, none of which go away or heal themselves.

A modern pressurized cooling system with overflow tanks should need little, if any, added fluid for as long as a year. Water in the coolant mixture can't boil away because it condenses in the overflow reservoir. Consider any change in the amount of loss an advance warning that problems are brewing.

Perhaps all you have to do to stop this loss is to tighten hose clamps—a good thing to do periodically anyway. If you can't see any leaks, try observing all connections just after starting the cold engine because this is when leaks usually occur. While pressure is starting to build, and before various parts expand from heat, you may be able to spot where you're losing coolant.

Any sign of air bubbles in your overflow tank is an indication of leakage in the head gasket. The trouble must be found and fixed immediately because if antifreeze gets into the oil, bearings seize very quickly.

Be faithful about changing permanent antifreeze at least every second year because rust and corrosion inhibitors wear out in time. Usually the system needs a good flush by then anyway to wash away abrasive particles that have broken loose.

With the engine cold, open all drains. Usually there are several on the block and one on the bottom of the radiator. While the old coolant is draining (into a suitable container for whatever waste disposal or recycling is practiced in your area), remove and clean the overflow tank if there's any sign of sludge or scale. Then stick a water hose into the radiator opening and let the water flow through freely for several minutes.

Now, with the water flow adjusted so that it just keeps the system full (you may have to close one or two of the drains to maintain the water level), start the engine and let it idle for ten minutes while fresh water flows through it. Watch to make sure that the water flow continues to be adequate.

Finally, turn off the engine, turn off the water, drain thoroughly, and let the engine cool. You don't want to shock a hot engine by filling it with cold coolant.

Then close all the drains and pour in a 50-50 mix of water and the coolant recommended by your engine manufacturer. If the local water has a high mineral or chlorine content, use distilled water to cut down on sediment and corrosion in the future.

Oil

Oil, like coolant, is a critical protector for your expensive engine. Many manufacturers now specify long periods between oil changes—perhaps as long as every 6,000 miles. It's not just a matter of cost and convenience; oil disposal has become a problem and lubricants have become better and last longer. In the old days, engines were engines and oil was oil. However, to get maximum protection and oil effectiveness today, it's important to select the right, manufacturer-recommended oil for *your* engine.

When you drive for long periods at a time, impurities and condensation are cooked out of the oil, making it more effective longer. If, however, your RV stands idle a lot and is used only for short hops, consider changing the oil and filter more often, especially if the RV is equipped with a turbocharger, whose bearings are very sensitive to contaminants in the oil.

Because most RVs won't fit on a standard gas station lift and must be taken to a special garage for service, consider doing your own oil changes. The savings are several. First, you buy the oil at a discount store or at sale prices instead of paying what the garage charges. Filters too can be bought at discount stores. While you're there, pick up a strap-type wrench if you don't have one. You will save time, too, because you can do the job when and where you choose. And you may save on cleanup, because if oil must be added inside your motorhome's cab, you may be more fastidious than a stranger would be.

If you change your own oil and other automotive fluids, be sure to collect and dispose of waste products properly. (Gordon Groene)

When you change oil, do it at the end of a long day's drive, while the oil is hot and contaminants are in suspension. It isn't enough just to start the engine and warm it up. The more impurities you can flush out with the oil, the better. Be sure to dispose of used oil in accordance with state and federal laws.

After the oil has drained, replace the drain plug and refill the system with oil. Now start the engine, which is still warm, to get the new oil circulating through the engine and the new filter. If you wait until the next morning, when everything is cold, the oil won't start circulating as readily.

Whatever oil you choose, try to use the same brand consistently. When you're a full-time rover, it's best to start with a brand that is sold internationally (Shell, Castrol) so you'll be able to get it throughout the United States, Canada, Mexico, and other countries you may visit.

Gear oil and automatic-transmission oil are also available in discount auto-parts stores, so you may as well start changing them yourself too. Your driver's manual will tell you what grade to buy.

Exhaust Manifold

Only a few years ago you could exit the interstate into a rest stop, turn off the engine without a thought, and go off to make a phone call. However, today's exhaust manifolds are usually made out of a low-quality iron that expands and contracts at a rate different from that of the high-quality iron or aluminum cylinder heads they're bolted to. If your RV is running red-hot and you turn off the engine abruptly, the engine parts will cool at different rates, placing undue stress on the manifold. It's just a matter of time until a weak spot in the casting fails. A cooldown period of 5 to 10 mintues before shutoff is a safety precaution (for turbocharged engines it's essential). If you do have to replace the manifold, look into high-quality, jointed manifolds, which are less likely to crack. They are sold in the aftermarket.

Engine Gauges

Although today's cockpit panels are filled with gauges and indicator lights, here are additional gauges we consider important. We suggest you or your mechanic add any that you don't already have.

Coolant temperature gauge. A warning light will tell you only when the coolant overheats. A gauge, on the other hand, indicates whether the coolant is too hot or too cold (which usually means the thermostat has failed).

Oil pressure gauge. An idiot light tells you you've lost oil pressure and must shut down immediately or die. However, earlier warning of falling pressure gives you more time to get out of traffic and into a safe area before shutting down.

Battery voltage gauge. You may have a stock ammeter, but a battery voltage gauge will tell you more about the general condition of your electrical system and voltage regulator. This information is especially important when your "house" is operating on battery power.

Transmission oil temperature gauge. When transmission oil gets too hot, its lubricating abilities diminish rapidly. With a gauge, you always know when to ease up on the load. If overheating is chronic, you know that you need more transmission cooling capacity.

The Drive Train

Wheels

When things come in sets, suspect the entire set if one part fails. Our RV's rear wheels crack radially about every 30,000 miles. When the first one cracked, we guessed that its twins would probably crack soon too. We replaced them all at once and were proved right. When we replaced them the second time, two had already started to fracture.

Bearings

Wheel bearings need regular service, which is an easy, straightforward job (on non-drive wheels) requiring only a few tools, cotter pins in the proper size, and, in most cases, new dust seals. Drive wheels get more complicated, so refer to a manual before opening them. We've had excellent luck with Lubriplate's waterproof wheel bearing grease.

It's especially important to keep close tabs on trailer wheel bearings because some brands wear quickly. If bearings themselves show any signs of wearing or scoring, replace them with one of the better brands, such as Federal-Mogul or Timken.

To adjust any type of wheel bearing that uses a cotter pin, tighten the nut by hand until all play is gone and the wheel rotates freely. Then back the nut up to the next hole. On infinitely adjustable axle nuts, tighten down snugly and then back off just until the wheel rotates freely with no discernible play in the bearings.

To repack bearings, first clean them thoroughly and give them a final rinse in clear kerosene or diesel fuel. Never dry a bearing by rotating it with compressed air, which could magnetize it. Bearings can best be packed by hand. Just put a glob of grease in the palm of one hand and scrape at it with the edge of the bearing cage, forcing grease up between the rollers until the bearing is completely full. This is usually all the grease that is needed unless manufacturer directions call for a specific amount in the hub.

After packing inside bearings, you'll have to replace dust seals. Be sure the new seals are seated squarely in their grooves, with the lip facing the bearing. As you finish the job, be sure the dust cap fits snugly. A wheel should never be operated with a missing dust cap because even the slightest bit of grit in a roller bearing can cause failure. In a pinch, make a temporary cap out of a tin can. Keep a special eye on boots on constant-velocity joints. The joints are expensive and can quickly be ruined if dirt or water gets to them.

One more point: Never replace just part of a bearing. Drive or press out the old outer race and put in a new one.

The easiest way to pack wheel bearings is by hand. Fill one palm with a good wheel–bearing grease and scoop the grease into the bearing cage. (Gordon Groene)

Greasing the RV

Few vehicles today have grease fittings. If yours does, you're lucky. Using them faithfully over the long run will assure longer wear than you'll get with the so-called permanently packed joints. Your owner's manual will tell you where these fittings are and how often they should be greased.

A few years ago a popular coach manufacturer neglected to mention in its owner's manual that inner-drive axle bearings should be lubricated every 24,000 miles. When failures started to occur, owners found themselves facing repair bills in the $4,000 range. To protect yourself from this type of disaster, know your RV and its needs as thoroughly as possible by talking to owners of similar rigs and reading RV magazines for reports of a pattern of failures in units like yours.

The only thing you need to do the job yourself is a grease gun, preferably the cartridge type, and grease cartridges. Use a high-pressure, lithium-type grease for chassis fittings and universal joints unless the manufacturer directs otherwise (see top photo, page 158).

Take two precautions. First, any suspension parts that carry the weight of the vehicle should be unloaded before greasing, if possible. (This doesn't include tie-rods.) Second, universal joints should be filled very slowly so that seals aren't forced out.

While you're lubricating, put a drop of oil on all hinges, including those on the service doors, the entry doors, the carburetor linkage, and the emergency brake linkage. We always keep handy an oil can filled with engine oil, and for lighter duty we keep a household-type, multipurpose oil.

Tires

One of the most important elements in tire care is to maintain the right pressure. As a bonus, you'll get better fuel mileage and safer handling. Your owner's manual will tell you which pressures are best for your tires. Keep in mind that this is a reference; some fine-tuning should be made to accommodate your load and your driving habits. The pressure should always be checked when the tires are cold. After about a mile of driving, pressures start increasing and you won't get an accurate reading.

Always check tire pressure when the tires are cold. Correct pressure is essential to tire wear and handling safety. (Gordon Groene)

For best wear, duals should always be within a pound of each other. An old truck driver's trick for checking duals is to "sound" them with a billy club. You'll soon learn to tell by the sound whether one tire's pressure is lower than that of its mate. This is the cleanest, most dependable way to check hot duals.

If the tread is wearing around the edges, you're underinflating. Tread worn in the middle (cupping) usually means that the wheels are out of balance or the shock absorbers are wearing out. Uneven wear on the front tires indicates misalignment. Because RV tires can be very expensive, you'll save greatly by watching for early wear and correcting it at once.

Even when you're not on the road, your RV's tires continue to take a licking from the sun. Try to keep them shaded; if the RV doesn't have covers or awnings for this purpose, have some made. A good spray-on coating, such as Star brite's Protector, which has ultraviolet absorbers, will help shield tires.

Brakes

Unless you have a complete set of tools and equipment for brake work, it's best to leave overhauls to a specialist. You can check the hydraulic-fluid reservoirs regularly and change the fluid as recommended by the vehicle manufacturer, inspect brake hoses for signs of deterioration and cuts, and keep tabs on the thickness of brake linings.

If your brakes are not self-adjusting, adjustment is covered in your owner's manual. Any time brake drums are removed, be sure to clean all dust and rust out of them to ensure smoother operation. If you have an older vehicle, this debris may be asbestos, so don't breathe or handle it. Always make sure that no oily substances get near brake linings.

A Few Cautionary Words

"I'm 63, about to retire, and a woman alone," wrote one of our readers. "Fulltiming has been my dream, and I'm about to take off, but I've heard a lot of horror stories about mechanics cheating and overcharging women. Do you have any advice?"

This dilemma applies to all of us—we can all be "taken for a ride." No matter your area of expertise, we all have blind spots. The one defense we all have against scams and con artists is to know as much as possible about our RVs, how they work, what harms them, and what sort of service they need when. It's a tall order, to be taken seriously, not something to be put off until you run out of other things to do.

First, we'll make a Pollyanna observation. We find most of our fellow citizens to be honest, fair, and hardworking. Sure, there are service station attendants who sell you oil you don't need or who will slash a tire so you'll have to buy a new one. There are also those who give a break to the elderly, the stranded, and the handicapped. Moreover, the customer is not always right. Sometimes he or she is demanding, cheap, or unwilling to admit that the breakdown was his or her own fault. The customer may be late for workshop appointments or think that he knows more than the mechanic does.

Assuming that you're an honest and considerate customer, here are some defense strategies.

■   Begin by studying all the manuals that came with the RV, even if you don't understand half of what is being said. Even if you're sure you already know how to put a tape in the stereo, adjust the furnace, light the oven, or check the oil, read these books until you know them forward and backward. Most of the time you can solve a problem just by going through the troubleshooting guide.

■   Talk to others in campgrounds, especially to people who have RVs like yours, but don't take one person's advice as gospel. The less you know about RVs, and the more intimidated you are by technobabble, the more advice you'll get from "experts."

■   Try to get a consensus from people who have similar vehicles, loads, mileage, and driving habits about such things as whether you really need new shock absorbers after 45,000 miles, or how long brake pads should last in your unit, or how your tire wear compares. Keep notes, and soon you'll have a good feel for how long things should last and how they feel or sound or look when they're nearing the end.

■   Among those components you can *see* nearing boot hill are fan belts, hoses, tires, shock absorbers (you can tell when they start leaking oil), and oil seals. Those you might *hear* as they start to fail include fan belts, tires, universal joints, wheel bearings, windshield wiper motors, and the exhaust system. Your *nose* is a good tool in sensing leakage in fuel, oils, or sewage; transmission overheat; electrical problems; or dragging brakes.

■   Fill your gas tanks yourself. Check and fill your own tires, oil, cooling system, batteries, drinking water, and automatic transmission oil. In doing them yourself you save money, make sure they're done right (even an honest mechanic could do the wrong thing for your particular RV), and avoid a chance of being cheated. Even if you're not filling propane tanks yourself, you can observe that the meter and scale are set properly.

■   No outsider can know as much as you do about your driving habits, your maintenance history, and your needs. Armed with common sense, regular reviews of your RV's manuals, and an ever-increasing knowledge that builds like a snowball, you will be a better mechanic than you ever dreamed possible.

In short, learn to look, listen, and sniff for abnormalities. The best mechanic in the world can't have the ear for your engine that you'll have. By keeping attuned to the everyday look, sound, and feel of your own rig you'll become your own best diagnostician. Even if you don't know what's wrong or what to do about it, you'll at least know to have it investigated.

Mechanical troubles almost never recover by themselves, so any early warnings may indicate that you need preventive maintenance well in advance of a highway breakdown. This will allow you to shop around for the right price, time, and place to have work done. Keep careful records, and soon you'll see a pattern developing, alerting you to maintenance tasks every so many months or every so many miles.

For the want of a shoe a horse was lost. For the want of a horse the battle was lost. Your battle against highway breakdown, equipment failure, and accelerated wear begins with preventive maintenance, most of it simple to do, at your leisure, with minimal equipment.

If you have an equipment failure, such as a cracked wheel, assume the worst—that similar failures will happen again after you've gone the same number of miles. (Gordon Groene)

Your Maintenance Log

New RVs usually come with a maintenance log. Or you can choose your own format; we use a small looseleaf notebook. Fill it in as you go, not just for your own records, but to validate any warranty claims. (If you're lucky in buying a used RV, it will come with a complete record of what maintenance and repairs were done, when, and by whom.)

Note which maintenance tasks have to be done when; refer to these guidelines so you can plan ahead for the next task:

According to mileage. This includes oil changes, tire rotation, grease jobs, and changing the fluid in the differential and transmission.

By the calendar. Battery maintenance, new radiator coolant, and brake fluid replacement are usually done every few months, regardless of mileage.

By the season. Items to list here might include changing air filters and air cleaners.

Once you've been keeping records for a while, you should be able to predict the mileage intervals between certain tasks. For example, if your tires needed replacing after X miles, you'll probably need to replace them after you've gone X miles again.

The Circle Check

Every time you start up, no matter whether you've spent a month at a campsite or two minutes in a roadside phone booth, take a walk all the way around the RV. This kind of routine is a religion with truckers and other professional drivers. Aside from helping you nip problems in the bud, it will give you peace of mind. You'll know for sure that you remembered to lock the bumper, that you didn't leave loose lashings that would allow a rooftop tarp to flap in the wind while everything else got drenched in the rain, that you did pick up the cooler from under the picnic table . . .

Here's what to look for:

- Inspect all tires to see if they've softened, been cut, or picked up nails.
- Check under the rig for leakage of fuel, oil, or water.
- Make sure you've shut all windows that should be closed when you're underway.
- Check every accessory door (don't forget the refrigerator!) to make sure it's securely fastened, and the fuel cap to make sure it's screwed on tight.
- Check the roof rack, tie-downs, bike racks, and hitches.
- At night, make sure all the lights are working. Occasionally have someone check the backup and brake lights for you.
- Mentally list everything you took out of the RV. Did you bring it all back aboard?
- Is the way clear ahead? behind? overhead? (You should know your rig's highest point in exact feet and inches.) Pay special attention to curb drop-off angles, choosing your route so your overhang won't scrape on the slope.
- As a last step before takeoff, you may want to record in a logbook such information as the name of the service station, the mile number of the rest stop, and the telephone number of the booth where you made a call. If you find later that you forgot something, or got cheated, or otherwise need to retrace your steps, this information may prove invaluable.

As you circle the RV, use the time not only to look for trouble spots but also to psych yourself up for the responsibility of taking the wheel and giving all your attention to the road. Some drivers use this time for meditation or a short prayer.

Now, confident that the way is clear, relax and enjoy the view.

TWENTY-THREE

Maintaining Your RV's Utility Systems

Here's a sobering thought: all the utilities you took for granted while living in a house are now yours to provide, fuel, maintain, and regulate. It's a tall order even for the most accomplished, longtime campers.

The owner's manuals that came with your RV should provide all the information you need for your systems. You can also order publications and how-to videos on maintaining your RV from RVIA, Box 2999, Reston, VA 22090; www.rvia.org.

Each of your utilities is supplied in two or more ways, which means that your maintenance duties are doubled, but so are your conveniences and backups. At a full-hookup campsite you get water through a hose and electricity through a heavy-duty extension cord. Waste water goes directly into your campsite's sewer outlet via a hose you supply. In fancier campgrounds you may also have telephone and cable TV hookups too. It sounds simple, and except for a few caveats, it is.

Away from the campground things get more complicated. Your electricity is supplied by generator, battery, and/or alternator. You have water in your own tanks, but you have to supply the water pressure and keep track of your reserves so that you don't run out in the middle of a soapy shower.

Waste water accumulates in two tanks, one for "black" water (sewage) and the other for "gray" water (sink and shower drains), which you'll have to empty eventually. And the propane you use at all times to run the stove now also cools the refrigerator.

163

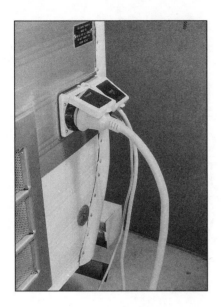

Umbilicals should be the best, heaviest, most waterproof and bugproof available. Shown here are electrical, telephone, and cable TV umbilicals. (Gordon Groene)

The Water System

When you're using campground umbilicals there are only a couple of things to worry about. First, the water may have an unpleasant taste, or you may be concerned about its safety. A light-duty filter can be added to sieve out particulated matter at the point of entry into the RV. You may also want to plumb in a heavy-duty filter at the kitchen sink.

The more serious filtration, treatment, or reverse-osmosis systems have their own faucet; you filter or treat only water to be used for drinking and cooking. Otherwise, you'll spend a fortune on replacement media.

Your second concern is "city" water pressure, which varies widely from campground to campground. If you hook into a system whose pressure is too high, your RV's plumbing can be damaged. Invest in a pressure regulator valve for the hose, and never hook up without it, not even when the pressure reading is in the safe range. We've seen pressure shoot up at the whim of a campground's water system.

On the road, when you are supplying your own water, your concerns include monitoring the water level so that you'll have adequate reserves, pump maintenance (read the manual; water pumps are fairly care free), and taking care of the water gauges. Most class A motorhomes have a control panel in the galley area that shows tank levels.

Some older RVs have no water pump but use an air pump to build air pressure in the water tank, forcing water to the faucets. If you have such a system, replace it. You can carry more water in less space and at less weight with a new, lightweight plastic tank and water pump. (An air pressure system can't be used with a thin-walled tank.)

One problem with many RV water pressure systems is that the pump runs on demand, even if you are drawing only a teaspoon of water for a recipe. The more jerks and starts, the more wear to the pump. To even things out, many systems are equipped with an accumulator tank, which maintains a reserve head of air. The larger the accumulator tank, the less often the pump has to run. If your water pump zzzzts off and on every few seconds, see an RV plumbing specialist who will know how and where

Most fulltimers use inline water filters for health reasons and to ensure uniform taste. (Camping World)

to plumb in an accumulator. And if you have a problem with pipes rattling when a washing machine or a dishwasher shuts off abruptly, the plumbing specialist can add what is called a water hammer eliminator.

Always turn off the water pump before leaving the RV. If you don't have a separate switch, use the circuit breaker. If the pump is on and a pipe or hose breaks, water will continue to pump until your tanks are empty or the battery is dead, flooding the RV.

Among the equipment we recommend are a white, drinking-water-quality hose that won't impart an unpleasant taste to the water; a Y fitting in case you have to share a water outlet with another camper; and quick-release fittings, described on page 166. You also will find it handy to add a simple, inexpensive water shutoff valve to the hose so you can have off-and-on water control in your hand rather than having to go back to the faucet when you're working with the hose.

Drain the hot-water tank regularly to get rid of accumulated scale and debris. (Gordon Groene)

Two types of hot-water systems are commonly used in RVs. One is a gas unit, a miniature version of a household gas water heater. The other is an all-electric system. Both systems sometimes incorporate a heat exchanger that captures engine heat. On the road, engine-heated water is stored in the hot-water tank. At rest, a gas flame or 110-volt heating element is used. Don't buy a cheap or jury-rigged system. The best ones are expensive, using the finest materials to eliminate any danger of getting antifreeze into your drinking water or drinking water into your coolant.

All hot-water tanks are equipped with a drain valve and should be flushed every few weeks. Even if you use a particle filter on your hose, some sand and scale gets through and settles. If you see any signs of soot on the tank or on the RV, the gas flame isn't adjusted properly. It could be running rich because the air shutter jiggled closed or bugs got into it. Clean and readjust it.

Waste Water

Your owner's manual tells you how to flush sewer tanks and hoses. It's a nasty job, but some steps can make it less onerous. First, add a shutoff valve and a quick-release fitting to your hose, as well as matching quick-release fittings where the hose connects to the RV and on an adjustable, trigger-type nozzle. You can now flick the hose off the RV, hook up a nozzle, and adjust the water spray and pressure for whatever cleanup tasks are at hand.

If your RV doesn't have a built-in flush system that allows you to blast water through pipes and into the black-water tank, add one or have an RV plumber do it for you. It's a fairly simple matter of tapping into a vent pipe from the outside of the RV and sticking the hose into an exterior fitting. Water flows through the pipes and tank

These are the parts you'll need to tee into the sewer line: adhesive for plastic pipe, a threaded adapter and screw cap for the outside of the RV, and an elbow and a 45–degree fitting to tap into the vent pipe. (Gordon Groene)

Locate a spot outside near the holding tank vent pipe. (Your additions won't show since the vent pipe is probably inside a closet or cabinet.) For the best flushing action, locate the fitting as high as possible on the side of the RV. Make a wood spacer block to fit between the inner and outer panels. Cut a hole to make a snug fit around the elbow and threaded adapter. Flare the outer skin of the RV into the wood block and seal it with silicone. (If the outer skin of your RV is fiberglass, seal it with epoxy.) (Gordon Groene)

and out the sewer hose, giving everything a thorough washdown.

Home centers and RV suppliers carry do-it-yourself plumbing fittings that allow even the most inexperienced plumbers to customize or expand plastic and copper plumbing, such as adding a holding tank flush, a water filter, a sink hose or an icemaker. Brand names include Genova's Uncopper, and Flair-It. Explain your needs to a knowledgeable salesperson who will be able to find all the fittings needed for plastic-to-plastic or plastic-to-metal additions.

An excellent guide to plumbing with the new plastics is *Do-It-Yourself Plumbing* by Richard Day (Genova). Although it's written for homeowners, the book explains the various types of plastic piping and how to join them and covers many plumbing basics that apply to the RV. A simpler, more basic help for the beginner is *The All-Thumbs*

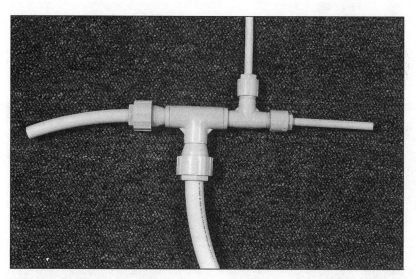

New plumbing fittings are designed for do-it-yourself installation on plastic or metal pipes. (Genova)

Guide to Home Plumbing by Robert Wood (TAB Books). Two others to try are *The Complete Guide to Home Plumbing* (Black & Decker) and *Cottage Water Systems* by Max Burns (Cottage Life Books).

It's important that the wrong things don't get into your tanks—grease, caustic chemicals that could damage your RV's system, and sewage treatment chemicals that could damage the campground's septic system. Grease could also gather on sensors inside tanks, resulting in false readings.

Biodegradable toilet papers are available, but we have never used them or any chemicals, and we've never had a problem with our straight-through flush system. Today's high-efficiency, low-water flush toilets have all the odor-free, clean-water-flush convenience of a home toilet.

Empty the tank immediately after parking, before solids have a chance to settle and compact. Periodically take a bumpy ride with nothing in the waste tanks but a few gallons of water and a cup of baking soda. Then hook up immediately and flush out the tanks.

Don't flush tampons, disposable diapers, baby wipes, waste paper, or facial tissues, not only because they could hurt the tank but because they probably won't get that far. Most RV toilets aren't designed to swallow things that swirl easily down a household john, such as flushable tampons, wipes, and tissues. When yours chokes up, repairs can be a nightmare.

When you have guests aboard who are not campers, make sure they know the rules. We posted a sign with the old sailor's saying, "Never put anything into the toilet that you haven't eaten first," and it gives everyone a smile as well as a lesson.

One more maintenance tip: if your RV manufacturer has supplied a steel storage

Gordon Groene

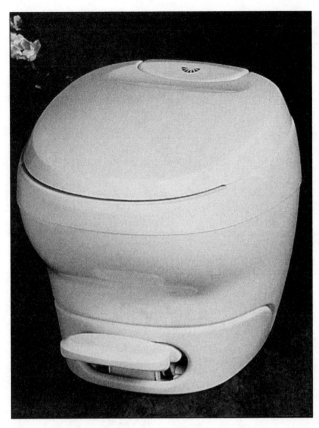

New toilets provide a pulsating flush, easy–to–replace blade and hub seals, and more clog–free action. (Camping World)

compartment for the sewer hose, replace it with a plastic one (a steel one will soon rust out from constant wetting). A length of 4- or 5-inch-diameter PVC pipe hung somewhere under the RV is ideal. We left ours open on both ends for the best air flow. The ends do need some sort of clip or pin closure, though, so the hose doesn't slip out.

The Propane System

Propane, which is efficient and easily available, provides you with cooking, baking, heat, hot water, refrigeration, and perhaps an outdoor barbecue—all without the noise and stink of a generator.

The gas pipes in your home might be neglected for years, but your house doesn't move. Because your RV bounces, twists, and vibrates, a lot more vigilance is needed. Always be on the lookout for loose or leaky fittings and chafed or damaged tubing. About twice a year, inspect the fittings by painting them with a soapy solution. If it bubbles, you can see the leak.

Don't allow rust to build up on your propane tanks. The more dampness and road slop they're exposed to, the quicker they'll corrode. When the tanks are empty, keep them tightly closed so that air and dampness can't get inside and start rust there. In case any air does get in, purge the tank with a little gas before recharging it. Make sure the tanks are well secured in the vehicle so that they can't shift and damage nearby pipes.

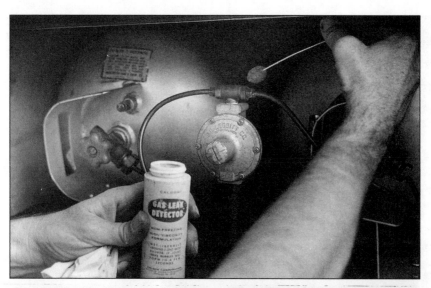

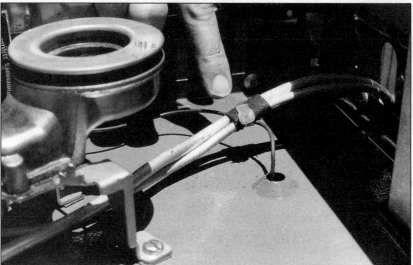

Propane connections can weaken and fail due to vibration and fatigue. Check for leaks periodically (top). Propane lines should be protected from vibration and abrasion (bottom). (Gordon Groene)

Propane use on an RV also requires some common sense. Don't drive with any propane flame or pilot light lit. In a fuel station, or if you come upon a highway accident in which fuel has spilled, it could cause an explosion. Don't leave the gas stove unattended on a windy day. If the flame blows out and gas continues to flow, an explosion could result.

If your RV didn't come equipped with a sniffer and an automatic solenoid shutoff, consider adding them.

Refrigeration

Most RV refrigerators are the absorption type, not the compressor type used in household refrigeration, so they require special treatment. For one thing, they're comparatively inefficient, able to keep foods at only 40–45° below ambient temperatures.

When starting the refrigerator, give it eight to twelve hours to cool down and stabilize. Don't overwhelm it with too many new room-temperature foods at once, and don't load it with leftovers until they've cooled off.

Hang a refrigerator thermometer right inside the door and glance at it each time you open the door. When temperatures rise above 40°, foods begin to spoil more rapidly. So keep a close eye on refrigerator temperatures, especially in hot weather.

Any RV supply house or catalog should have a small, battery-operated fan that will improve air circulation inside the unit. On hot days try to keep the RV shaded so that the sun doesn't shine on the area containing the refrigerator's works, and try to increase the air flow to the coils.

If you find that the refrigerator won't cool, especially after being in storage for a while, check first to see that the flame or heating element is working. If it is, and the unit still won't cool down, try driving on a bumpy road, which sometimes gets the circulation going. If that doesn't work, remove the refrigerator from the RV and turn it upside down for a day or two.

Another surprisingly common problem is that spiders love to nest in the chimneys of gas refrigerators. If the refrigerator doesn't cool, check the chimney for spiders, debris, or soot. If heat can't go up the chimney to heat the boiler, no cooling is achieved. Soot, by the way, shouldn't be a problem if the flame is adjusted properly.

Lights and Wiring

Most RVs are wired for both 12-volt and 110/120-volt service. It's likely that some or all of your lights, entertainment electronics, and some other accessories, such as the furnace blower and the exhaust fan over the stove, will be 12-volt only.

Most refrigerators work on 12 or 110 volts. Some are three-way and work on gas and 12- and 110-volt service. Be very careful about shutting off the flame when fueling, or leaving the fridge on 12-volt service after the engine is shut down, which could drain the battery fairly quickly.

Because of the danger of running down the start battery accidentally, it's best to have two separate electrical systems, one to start the engine and a second to run the "house." The more you know about battery management, the more you can fine-tune the system. For example, we can gang up both systems, or use the "house" battery to start the engine in a pinch. This is a dangerous game to play, however, because if you confuse the switching arrangements, you may find yourself with two dead batteries instead of one. Again, your best guide is your RV manual.

Two recent aids to your electrical management are available. Heavy-duty AC alternators that work off your main engine can supply as much as 5 kilowatts underway. And a new inverter technology allows higher output from more compact, more efficient units.

If you have plenty of battery power in reserve and would like to be able to run a hair dryer, a vacuum cleaner, a heavy-duty drill, or a microwave oven by convert-

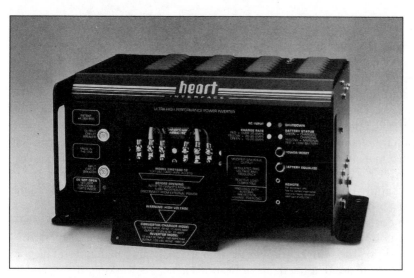

Sophisticated new inverter/battery charger units give you full-time energy management.
(Heart Interface)

ing 12-volt juice to 110/120-volt power, ask your RV supplier what's available in inverters.

Keep in mind the limitations of your batteries before putting a 20-pound turkey into the microwave oven. A 1,200-watt hair dryer draws about 12 amps when it's in the AC plug, but when it is running off an inverter it draws 100 amps from the battery. Even if your inverter is 100 percent efficient (which it isn't), and even if your battery delivers its full charge of 600 amps per hour from start to finish (which it won't), it will not be long before the battery is stone-cold dead.

Unless you're savvy about electricity, it's best to have repairs and troubleshooting done by a professional, especially when you're dealing with household current. You could electrocute yourself or set your RV up for a future fire. Working with 12-volt systems is somewhat simpler, but it's still important to play by the safety rules. Very good 12-volt how-to manuals, usually designed for use on boats or cars, are available, especially *RV Electrical Systems* by Bill and Jan Moeller (Ragged Mountain Press) and *The 12-Volt Bible for Boats* by Miner Brotherton (International Marine). Even the non-techie can find failures in the 12-volt system by using a multimeter. If you have a failure in a 12-volt fan, light, or television, start checking at the item itself, and keep working backward toward the battery until you find the problem—usually an open wire, a blown fuse, or a loose connection at the battery end. When a light fails, check the bulb first, then the socket, which could be corroded.

The Generator

Because generators come in so many types and sizes, for use with diesel, gasoline, or propane fuel, we'll concentrate here on some general guidelines. Again, the owner's manual that came with your generator is the best guide to its use and maintenance.

Just as your odometer is an essential log for engine and drive-train maintenance, the generator's hour meter will tell you when routine inspections and maintenance should be done. If it doesn't have one, keep a log manually.

First, know the unit's capacity and don't try to exceed it. The generator could be damaged; so could an expensive air conditioner or appliance. The safest procedure is to note the electrical draw listed on each of your appliances so that you'll always have an idea of what demands are being made on the generator.

Your generator is rated in watts; for example, a 4.5 kW (kilowatt) generator puts out 4,500 watts. Add up the wattage of all the 110-volt items that you might be using on generator power. You'll find the wattage given somewhere on each item. Don't forget the battery charger, the electric water heater, or anything else that kicks in automatically when the generator goes on.

If an item is rated only in amps, as many power tools are, figure wattage by multiplying amps by volts. For example, 3 amps × 110 volts = 330 watts. If the item is rated only in horsepower, figure about 750 watts per horsepower. If there are two ratings, one for starting load and one for running, list the higher one.

Generators let you camp without hookups. (Gordon Groene)

If you have motors that are rated only in horsepower, here are their approximate wattages:

HP	STARTING LOAD (Watts)	RUNNING LOAD (Watts)
¼	600	275
⅓	800	400
½	1200	500
¾	2100	500
1	2500	1200
2	3500	2200

If you have a marginally sized generator (which isn't a bad idea because you want to keep generator cost, weight, and fuel costs at a minimum), and don't have sufficient juice to run everything at once, you'll soon develop a sixth sense about generator juggling. For example, you'll turn off the air conditioner before using the heavy-duty drill; or you'll turn off the electric skillet before using the hair dryer.

Regardless of your generator's output, conservation is the key. *Every watt will cost you fuel dollars.* Don't assume that just because the generator is running anyway, all the juice is free.

Campground Electricity

Electrical hookup can mean many things. We've been at campgrounds where the wiring was so old and flimsy that there wasn't enough juice to run the battery charger. At others there wasn't enough power to handle the starting load of our medium-size air conditioner.

If you have a voltmeter and can see that incoming juice is not adequate, don't try to use any motorized equipment. At or below 90 volts, motors will overheat and eventually burn out. If you know the power demand of each electrical item you have aboard, as described above, and know what amperage the service is (usually 15 or 30 amps), you can stagger appliance use so that you don't damage anything.

You will need an adequately sized power cord. Try to keep it 25 feet long or less because the longer the cord, the more electrical potential is lost. If your service cord feels warm, it's too light for the duty. If plugs feel hot, it's time to clean and brighten the contacts.

If your plug won't fit the campground's receptacle, ask at the office to borrow a pigtail adapter (a deposit is usually charged). If you find yourself constantly encountering the same receptacles, buy your own pigtail in that size.

You'll also need a polarity tester, which will show whether the polarity to the two power connectors is reversed and whether there is current to the safety ground, which would mean that the entire RV, including doorknobs and metal steps, could zap you with up to 110/120 volts. Always test before plugging in.

It's also a good idea to have a portable ground-fault interrupter or two. Say you're using a power tool outdoors in wet grass, and it's plugged into the receptacle on the side of the RV. If you have used a ground-fault interrupter, the current will cut off the instant any shorted current is sensed.

RVIA photo archives

Exterior

Your RV is a big financial investment, and because it's also your home, it's an emotional investment too. It deserves the best care you can give it.

No matter whether its skin is fiberglass, steel, or aluminum, your biggest enemy, second only to road damage, is the sun. Use the best polishes and protective coatings, which not only coat the finish but contain ultraviolet inhibitors that keep harmful rays from getting through to the paint.

Underneath the RV, rust is the chief destroyer. If you drive salted roads in winter or drive along beach roads where you're throwing up salty sand and the wind is filled with ocean spume, wash off the salt as soon as possible. Salt is a quick, formidable destroyer.

Some RVs require annual recoating of roof seams. Your owner's manual will tell you where, why, and what to use. Since so many RVs are "stick" built, with a metal skin over a wood framework, leaks in the roof or skin should be dealt with immediately. Wood rot starts easily, spreads fast, and consumes rapidly.

We've seen RVs with frames so completely rotted away that nothing was left but a thin shell. Kitchen cupboards fell down, and when a few screws were removed, the entire back end fell off the RV. Just the merest whiff of dry rot should send you off in search of the source of the leak. In the case of the RV mentioned above, cabinets had been hung using screws through the roof. Leakage around these screws wept through the entire structure. We once had a leak around a roof seam that led to a strip of dry rot under the carpeting.

Dry rot has no easy cure. First, the leak(s) must be found and eliminated. Second, the wood has to be exposed and dried. Softened wood must be dug out and replaced with sound new wood. Third, a constant check should be kept on seals and bedding compound at every joint, rivet, screw, or other point where water could enter. Such seals can crack, dry out, or shrink. Again, it pays to buy the best, most ultraviolet-resistant sealants for exterior use.

Heat and Air

Heating and air-conditioning systems differ, so once again, the owner's manual for each unit is the most reliable guide. Among universal rules: Change filters often; restricting air flow reduces efficiency. Check over the furnace at the start of each cold season. Clean the grills, touch up rust with high-temperature paint, check the pilot light or ignition and main-burner flame, and clean the fan blades.

If manufacturer instructions call for oiling the fan motor, do it now. (Some motors are sealed and don't normally require additional oil.) An RV is a small area that can fill rapidly with carbon monoxide when things go wrong. A wise addition to any RV is a good electronic carbon monoxide detector.

Inspect wiring bundles to make sure they haven't been damaged by chafe, working, or contact with stowed items. Look over the ductwork for signs of leaks, twisting, or dents. If it runs through storage areas, the ductwork may have taken some knocks.

Check exhaust and intake ports for restrictions (mud dauber nests, for example). And if you ever camp in snow, make sure these ports are kept free of blockage.

Twenty-Four

Safety and Security

You can drive away from a tiresome job, loud neighbors, and city pollution, but there is no escape from crime, highway hazards, and everyday household dangers.

Buckle Up

Seat belts are still the most important defense against being killed or injured on the highway. Even if you have air bags, they must be used in concert with the time-tested seat belt. If you don't believe buckling up is important, here are a few things to consider.

■ Your fears of being burned alive are not justified. Fire occurs in only one crash in ten. If your vehicle does burn, you are more likely to be able to extricate yourself and your loved ones if you were protected by a seat belt from being knocked out in the crash.

■ The same goes for drowning in a vehicle that drops off a bank or a bridge. In Holland, a land laced with canals, special courses in driver safety emphasize the importance of wearing a seat belt. You're less likely to be injured on impact; more likely to be able to get yourself out of a submerged vehicle.

■ Many drivers think that they are protected by the steering wheel, but the worst injuries of all are sustained by the driver who is impaled on the steering column before being thrown against the windshield. As the captain of this land yacht, your primary duty is to stay at your station and in control of the vehicle until it comes to a stop. If

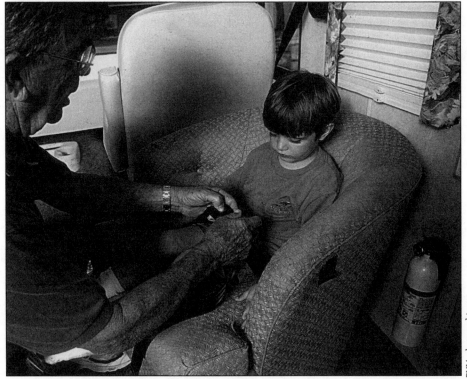

you're thrown out of the driver's seat by an impact, whatever control you might have exercised has been snatched from you. The driver needs a seat belt as much as anyone.

■   Seat belts are required by law in many states, and those laws are getting stiffer. States that formerly required seat belts but did not cite violators unless they were stopped for some other reason are now writing tickets for seat belt noncompliance as a primary offense.

■   Baby on board? According to Evenflo, a baby products manufacturer, four out of five child safety seats are installed improperly. For information on child passenger safety contact the Evenflo Parent Link Consumer Resource Center at 800-233-5921, www.evenflo.com. Ask for the free booklet *Safe Passage*. To find out how to properly install a safety seat and whether your seat has been recalled, contact the U.S. Government Auto Safety Hotline at 800-424-9393, www.nhtsa.dot.gov.

Do you still feel that seat belts are wimpy? Pilots, professional race car drivers, and thousands of highway crash survivors do not agree.

Firearms

Should you carry a gun aboard to ensure personal safety? It's a very personal decision. The major difference between keeping a gun in your home and carrying one in your RV is that your RV usually comes under laws covering vehicles, not residences. Even in states where it's legal to have a gun in your house you can be arrested for having one in your rolling home even if you are merely passing through and have no intention of making so much as a fuel stop.

In transit, guns must be unloaded and locked away somewhere other than the glove compartment or any place where they could be reached by the driver. National parks generally prohibit firearms, while national forests usually adhere to state law, as of course do state parks. Be sure to check the law before you enter a new state.

If you cross into Canada, you'll need a permit to bring in a sport gun. Call the Canadian Firearms Center at 800-731-4000 for a recorded message; forms can be found at www.cfc.gc.ca.

It's very difficult to bring any firearm into Mexico, where possession of a gun or even ammunition is illegal; the penalty is jail. Call 202-736-4000 for more information.

For more information on gun laws that apply to you as you travel, go to www.nraila.org and click on Firearm Laws. Or write the National Rifle Association Publications Division, 11250 Waples Mill Road, Fairfax, VA 22030.

Other Personal Safety Tips

■   Paint a huge number or symbol on the roof of your RV. It will help rescuers find you if you radio for help in an emergency, and it will help officials find the RV if it's stolen.

■   Guard against being hit at the roadside when you're stopped for a tire change or other breakdown. Get everyone out of the RV and to a safe spot well off the road. You might make an occasional announcement on the CB alerting drivers that there is a stopped vehicle at mile marker such and such.

■   Set flares, or better still, xenon strobe lights. Such strobes are available through dive shops, marine stores, and emergency-supply houses. Firefighters use them for marking a route through smoke-filled buildings; scuba divers use the waterproof versions in cave and wreck diving.

■   As folksy and friendly as it seems to be, it's not wise to hang a sign on your RV announcing your name. A stranger who wants to catch you unawares in the wee hours can pound on your door, calling your name. Assuming it's a campground neighbor, or the manager bringing you an emergency message, you open the door and . . .

Theftproofing

There are three primary ways to theftproof your RV: vigilance, locks, and electronic security devices.

Often the simplest steps are the most effective, such as simply closing the curtains securely when you're not aboard. If you don't, a thief can easily see your TV, cameras, radios, purse, and other valuables, size up the situation, smash a window, grab something, and run.

We installed extra light switches over the bed so that we can maintain darkness inside and yet turn on bright outdoor lights around the RV if we hear anything suspicious outside. You might also want to be able to use a bullhorn, a siren/strobe, or a CB radio from your bed.

When you leave the RV, close and lock all doors and windows. For ventilation, open only overheads. If your RV has no locks on its service doors, buy and install them (except on propane doors, which should not be locked). If your original service door locks were the cheap, flimsy type that soon corrode away, get new, rustproof locks. Padlock the spare tire and add a locking fuel cap. Various types of tongue locks are available to secure travel trailers.

If you're ordering a new RV, ask what security features are provided as standard equipment or as optional extras. By planning such devices early in the construction of an RV, you can assure the best installation, the most efficient wiring, the most convenience and concealment, and the components most compatible with the RV and its systems.

So many alarm systems are available in the automotive, household, and marine market that it's just a matter of shopping for what best suits your needs. It all depends on how much money you want to

We mounted a remote–control, swiveling spotlight on the top of our cab. (Gordon Groene)

Top: *Protect fuel and water tanks with heavy–duty locks.* (Jerry Martin Company) **Right:** *Various locks are available to hinder trailer theft. This Safe–T–Hitch also prevents accidental unhitching underway.* (Flushette Manufacturing Company)

spend and how much electronic gamesman- ship you are willing to play. Specialists in RV security systems include Brink's Home Secu- rity, 845 S. Milliken, Suite A, Ontario, CA 91761, 909-390-7555; and Trekmate, Inc., Box 2010, Sparks, NV 89431, 888-941-3404 or 760-941-3444, www.trekmate.com.

Warning Devices

Sometimes the greatest dangers come from within. They include carbon monoxide, gasoline fumes, propane, overheat, and smoke. One or two smoke alarms are a must, but keep in mind that they can't "see" other dangerous fumes. For those, you'll need other detectors.

You might put a gasoline fumes detector and perhaps an automatic fire alarm in the engine compartment; a high-temperature alarm in the generator compartment; and another temperature alarm, set to a low temperature, to warn you if the refrig- erator or the freezer warms up above food-safe temperatures. We also have a small, battery-operated water alarm the size of a deck of cards. Placed on the bathroom floor, it buzzes if it gets damp, giving ample warning that water is leaking or the toi- let is flooding.

Fire Safety

Among fire safety suggestions we recommend are:

■   Know how your emergency exits work. Try them. If you need a wrench, gloves, or other aids to open a sticky, seldom-used escape hatch, keep them near the exit. Discuss alternate escape routes, including escape means if you're involved in an accident in which the RV lands on its roof or sides.

■   Test the smoke and carbon monoxide alarms regularly. Don't just rely on a signal light to tell you it's operating or a buzzer to tell you that a battery is getting weak.

■   Check fire extinguishers regularly. If they are dry powder, drive with them on their side occasionally to dislodge and loosen the powder. Otherwise, it can pack down from road motion and you may not get a full charge. If the gauge reads "low" or the extinguisher is out of date, have it recharged. The local fire department should be able to steer you to a fire-extinguisher service station.

■   Damp charcoal can ignite from spontaneous combustion. Carry charcoal in a sealed can.

■   Keep a box of baking soda handy for extinguishing minor flareups in the galley.

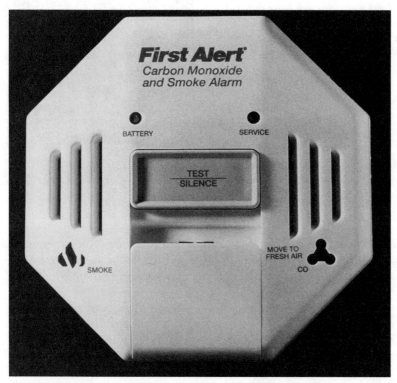

A combination smoke and carbon monoxide alarm provides extra protection.
(Jerry Martin Company)

■   With your family, have a "scramble" drill so you'll all know how to get your-selves and your RV to safety in case of a forest fire or a fire in a neighboring RV.

■   Don't leave an open flame unattended. Keep combustibles well away from the stove, grill, or campfire.

■   Fix fuel leaks immediately. Propane is explosive, and it settles in heavy, in-visible pools where you least expect them. Gasoline evaporates quickly, but its fumes too sink into lethal, unseen puddles. Diesel is less explosive, but it soaks into every-thing and lingers there, posing a fire hazard for a long time. Any leak is dangerous.

■   Keep battery terminals and fuse blocks clean. Corrosion creates heat creates fire.

■   A dragging brake can start a fire in brake fluid. A dual tire that goes flat and remains unnoticed as it drags on for miles can catch fire. A stuck V-belt can ignite. A fire can also start under the chassis if you drive through high, dry weeds with a hot cat-alytic converter.

TWENTY-FIVE

The End of
the Road

Every story has an end, so even if you're just beginning your full-time journey, it's not too soon to give some thought to the rest of the tale. For some fulltimers the roaming life ends suddenly and dramatically with death, divorce, illness, or a family crisis. For others, the RV life just grinds to a stop; they find that all the magic and motion has gone out of fulltiming. As long as you and your travel partner(s) keep communicating and caring about each other, the transition out of fulltiming can be just as exciting as the move into your RV.

One of the best things about fulltiming is that it can give you a lingering look at every part of the country. Instead of making a hurried choice of a place to settle down, you can reside temporarily in one community after another. Join a church and clubs, make friends, perhaps find a job, look over the different neighborhoods in town, and get a sense of local politics. As long as you're living in your RV, you're free to move on the minute you don't like the setup.

We spent one summer in a state that we thought would be our eventual home. For months we made the rounds with real estate agents, looking at property. We loved the community for its symphony and good libraries, nice folks, and good shopping. The climate was perfect in summer, with warm days and cool nights. But gradually disenchantment began to set in. With fall came north winds bearing the odor of a pulp mill on the other side of the next mountain. The weather turned colder, and we began to feel stiffness in joints we'd forgotten we had. Our statement from a local bank reflected a debit for a state tax we didn't know existed. Then a local widow told us how she was struggling to pay her taxes. She'd owned her home jointly with her husband, and when he died, she had to pay inheritance taxes on half of her own home. We ruled out that state as a future home.

Another time we found a beautiful piece of acreage in the pine woods of north-central Florida. With the owner's permission, we parked our RV on it for a few nights while we looked it over. One night, when the wind shifted, we realized the land was just downwind of a landfill. Camping on another piece of land we were close to buying, we realized it was on a seven-year floodplain. What was now a lovely trout stream could become a raging torrent in a wet spring. We left another state when we learned that the high sales tax also applied to food. In some areas, we discovered that local well water was so bad that we'd always have to buy our drinking water. And in one locale, to our complete amazement, there were lots for sale that had no water at all. There was no rain, no river, no well water. Every drop would have to be trucked in.

No state or climate is perfect, but when you're fulltiming, you can experience all climates, all seasons, and many different communities before settling down. You can live temporarily among the people who may be your permanent neighbors, read local papers, sit in on local council meetings, and learn about local and state taxes and license fees. And while you're investigating all this, you'll be living comfortably in your own rolling home, ready to move along whenever you like.

When we first went fulltiming, it was a step taken over many months, with lots of thought and planning. When you decide to leave fulltiming to buy a house, enter a retirement community, resume a career, or adopt any other new lifestyle, that transition too should be taken slowly and carefully. If you wait until you're too fed up, too broke, too cold, too hot, or on the verge of divorce, it's too late to act with restraint, prudence, and economy.

It was with a sense of adventure and joy that we eased out of fulltiming, first by buying acreage and returning to it once or twice a year to camp under our trees, listen to our land, and meet our neighbors. After a few years we knew it was right, so we built a small house. Later, we added another house and more acreage. We continue to slip away, still in the same RV, knowing that we now have the courage and know-how to become fulltimers again any time we choose.

To break away was tough. To stay away was sometimes even tougher. What we gained, though, was ten years of travel that nobody can ever take away from us, no matter what the future holds. As the saying goes, just do it.

Appendix 1

Useful Addresses

American Association of Retired Persons. AARP, a nonprofit organization open to people aged 50 and older, offers group health insurance, a discount pharmacy, and other benefits. For information write AARP Membership Processing Center, 3200 E. Carson Street, Lakewood, CA 90712; www.aarp.org.

Catalogs. For free, helpful catalogs write **Camping World**, Box 90018, Bowling Green, KY 42102, www.campingworld.com; **Cabela's**, 812 13th Avenue, Sidney, NE 69160, www.cabelas.com; **L.L. Bean**, Freeport, ME 04033, www.llbean.com. Also pick up some **Sears** specialty catalogs for camping, boating, health and handicap, big and tall sizes, RV furnishings and accessories, and other hard-to-find items. They are available free at any Sears store and www.sears.com. **Penney's** seasonal catalogs cost $5 (some specialty catalogs are free) and are available in their stores and at catalog centers and www.jcpenney.com.

Closet heaters. Golden Rod closet heaters are electrically heated bars that install easily, emit a constant glow of heat, and reduce or eliminate mildew in closets and other small, enclosed areas. Contact Buenger Enterprises, 3600 South Harbor Boulevard, Oxnard, CA 93035; 800-451-6797, 805-985-0541; www.goldenroddehumidifiers.com.

Customs service. Make sure you don't run afoul of the law when returning from another country. The pre-Columbian antique you bought in Mexico or the whalebone artifact from Canada may be confiscated at the border. Travel with pets, firearms, large amounts of cash, cigarettes and alcohol, plants, and certain souvenirs can be complicated if not illegal. Request the booklet *Know Before You Go* from the U.S. Customs Service, Department of the Treasury, 1301 Constitution Avenue N.W., Washington, DC 20229; www.customs.ustreas.gov.

Disabilities. For books on all aspects of travel with any type of physical limitation, contact The Disability Bookshop, Box 129, Vancouver, WA 98666; 360-694-2462; www.disabilitybookshop.virtualave.net.

Driver rehabilitation. If you have to learn to drive with a physical impairment, contact Memorial Hospital Driver Education Center, 615 N. Michigan Street, South Bend, IN 46601; www.qualityoflife.org.

Emergencies. Travel-es is a new program from the RV America Association (see also that entry) that is available through RV dealers. It offers pretrip help (currency exchange, weather forecasting, etc.), on-the-road assistance (like that from auto clubs), plus medical evacuation (if needed, they'll provide a driver for your RV and transportation for your family or a pet), 24-hour medical service via its Nurse Help Line, emergency message relay, and more. Contact your RV dealer or go to www.irvamerica.com/traveles/index.cfm.

Escapees. This organization of fulltimers operates campgrounds, one of the most comprehensive mail forwarding services, and defends fulltimers' rights. Contact them at 100 Rainbow Drive, Livingston, TX 77351; 888-757-2582; www.escapees. com.

International RVing. We have rented RVs in Europe, New Zealand, and Australia. For rental sources, contact major international rental car companies, such as Auto Europe, 800-223-5555, www.autoeurope.com. An excellent book on car camping in Europe is *Camping Europe*, second edition, by Carol Mickelsen (Carousel Press).

Mattresses. Mattresses made to custom specifications feature innerspring construction and come in any shape and size you need. They fold for easy installation and can be made with a hinge for easy access to under-bed storage. Handcraft Mattress Company, 531 E. Goetz, Santa Ana, CA 92707; 714-241-7751; mkboatbeds@aol.com; www.boatbeds.com.

Plumbing products. Incinolet toilets, which require no plumbing because all waste is burned, can be researched at www.incinolet.com. Call 800-527-5551 for a free brochure. Tankless water heaters are available from 800-211-6888, www.manglesandmarbles.com; or AquaStar, 800-642-3199, www.ControlledEnergy.com.

RV America Association (RVAA). RVAA is a growing Internet-based advocacy group and social network of RV owners. Its Web sites include www.rvamerica.com and www.rvamericacoalition.org. To chat with other RVers, try www.rvforums.com, www.fulltimerving.com, and www.womensrvforum.com. You can also contact them at 408 E. Southern Avenue, Tempe, AZ 85282, 480-784-4771. See also the Emergencies entry.

Recreational Vehicle Industry Association (RVIA). For information on RV rental sources, RV camping clubs, industry standards, RV publications, and much more, contact RVIA at Box 2999, 1896 Preston White Drive, Reston, VA 22090-0999; 800-336-0154, 703-620-6003; www.rvia.org.

RV Web sites. If you've never owned a RV before, try www.firstrv.com. To shop for a RV or RV accessories, go to www.rv-classifiedads.com. You can find rentals at www.rv-rentals.net and dealers at www.rv-dealers.com.

RV publications. For a list of books and pamphlets on RVs contact RVIA, Box 2999, Reston, VA 22090; www.rvia.org.

Refrigerator replacement parts. Midwest Products repairs RV cooling units and supplies spare parts. Contact them at 2280 Avenue of Industries, Corning, IA 50841, 800-331-7698, www.mwpcool.com.

Road conditions. The following states will supply highway reports, some of them year-round and others just in winter. Conditions are: R1, snow tread allowed or chains required; R2, four-wheel drive allowed, others require chains; R3, chains required on all vehicles. Note that some numbers answer only during business hours. (Information is also available on the Internet, but not all states have easily accessible, up-to-date highway information. Try a search on "highway + conditions + [state name]". An excellent source for information on road construction is www.randmcnally.com.)

Alabama, 334-242-4378
Arizona, 602-651-2400, ext. 7623; construction information, 602-255-6588
Arkansas, 501-569-2374
California, 916-445-7623 or 445-1534
Colorado, 303-639-1111

Connecticut, 860-865-2650

Florida, 800-475-0044

Georgia, 404-635-6800

Idaho, 208-336-6600

Illinois, 312-368-4636; winter conditions, 217-782-5730; construction, 800-452-4368

Indiana, 317-232-8298; construction, 317-232-5533

Iowa, 515-281-5824

Kansas, 785-291-3000 or 800-585-7623

Kentucky, 800-0459-7623

Louisiana, 225-379-1541

Maine, 207-287-3427

Maryland, 800-327-3125

Massachusetts, 617-374-1234

Michigan, 800-337-1334

Minnesota, 800-542-0220

Mississippi, 601-987-1212

Missouri, 800-222-6400

Montana, 406-444-6339 or 800-332-6171

Nebraska, 402-479-4545; winter, 402-471-4533

Nevada, 702-486-3116 (south), 775-793-1313 (northwest), 775-738-8888 (northeast)

New Hampshire, 603-271-6900

New Jersey, 732-247-0900 (Turnpike), 732-727-5929 (Garden State Parkway)

New Mexico, 505-827-5154 or 800-432-4269

New York, 800-847-8929 (Thruway only)

North Carolina, 919-549-5100, ext. 7623

North Dakota, 701-328-7623; construction, 701-328-2565

Ohio, 888-876-7453 (Turnpike), 614-466-7170 (elsewhere)

Oklahoma, 405-425-2385

Oregon, 503-588-2941; winter, 800-977-6368

Pennsylvania, 800-331-3414 or 888-783-6783

Rhode Island, 401-222-2468

South Carolina, 803-896-9621

South Dakota, 605-367-5707

Tennessee, 800-858-6349

Texas, 800-452-9292

Utah, 801-964-6000

Vermont, 802-828-2648

Virginia, 800-367-7623

Washington, 800-695-ROAD (800-695-7623); construction, 360-705-7075; mountain passes in winter, 888-766-4636

West Virginia, 304-558-2889

Wisconsin, 800-762-3947

Wyoming, 888-996-7623 or 307-772-0824; construction, 307-777-4437

Social Security Administration. Call 800-SSA-1213 or go to www.ssa.gov.

Solar products. **RV Solar Electric**, 14415 N. 73rd Street, Scottsdale, AZ 85260, 800-999-8520, www.rvsolarelectric.com (full range of solar products as well as a book, *The RVer's Guide to Solar and Inverter Power*); **Atlantic Solar Products**, 9351-J Philadelphia Road, Baltimore, MD 21237, 410-686-2500, www.atlanticsolar.com; **Solar City**, 1 Moon Mountain Road, Quartzsite, AZ 85346, 800-255-7652; **RV Solar**, 45 S. Central Boulevard, Quartzsite, AZ 85346, 888-RV-SOLAR, www.rvsolar.com; **Go Solar**, 1446 Flanders Road, Riverhead, NY 11901, 631-777-2224, www.gosolar.com; **Northern Arizona Wind & Sun, Inc.**, 2725 E. Lakin Drive, #2, Flagstaff, AZ 86004, 800-383-0195 (for ordering), www.solar-electric.com; **Sun Amp Power Company**, 7850 E. Evans, Suite 104, Scottsdale, AZ 85260, 800-MR-SOLAR, www.sunamp.com; **RV Power Products**, 1058 Monterey Vista Way, Encinitas, CA 92024, 760-944-8882, www.rvpowerproducts.com; **SolarElectric.com**, an online catalog.

Superintendent of Documents. The U.S. Government Printing Office, Washington, DC 20402, www.gpo.gov, publishes a long list of advisory books and pamphlets on all phases of camping, consumerism, and lifestyle.

Tax forms. The most commonly used forms are available at post offices and libraries at tax time or at www.irs.gov/forms_pubs/index.html.

Appendix 2

What's Available in RVs

Dozens of manufacturers and hundreds of RV retailers compete for the dollars the fulltimer will spend on his or her dream house. Visit dealers in your hometown and step aboard as many models as possible in order to get a feel for construction, size, livability, and special features. Then write to the manufacturers listed here to find out what else is available.

RVIA provided the following contact information for manufacturers. Also included, where available, are the types and brands of RVs offered.

A & J Vans, Inc., 333 Washington St., Valders, WI 54245; 920-775-9333. Van conversions, conversion vehicles for disabled, pickup truck conversions, sport utility conversions.

Action RV Specialists dba Action Leisure Conversions, 6701 Jefferson N.E., Albuquerque, NM 87109; 505-294-1654. Travel trailers, horse trailer conversions. Action Leisure.

Advantage Enterprises, 104 Miller Dr., White Pigeon, MI 49099; 616-483-9659. Van conversions. Advantage, Rockwood Vans, Cobra.

Advantage West Corp., 1502 E. Buckeye Rd., Phoenix, AZ 85034-4109; 602-254-1364; www.advantagewest.com. Van conversions, pickup truck conversions, sport utility conversions.

Aero Manufacturing, Inc., 1018 W. Brooklyn St., Syracuse, IN 46567; 219-457-8787; www.aero-rv.com. Fifth-wheel travel trailers, travel trailers.

Airstream, Inc., 419 W. Pike St., Jackson Center, OH 45334-0629; 937-596-6111; www.airstream-rv.com. Class A motorhomes, van campers, travel trailers.

Alfa Leisure, Inc., 13501 5th St., Chino, CA 91710; 909-628-5574. Fifth-wheel travel trailers, specialty trailers. Alfa Gold, Gold, Ideal, See Ya.

Alfa Motorhomes, Inc., 1612 S. Cucamonga Ave., Ontario, CA 91761; 909-628-5574. Class A motorhomes.

American Vans, Inc., 226 E. Jones Chapel Rd., Danielsville, GA 30633; 706-795-3344; www.americanvansinc.com. Van conversions, pickup truck conversions.

Anaheim Industries, 2305 Bennington Rd., Houston, TX 77093-8999; 713-697-3160; www.anaheimconversions.com. Van conversions, pickup truck conversions, sport utility conversions.

Archer Coach Corp., 1730 Gateway Ct., Elkhart, IN 46514; 219-266-5222. Van conversions, pickup truck conversions, sport utility conversions.

Arnold Engineering, Inc. dba Mountaineer, RR#2, Box 2084/5200 W. 3000 S., Roosevelt, UT 84066; 435-823-5160. Fifth-wheel travel trailers, travel trailers. Mountaineer.

Bigfoot Industries Inc., 4114 Crozier Rd., RR#3, Comp. 44, Palisades, Armstrong, BC V0E 1B6 Canada; 250-546-2155; www.bigfootrv.com. Class C motorhomes, truck campers, travel trailers. Big Foot.

Blue Bird Wanderlodge, 1 Wanderlodge Way, Fort Valley, GA 31030; 478-825-2021. Class A motorhomes. Blue Bird Wanderlodge, Wanderlodge LX, Wanderlodge LXi.

Bonair Leisure Products Ltd., 2885 Smith Blvd., N. Thetford Mines, QC G6G 6P6 Canada; 418-335-5259; www.bonair-rv.com. Folding camping trailers, fifth-wheel travel trailers, truck campers, travel trailers. Bonair, Master Coach, Oxygen.

California Comfort Vans, Inc. dba El Kapitan Van Conversions, 15040 Goldenwest Circle, Westminster, CA 92683-5220; 714-896-8267; www.elkapitan.com. Van conversions.

Carriage, Inc., #5 Industrial Park, Millersburg, IN 46543; 219-642-3622; www.carriageinc.com. Fifth-wheel travel trailers, travel trailers. Cameo, Carri-Lite, Carriage, Carriage LS, Royals International, Carri-Go.

Centurion Vehicles, Inc./Advantage Enterprises, 69651 U.S. 131 S., White Pigeon, MI 49099; 616-483-9659; www.centurionvehicles.com. Van campers, van conversions, pickup truck conversions. Austin, Cimarron, Classic 150, Classic 350, Laredo, Laureate, Legion, Mirage, Monterey, Outland, Pacifica, Sedona Sport, Tribunal, Starcraft.

Chariot Vans Inc., 28829 Paul Dr., Elkhart, IN 46514; 219-264-7577. Van conversions, pickup truck conversions, sport utility conversions. Chariot Vans, Midway Coach, Roman Wheels, Timeless Vans, Unique Motor Coach.

Classic Manufacturing Ltd., 10026 Marquis Ave., N. Battleford, SK S9A 3W2 Canada; 306-445-5510. Folding camping trailers, truck campers. Explorer, Sundance.

Coach House, 3480 Technology Dr., Nokomis, FL 34275; 941-485-0984, 800-235-0984; www.coachhouserv.com. Van campers, class C motorhomes. Coach House, Platinum.

Coachmen Industries, Inc., 2831 Dexter Dr., Elkhart, IN 46515; 219-262-0123, 219-262-0123; www.coachmen.com. Folding camping trailers, fifth-wheel travel trailers, class A motorhomes, class C motorhomes, van campers, truck campers, travel trailers. Catalina, Catalina Imperial, Catalina Sport, Cheyenne, Clarion, Classic, Countess, Cross Country, Cruiseair, Cruisemaster, Crusader, Custom, Dearborn, Encounter, Epic, Executive, Fan, Flite, Freeport, Frolic, Jimmy, Kingston, Legend, Leprechaun, Marquee, Marquee LX, Mirada, Palm Beach, Phoenix, Pompano, Prestige, Prospera, Pursuit, Ranger, Regency, Revere, Roadmaster, Royal, Royal Coachmen, Saga, Santara, Savannah, Shasta, Signature, Spirit, Sport, Sportscoach, Sprite, Starflyte, Swinger, Travelmaster, Van Camper, Van Traveler, Viking, Vision.

Colorado Custom Center, Inc., 23445 County Rd. G, Cortez, CO 81321; 970-564-9435. Van conversions, pickup truck conversions, sport utility conversions.

Colorado Two J., Inc. dba K&J Trailer Sales, 815 N. Van Buren St., Shipshewana, IN 46565; 219-768-7707. Travel trailers, horse trailer conversions. Jamco, Kiefer Built.

Columbia Northwest, Inc., Main St. Kecksburg, Mammoth, PA 15664; 724-423-7440, 724-423-7440; www.aliner.com. Folding camping trailers. A-Lite, Aliner.

Companion Vans, Inc., 711 E. Jefferson St., Kosciusko, MS 39090; 662-289-7711; www.companionvans.com. Van conversions, pickup truck conversions, sport utility conversions, conversion vehicles for the disabled. Companion.

Conquest, 1701 Century Dr., Goshen, IN 46526; 219-533-3121. Fifth-wheel travel trailers, class C motorhomes, travel trailers.

Contract Manufacturer, Inc. dba CM Trailers, 300 Industrial Rd., Madill, OK 73446; 580-795-5536. Fifth-wheel travel trailers, horse trailer conversions.

Cook & Reeves Cars, Inc. dba Superior Van, 4443 Dixie Hwy., Louisville, KY 40216; 502-447-8255; www.superiorvan.com. Van conversions. Superior Van.

Country Coach, subsidiary of National RV Holdings, 135 E. First St., Junction City, OR 97448; 541-998-3720, 800-547-8015; www.countrycoach.com. Class A motorhomes. Affinity, Allure, Concept, Country Coach, Country Coach Conversion, Intrigue, Magna.

Crossroads RV Inc., 1115 W. Lake St., Topeka, IN 46571; 219-593-3850; www.crossroadsrv.com. Fifth-wheel travel trailers, travel trailers. Crossroads RV.

Custom Campers, Inc., P.O. Box 965, Chanute, KS 66720; 316-431-3990. Fifth-wheel travel trailers. Hitchhiker II.

Custom Interiors & Designs Inc., P.O. Box 526, Caddo, OK 74729; 580-367-2603, 580-367-2603; www.redriverok.com/custominteriors. Travel trailers, horse trailer conversions.

Custom Vans of Houston Inc., 50 W. Canino, Houston, TX 77037; 281-448-8183. Van conversions, pickup truck conversions, sport utility conversions.

Customizers Inc., 14133 Pennsylvania Ave., Hagerstown, MD 21742; 301-797-7727. Van conversions, pickup truck conversions, sport utility conversions.

D'Elegant, Inc., 11847 Shaver Rd., S. Schoolcraft, MI 49087; 616-679-2813; www.delegant.com. Van conversions, pickup truck conversions, sport utility conversions. D'Elegant.

D. M. Conversions Ltd., 12651 W. Silver Spring Dr., Butler, WI 53007; 262-781-1170. Van campers, van conversions, pickup truck conversions.

D. M. Conversions of Florida, 2033 Belcher Rd. S., Largo, FL 33771; 813-530-3691. Van conversions.

Damon Corp., 2958 Gateway Dr., Elkhart, IN 46515; 219-262-2624, 800-577-5692; www.damonrv.com. Class A motorhomes. Challenger, Day Break, Escaper, Intruder, Ultrasport.

Debut Automotive Design, Inc., 8175 Gratiot Rd., Saginaw, MI, 48609; 517-781-0901; www.debutautomotive.com. Van conversions, pickup truck conversions.

Double B Trailers, LLC, 1124 S. MacArthur, Oklahoma City, OK 73128; 405-917-1800. Fifth-wheel travel trailers, horse trailer conversions. Elite.

Dream Catcher Interiors dba Cherokee Trailers, 11301 S. I-44 Service Rd., Oklahoma City, OK 73189; 405-691-8222. Fifth-wheel travel trailers, horse trailer conversions. Dream Catcher.

Duster Camper II, 2050 Bluebonnet Pkwy., McGregor, TX 76657-1333; 254-840-3770. Fifth-wheel travel trailers, horse trailer conversions.

Dutchmen Manufacturing, Inc., 58971 E. County Line Rd., Middlebury, IN 46540; 219-534-1224; www.dutchmen-rv.com. Fifth-wheel travel trailers, travel trailers. Dutchmen–Classic.

Dynamax Corp., 2745 Northland Dr., Elkhart, IN 46515; 219-262-3474; www.dynamaxcorp.com. Class A motorhomes, class C motorhomes. Carri-Go, Starflyte, Isata Sport Sedan, Isata Touring Sedan, Grand Sport.

Elk Automotive Inc., 3012 Mobile Dr., Elkhart, IN 46514; 219-264-0768. Van conversions.

Euro-Liner, LLC, 4251 Pine Creek Rd., Elkhart, IN 46516; 219-296-1550. Class A motorhomes.

Exiss Aluminum Trailers, 900 Exiss Blvd., El Reno, OK 73036; 405-262-6471. Fifth-wheel travel trailers, horse trailer conversions. Exiss.

Explorer Van Co., U.S. 30 W. & Fox Farm Rd., Warsaw, IN 46580; 219-267-7666. Van conversions.

Fleetwood Enterprises, Inc., 3125 Myers St., Riverside, CA 92503; 909-351-3500, 800-444-4905; www.fleetwoodrv-info.com. Folding camping trailers, fifth-wheel travel trailers, class A motorhomes, class C motorhomes, truck campers, travel trailers. American Dream, American Eagle, American Tradition, Angler, Avion, Bounder, Caribou, Discovery, Elkhorn, Flair, Jamboree, Oak Park, Pace Arrow, Prowler, Southwind, Terry, Tioga, Wilderness.

Fleetwood Folding Trailers, Inc., 258 Beacon St., Somerset, PA 15501; 814-445-9661, 814-445-9661; www.foldingtrailers.com. Folding camping trailers. Chesapeake, Coleman, Colorado, Columbia, Jamestown, Laramie, Newport, Redwood, Savannah, Sequoia, Shenandoah, Sun Valley, Tara, Williamsburg.

Fontaine Modification Co., 11400 Westport Rd., Louisville, KY 40241; 502-426-5450, 800-366-8246. Pickup truck conversions.

Forest River, Inc., 3010 College Ave., Goshen, IN 46528; 219-533-5934; www.forestriver inc.com. Fifth-wheel travel trailers, class A motorhomes, class C motorhomes, travel trailers, specialty trailers. All American–Sport, Cardinal, Cedar Creek, Cherokee, Flagstaff, Georgetown, Odyssey, Real-Lite, Reflection, Rockwood, Roo, Salem, Sandpiper, Sentinel, Shamrock, Sierra, Spinnaker, Summit Ridge, Sunseeker, Veri-Lite, Wildcat, Wildwood, Windsong.

Foretravel, Inc., 1221 N.W. Stallings Dr., Nacogdoches, TX 75964; 936-564-8367; www.foretravel.com. Equipped for disabled, class A motorhomes. Grand Villa, Travco, Unicoach.

Four Winds International Corp., 701 County Rd. 15, Elkhart, IN 46515-1486; 219-266-1111; www.fourwinds-rv.com. Class A motorhomes, class C motorhomes, travel trailers. Four Winds.

Frank Industries, Inc. dba Xplorer Motor Homes Division, 3950 Burnsline Rd., Brown City, MI 48416; 810-346-2771, 800-343-2771; www.xplorermotorhome.com. Van campers, class C motorhomes. Roamer, Xplorer.

Franklin Coach Co., Inc., 160 S. Oakland Ave., Nappanee, IN 46550; 219-773-4106. Fifth-wheel travel trailers, travel trailers. Franklin.

General Coach, 9th St. E., Oliver, BC V0H 1T0 Canada; 250-498-3471; www.gc-oliver.com. Fifth-wheel travel trailers, class C motorhomes.

General Coach, 73 Mill St., Hensall, ON N0M 1X0 Canada; 519-262-2600; www.gc-hensall.com. Fifth-wheel travel trailers, travel trailers.

Geneva SVS, Inc., 1070 Carey St., Lake Geneva, WI 53147; 262-248-0244, 800-248-0244; www.genevasvs.com. Van conversions, conversion vehicles for disabled. Delavan, Fontana, Geneva.

Georgie Boy Manufacturing, Inc., 69950 M62, Edwardsburg, MI 49112; 616-663-3415, 616-663-3415; www.georgieboy.com. Class A motorhomes, class C motorhomes.

Gerstner Manufacturing, Inc. dba Zephyr Van Conversions, 1950 Jimmy Daniel Rd., Bogart, GA 30622; 706-354-8067. Van conversions, conversion vehicles for disabled, pickup truck conversions.

Glendale RV, 145 Queen St., Strathroy, ON N7G 3J6 Canada; 519-245-1600, 519-245-1600; www.glendalerv.com. Fifth-wheel travel trailers, class C motorhomes, travel trailers. Glendette, Golden Falcon.

Gore's Trailer Manufacturing Inc., 305 Gore Trailer Rd., Whiteville, NC 28472; 910-642-4298, 800-334-3488; www.goretrailers.com. Travel trailers, horse trailer conversions.

Grand Touring RV Manufacturers Inc. dba GTRV-USA, #3 12320 Trites Rd., Richmond, BC V7E 3R7 Canada; 800-515-7007. Van campers.

Granite Bay, Inc., 1535 N. Mountain Springs Pkwy., Springville, UT 84663; 801-489-7214. Class A motorhomes. Granite Bay, Destiny, Serenity.

Great West Van Conversions Inc., 329 Parkdale Rd., St. Andrews, MB R1A 3N9 Canada; 204-338-9303, 888-498-8267; www.greatwestvans.com. Van campers. Classic Sport, Classic Royale, Classic Supreme.

Gulf Stream Coach, Inc., 503 S. Oakland Ave., Nappanee, IN 46550; 219-773-7761, 800-289-8787; www.gulfstreamcoach.com. Fifth-wheel travel trailers, class A motorhomes, class C motorhomes, travel trailers. Ameri-Lite, Conquest, Friendship, Gulf Stream, Innsbruck, Palm Breeze, Scenic Cruiser, Sea Hawk, Sun Sport, Sun Voyager, Tour Master.

Hi Lo Trailer Co., 145 Elm St., Butler, OH 44822; 419-883-3000, 800-321-6402; www.hilotrailer.com. Travel trailers. Bon Voyage, Fun Chaser, Fun Lite, Fun Maker, La Grand, Tele Casa, Voyager.

Holiday Rambler Alumascape, 1722 Mishawaka Rd., Elkhart, IN 46517; 219-295-8060. Fifth-wheel travel trailers, class A motorhomes, travel trailers.

Holiday Rambler RV Division, 606 Nelson's Pkwy., Wakarusa, IN 46573-0465; 219-862-7211, 800-650-7337; www.holidayrambler.com. Fifth-wheel travel trailers, class A motorhomes, travel trailers. Aluma-Lite, Alumascape, Endeavor, Imperial, Navigator, Vacationer.

Home & Park Motorhomes, 100 Shirley Ave., Kitchener, ON N2B 2E1 Canada; 519-745-1169, 888-762-3873; www.roadtrek.com. Van campers. Home & Park, Roadtrek.

Homette Corp., 1230 SW 10th St., Ocala, FL 32678; 352-622-2777.

Horton Vans Inc. RV Division, 101 Industrial Blvd., Eatonton, GA 31024; 706-485-8506. Fifth-wheel travel trailers, travel trailers, horse trailer conversions.

Hy-Line Enterprises Inc., 21674 Beck Dr., Beck Industrial Park, Elkhart, IN 46516; 219-294-1112; www.hylinetrailers.com. Fifth-wheel travel trailers, travel trailers. Hy-Line, Premier.

James Reeves Inc. dba J.R.'s Custom Auto, 1477 E. Hwy. 356, Irving, TX 75060; 972-438-4902. Pickup truck conversions, sport utility conversions.

Jayco Inc., 903 S. Main St., Middlebury, IN 46540; 219-825-5861, 219-825-5861; www.jayco.com. Folding camping trailers, fifth-wheel travel trailers, class C motorhomes, truck campers, travel trailers. Camper III, Camper IV, Camper V, Designer Series, Eagle, Hawk, Heritage, Jay Series, Jayco, LeisureStar, LumaStar, Minivan Super Sport, Sportster, Starcraft, Super Sport, XL Series, Shimera, Venture.

K-Z, Inc. dba Sportsmen, 9270 W. U.S. 20, Shipshewana, IN 46565; 219-768-4016; www.kz-rv.com. Fifth-wheel travel trailers, truck campers, travel trailers. Sportsmen.

Keystone RV Co., 17400 Hackberry Dr., Goshen, IN 46526; 219-642-4590; www.keystonerv.com. Fifth-wheel travel trailers, travel trailers. Big Sky, Bobcat, Cabana, Challenger, Cougar, Hornet, Laredo, Lighthouse, Montana, Mountaineer, Springdale, Sprinter, Tail-Gator.

Keystone West, 3000 Westgate, Pendleton, OR 97801; 541-276-6075. Travel trailers, fifth-wheel travel trailers.

King of the Road, 1313 Rd. G, York, NE 68467; 402-363-7460. Fifth-wheel travel trailers, travel trailers. King of the Road.

Kit Manufacturing Co., 412 S. Kit Ave., Caldwell, ID 83606; 208-453-2500, 208-453-2500; www.kitmfg.com. Fifth-wheel travel trailers, travel trailers. Companion, Espre', Millennium, Patio Hauler, Road Ranger, Sun Chaser.

Knighthill Automotive Ltd., 11631 Bridgeport Rd., Richmond, BC V6X 1T5 Canada; 604-273-1800. Van campers.

Komfort Corp. Division of Thor Industries, 12628 S.E. Jennifer St., Clackamas, OR 97015; 503-722-5199; www.komfort-rv.com. Fifth-wheel travel trailers, travel trailers. Komfort.

Kustom Car Creations dba Kustom Creations, 23180 Harper Ave., Charlotte Harbor, FL 33980; 941-625-9993. Van conversions.

L.A. West, Inc., 1995 U.S. 20, East LaGrange, IN 46761; 219-463-4060, 800-786-8267; www.lawest.com. Van conversions.

Lance Camper Manufacturing Corp., 43120 Venture St., Lancaster, CA 93535; 661-949-3322; www.lancecamper.com. Truck campers. Lance Camper.

Layton Travel Trailer, 425 S. Palm, Hemet, CA 92546; 909-925-0401. Fifth-wheel travel trailers.

Lazy Daze, Inc., 4303 Mission Blvd., Montclair, CA 91763-6052; 909-627-1219. Class C motorhomes. Lazy Daze.

Leisure Guide of America, Inc., 1543 Sandy Cross Rd., Royston, GA 30662; 706-245-7035. Van conversions, pickup truck conversions, sport utility conversions. Leisure.

Leisure Travel Vans 1999-Ltd., Hwy. 3 E. at Rd. 28 W., Morden, MB R6M 1B1 Canada; 204-822-3009; www.leisurevans.com. Van campers.

Majestic Van & Truck, 8241 Gratiot, Saginaw, MI 48609-4878; 517-781-0985. Van conversions.

Marathon Homes Corp., 4420 Pine Creek Rd., Elkhart, IN 46515; 219-294-6441, 219-294-6441; www.marathonhomes.com. Fifth-wheel travel trailers, travel trailers, specialty tow vehicles. Marathon, Olympian.

The MHC Group, 9550 Hermosa Ave., Rancho Cucamonga, CA 91730; 909-989-9399. Class A motorhomes, fifth-wheel travel trailers. Pinnacle, Residency, Traveleze, Summit.

Midwest Vans, Inc., 1801 Minnie St., Elkhart, IN 46516; 219-293-3395; www.midwestvans.com. Van conversions, pickup truck conversions.

Monaco Coach Corp., 91320 Coburg Industrial Way, Coburg, OR 97408-9492; 541-686-8011, 800-634-0855; www.monaco-online.com. Class A motorhomes. Diplomat, Dynasty, Executive, Monaco, Royale Coach by Monaco, Signature Series La Palma, Windsor.

Monaco Coach Corp. McKenzie Towables Division, 91320 Coburg Industrial Way, Coburg, OR 97408; 800-634-0855, 800-486-3995; www.monaco-online.com/Mck2/index.html. Fifth-wheel travel trailers.

Monroe Truck Equipment Co., 1051 W. 7th St., Monroe, WI 53566; 608-328-8127; www.monroetruck.com. Pickup truck conversions, sport utility conversions.

National RV, Inc. subsidiary of National RV Holdings, 3411 N. Perris Blvd., Perris, CA 92571; 909-943-6007. Fifth-wheel travel trailers, class A motorhomes, travel trailers, specialty trailers. Dolphin, Islander, Seabreeze, Seaview, Tradewinds, Tropi-Cal, Surfside, Splash, Palisades, Marlin, Caribbean.

Newmar Corp., 355 N. Delaware St., Nappanee, IN 46550-0030; 219-773-7791, 219-773-7791; www.newmarcorp.com. Fifth-wheel travel trailers, class A motorhomes, travel trailers. American Star, Dutch Star, Kountry Aire, Kountry Star, London Aire, Mountain Aire.

Nexus Management Corp. dba Custom Craft Trailer Outfitters, 114 E. 2nd St.,

Kanawha, IA 50447; 641-762-3611. Fifth-wheel travel trailers, travel trailers, horse trailer conversions. Kiefer Built.

Nomad Travel Trailer, 920 W. Mayberry, Hemet, CA 92546; Fifth-wheel travel trailers, travel trailers.

Nu Wa Industries, Inc., 3701 Johnson Rd., Chanute, KS 66720; 316-431-2088; www.nuwa.com. Fifth-wheel travel trailers, travel trailers. Hitchhiker, Nu Wa.

Osage Industries, Inc., Rt.1 Twin Ridge Rd., Linn, MO 65051; 573-897-3634. Van conversions, pickup truck conversions.

Outlaw Conversions, 1000 Airport Rd., Stephenville, TX 76401; 254-968-5733. Travel trailers, horse trailer conversions.

Pace American Corp., 11550 Harter Dr., Middlebury, IN 46540; 219-825-7223. Specialty trailers, horse trailer conversions. Explorer, Pace.

Peak Manufacturing Inc., 100 Canola Ave., N. Battleford, SK S9A 3M1 Canada; 306-445-6695. Truck campers, class C motorhomes, travel trailers, fifth-wheel travel trailers. Frontier, Kodiak, Vanguard.

Peterson Industries, Inc., RR 2, Box 95, Smith Center, KS 66967; 785-282-6825, 800-368-3759; www.petersonind.com. Fifth-wheel travel trailers. Excel.

Phoenix USA Inc., 52400 N. State Rd. 15, Bristol, IN 46507; 219-848-0207; www.phoenixusarv.com. Van campers, class C motorhomes. Phoenix.

Play-Mor Trailers, Inc., Hwy. 63 S., Westphalia, MO 65085-0128; 573-455-2387. Fifth-wheel travel trailers, travel trailers. Play-Mor.

Pleasure-Way Industries Ltd., 302 Portage Ave., Saskatoon, SK S7J 4C6 Canada; 306-934-6578, 800-364-0189; www.pleasureway.quadrant.net. Van campers. Pleasure-Way.

Pony Hills Conversions, 13456 S.E. 34th Ave., Blooming Prairie, MN 55917-5982; 507-583-2457. Fifth-wheel travel trailers, horse trailer conversions.

Prestige Motorcoach Corp. dba SECCA Corp., 400 W. Gardena Blvd., Gardena, CA 90248; 310-217-2300. Van conversions, pickup truck conversions.

Quality Coaches, Inc., 52743 Stephen Place, Elkhart, IN 46514; 219-262-3649. Van conversions.

R.C. Willett Co., Inc., 3040 Leversee Rd., Cedar Falls, IA 50613-9702; 319-233-3461, 800-367-3910; www.rcwillett.com. Truck campers. Northstar, Texson.

R-Vision, Inc., 1628 W. Beardsley, Elkhart, IN 46514; 219-262-0144, 219-268-2111; www.trail-lite.com. Fifth-wheel travel trailers, travel trailers, class A motorhomes, class C motorhomes. Bantam, Trail Harbor, Trail Lite, B-Plus, Condor, Trail Bay, Trail Cruiser.

Recreation By Design, LLC, 21746 Buckingham Rd., Elkhart, IN 46516; 219-294-2117; www.recreationbydesign.com. Fifth-wheel travel trailers, travel trailers. Backwaters, Belair, Capri, Coach Craft, Ledger, Royal Voyager, Vacation Aire, Vagabond.

Regency Conversions, Inc., 2800 Golden Triangle Blvd., Fort Worth, TX 76177; 817-847-7171; www.regencyvans.com. Van conversions, pickup truck conversions, sport utility conversions.

Rexhall Industries, Inc., 46147 7th St. W., Lancaster, CA 93534; 661-726-0565, 661-726-0565; www.rexhall.com. Class A motorhomes. Aerbus, American Clipper, Anthem, Rexair, Rose Air, Vision.

Riverside Vans, Inc., 57951 Farrand Rd., Colon, MI 49040; 616-432-3031. Van conversions, pickup truck conversions.

Rocky Ridge, Inc., 259 Westclock Extension, Franklin Springs, GA 30639; 706-245-5900. Van conversions, pickup truck conversions.

Royale Coach, 1330 Wade Dr., Elkhart, IN 46514; 219-262-9278. Class A motorhomes.

Schooley Custom Conversions, Inc., 204 Michael Dr., Longview, TX 75603; 903-234-8342. Fifth-wheel travel trailers, horse trailer conversions.

Sherrod Vans, Inc., 6464 Greenland Rd., Jacksonville, FL 32258; 904-268-3321; www.sherrodvans.com. Van conversions, pickup truck conversions. Evo Series, Executive, Gran Sport, Monterey.

Sherry Design, Inc., 1045 N. Nappanee St., Elkhart, IN 46514-1737; 219-266-1477. Van conversions.

Showtime Conversions, Inc., 12141 Industrial Pkwy. E., Middlebury, IN 46540; 219-825-1130. Fifth-wheel travel trailers, horse trailer conversions, specialty trailers, travel trailers. Showtime.

Skyline Corp., 2520 By-Pass Rd., Elkhart, IN 46515; 219-294-6521; www.skylinecorp.com. Fifth-wheel travel trailers, travel trailers. Aljo, Key Largo, Layton, Nomad, Nomad Century, Scottsdale, Seaview, Sun Haven, Tahoe, Layton/Celebrity.

Southern Coach, Carolina Custom Center, 960 Old Winston Rd., Kernersville, NC 27284; 336-996-6807; www.southerncoach.com. Van conversions.

Southern Comfort Conversions, Inc., 7769 Gadsden Hwy., Trussville, AL 35173; 205-655-0919, 800-745-6096; www.scomfort.com. Van conversions, pickup truck conversions, sport utility conversions.

Space Craft Manufacturing Inc., Rt. 1, West Hwy. 40, Concordia, MO 64020; 660-463-7520; www.spacecraftmfg.com. Fifth-wheel travel trailers, equipped for disabled, travel trailers, horse trailer conversions. Space Craft.

Sportsmobile, Inc., 250 Court St., Huntington, IN 46750; 219-356-5435. Van campers.

Sportsmobile Texas, 9805 Gray Blvd., Austin, TX 78758; 512-835-4409. Van campers.

Sportsmobile West, 425 N. Minnewawa, Clovis, CA 93611; 559-322-1562; www.sportsmobile.com. Van campers. Sportsmobile.

Stable Living Conversions, Inc., 7410 E. U.S Hwy. 60, Suite A, Rogersville, MO 65742; 417-753-5100. Travel trailers, horse trailer conversions.

Stage Coach Conversions, 10160 U.S. 62, Leesburg, OH 45135; 937-393-3035; www.reedstrailersales.com. Fifth-wheel travel trailers, travel trailers, horse trailer conversions.

Starcraft Conversions, 69651 U.S. 131 S., White Pigeon, MI 49099; 616-483-9659. Van conversions. Starcraft Conversions.

Starcraft RV, 536 W. Michigan St., Topeka, IN 46571-0458; 219-593-2550, 800-945-4787; www.starcraftrv.com. Folding camping trailers, fifth-wheel travel trailers, truck campers, travel trailers.

Sun Valley, Inc., 28868 Paul Dr., Elkhart, IN 46514; 219-262-1923, 800-327-7684; www.sunliteinc.com. Truck campers, travel trailers, fifth-wheel travel trailers. Apache, Hideaway, Sun-Lite, Sun Valley.

Sunline Coach Co., 245 S. Muddy Creek Rd., Denver, PA 17517-9773; 717-336-2858, 717-336-2858; www.sunlinerv.com. Fifth-wheel travel trailers, travel trailers. Sunline.

SunnyBrook RV, Inc., 201 14th St., Middlebury, IN 46540; 219-825-5250, 219-825-5250; www.sunnybrookrv.com. Fifth-wheel travel trailers, travel trailers. Mobile Scout, Sunnybrook.

T.A. Enterprises, Inc. dba Eclipse Conversions, 135 County Rd. 6, Elkhart, IN 46514; 219-262-1223. Van conversions, pickup truck conversions.

Teton Homes, P.O. Box 2349, Mills, WY 82644; 307-235-1525; www.tetonhomes.com. Fifth-wheel travel trailers. Teton Grand, Teton Prestige, Teton Expedition, Teton Tradition.

Thor America, 37 Old 522, Middleburg, PA 17842; 570-837-1663; www.thoramerica-rv.com. Fifth-wheel travel trailers, travel trailers.

Thor California Inc., 14255 Elsworth St., Moreno Valley, CA 92553-9013; 909-697-4190; www.thorcalifornia-rv.com. Fifth-wheel travel trailers, travel trailers.

Thor Fold Down Division, 925 W. Brooklyn St., Syracuse, IN 46567-1432; 219-457-8787; www.thorcampers-rv.com. Folding camping trailers, travel trailers.

Thor Industries, Inc., 419 W. Pike St., Jackson Center, OH 45334; 937-596-6849; www.thorindustries.com. Folding camping trailers, fifth-wheel travel trailers, class A motorhomes, class C motorhomes, travel trailers. Airstream, Aristocrat, Bambi, Breeze, Chateau, Citation, Corsair, Cutter, Dutchmen, Excella, Fifth Avenue, Four Winds, Fun Mover, Hurricane, Infinity, Komfort, Land Yacht, Legacy, Limited, Park Avenue, Prism, Safari, Signature Series, Skamper, Tahoe, Wanderer, Windsport, Zephyr.

Tiffin Motor Homes, Inc., 502 4th St. N.W., Red Bay, AL 35582; 256-356-8661, 256-356-8661; www.tiffinmotorhomes.com. Class A motorhomes. Allegro, Allegro Bay, Allegro Bus, Phaeton, Zephyr.

Timberland RV Co., 1482 N. Eel River Cemetery Rd., Peru, IN 46970; 765-475-9500. Fifth-wheel travel trailers, travel trailers.

TL Industries, 25876 Miner Rd., Elkhart, IN 46514; 219-264-3127. Travel trailers, fifth-wheel travel trailers. Country Charm, Elite, Kountry Comfort.

TowLite, Inc., 500 S. Main St., Bellville, OH 44813-0577; 419-886-0066, 800-321-6402; www.towlite.com. Travel trailers. Towlite.

Trail Boss Conversions, Inc., Rt. 2, S. Outer Rd., Bates City, MO 64011; 816-690-7133. Travel trailers, horse trailer conversions.

Trail Wagons, Inc., 607 E. R St., Yakima, WA 98901; 509-248-9026; www.chinookrv.com. Van campers. Chinook, Trail Wagons.

TrailManor, Inc., 135 Hulsey Lane, Lake City, TN 37769; 865-426-7426; www.trailmanor.com. Travel trailers. Trailmanor.

The Transit Authority Corp., 8020 Deering Ave., Canoga Park, CA 91304; 818-888-7549; www.thetransitauthority.com. Van conversions, conversion vehicles for disabled, pickup truck conversions, sport utility conversions. The Transit Authority.

Travel Supreme, Inc., 66149 State Rd. 19, Wakarusa, IN 46573; 219-862-4484, 219-768-7273; www.travelsupreme.com. Fifth-wheel travel trailers, travel trailers, class A motorhomes. Travel Supreme.

Travelmaster RV, 14489 U.S. 20, Middlebury, IN 46540; 219-825-8561. Class C motorhomes.

Triple E Recreational Vehicles, P.O. Box 1230, Winkler, MB R6W 4C4 Canada; 204-325-4361, 204-325-4361; www.tripleerv.com. Fifth-wheel travel trailers, class A motorhomes, class C motorhomes, travel trailers. Commander, Embassy, Empress, Senator, Topaz, Topaz Touring Edition.

Trojan Vans, Inc. Kustom Kreations, 190 Industrial Park Rd., Oneonta, AL 35121; 205-274-2900; www.kustomkreations.com. Van conversions, pickup truck conversions. Kustom Kreations, E-Z Ride.

Unique Conversions, Inc., 1502 Hwy. 157 N., Mansfield, TX 76063; 817-477-5251. Van conversions.

Vanguard Industries of MI Inc., 31450 M86 W., Colon, MI 49040; 616-432-3271. Folding camping trailers, truck campers. Palomino.

Vanworks, Inc., 900 E. Lincoln Ave., Fort Collins, CO 80524; 970-484-5344, 970-484-5344; www.vanworks.com. Van conversions.

Viking RV, 580 W. Burr Oak St., Centreville, MI 49032; 616-467-6321, 616-467-6321; www.vikingrv.com. Folding camping trailers.

Wagner Trailer Interiors, Inc., 7575 Hwy. 177, Shawnee, OK 74804-0614; 405-964-4242. Fifth-wheel travel trailers, horse trailer conversions.

Waldoch Crafts Inc., 13821 Lake Dr., Forest Lake, MN 55025; 651-464-3215. Van conversions, conversion vehicles for disabled, pickup truck conversions, sport utility conversions. Waldoch Crafts.

Warrior Manufacturing Weekend Warrior Trailers, 1320 Oleander Ave., Perris, CA 92571; 909-940-5556. Fifth-wheel travel trailers, travel trailers, specialty trailers. Weekend Warrior.

West Coast Leisure Homes Ltd., 316 Dawson Ave., Penticton, BC V2A 3N6 Canada; 250-493-1535. Fifth-wheel travel trailers, truck campers, travel trailers. Okanagan.

Western Recreational Vehicles, Inc., P.O. Box 9547, Yakima, WA 98909-0547; 509-457-4133, 509-457-4133; www.wrv.com. Fifth-wheel travel trailers, class A motorhomes, truck campers. Alpenlite, Alpine, Alpine Coach.

Whinny Cargo Conversions, 273 Goldenrod Rd., Ozark, MO 65721; 417-581-6575. Travel trailers, horse trailer conversions.

Winnebago Industries, Inc., 605 W. Crystal Lake Rd., Forest City, IA 50436; 641-585-3535; www.winnebagoind.com. Low-profile motorhomes, equipped for disabled, class A motorhomes, class C motorhomes, van campers. Eurovan Camper, Itasca Horizon, Itasca Spirit, Itasca Suncruiser, Itasca Sundancer, Itasca Sunflyer, Itasca Sunrise/Sunrise S.E., Rialta, Ultimate Advantage, Ultimate Freedom, Winnebago Adventurer, Winnebago Brave, Winnebago Chieftain, Winnebago Journey, Winnebago Minnie, Winnebago Minnie Winnie.

Index

Numbers in **bold** refer to pages with illustrations